Information Age Economy

Information Age Economy

F. Rose
The Economics, Concept, and Design
of Information Intermediaries
1999, ISBN 3-7908-1168-8

S. Weber
Information Technology in Supplier Network
2001, ISBN 3-7908-1395-8

K. Geihs, W. König and F. von Westarp (Eds.)
Networks
2002, ISBN 3-7908-1449-0

F. von Westarp
Modeling Software Markets
2003, ISBN 3-7908-0009-0

Dennis Kundisch

New Strategies for Financial Services Firms

The Life-Cycle-Solution Approach

With 50 Figures
and 10 Tables

Physica-Verlag
A Springer-Verlag Company

Dr. Dennis Kundisch
Universität Augsburg
Lehrstuhl für Betriebswirtschaftslehre,
Wirtschaftsinformatik & Financial Engineering
Kernkompetenzzentrum IT & Finanzdienstleistungen
Universitätsstraße 16
86135 Augsburg, Germany
dennis.kundisch@wiwi.uni-augsburg.de

ISBN 3-7908-0066-X Physica-Verlag Heidelberg New York

Cataloging-in-Publication Data applied for
A catalog record for this book is available from the Library of Congress.

Bibliographic information published by Die Deutsche Bibliothek
Die Deutsche Bibliothek lists this publication in the Deutsche Nationalbibliografie; detailed bibliographic data is available in the Internet at *http://dnb.ddb.de*.

Physica-Verlag Heidelberg New York
a member of BertelsmannSpringer Science + Business Media GmbH

http://www.springer.de
© Physica-Verlag Heidelberg 2003
Printed in Germany

Cover design: Erich Kirchner, Heidelberg
SPIN 10927304   88/3130 – 5 4 3 2 1 0 – Printed on acid-free paper

*This book is devoted to my family
and particularly to my dear nieces
Annika and Katharina.*

Foreword

The theme of this book "New strategies for financial services providers" is an equally relevant and important topic in science and practice. In the (post) information age economy, the German financial services market and many big financial services providers are in a deep crisis. Increasing competition due to deregulation and improved transparency through new means of communication on the one hand, and empowered customers demanding individualized solutions for their financial problems e.g. because of new working circumstances, increase the pressure on the market participants to alter their strategies according to these new challenges. Many firms have reacted defensively either by merging in the hopes of realizing scale effects – a high-risk venture considering the last few years – or by adapting "me-too-strategies" (also known as "lemming-banking") that do not provide for a sustainable competitive advantage.

Based on a profound analysis of developing mega-trends in the years ahead, especially in information and IT-intense market, Dr. Kundisch develops a new anticyclical strategy that aims at using IT as an enabler to strengthen customer relationships and focus on individualized solutions wherever it seems economically sound to do so.

However, he does not stop after the development of the strategy, but provides two important concepts that may help turn this vision and strategy into reality. Thus, he favorably and refreshingly differentiates against many contributions that stop at the fairly abstract strategic level.

The results of this examination are a highly valuable input for the multi-year project efficient coordination in the services sector funded by Deutsche Forschungsgemeinschaft.

It is noteworthy that the finished content model (Chap. 6) not only found recognition in scientific journals and conferences, but its central ideas were put to practical use at a large German multinational bank. Moreover, the product model is an excellent tool to streamline the process of customer consultation while simultaneously improving the quality of the recommendations. Based on methods in artificial intelligence, Dennis Kundisch presents an IT-based approach showing how solutions can be structured and configured that satisfy specific customer constraints. This new concept includes uncertainty and risk in the formal representation of financial problems and solutions. Hence, a gap between finance and distributed artificial intelligence – so far mostly unrelated scientific areas – is bridged.

The author manages to integrate current research questions in finance and the financial services market with practical recommendations concerning the implementations of these findings using modern concepts of information processing. He closes an existing gap between economic, business and IS literature. My hopes for this book are for widespread readership and debate among scientists and practitioners in the community.

Hans Ulrich Buhl
University of Augsburg
2003

Preface

The following fulfills a longstanding dream of mine – to write a preface for a book.

Interpreting and understanding market functions has fascinated me for years. My research has focused on a market that nearly everyone experiences at virtually every stage of his or her life – the financial services market for the private customer. The challenge to studying markets is that the moment you think you understand how forces are interrelated, the markets change and you are proven wrong. Nevertheless, I am optimistic that I can provide a basic understanding about the financial services market and improve efficiencies in this (German) market as well.

This text evolved during the multi-year project efficient coordination in the services sector funded by Deutsche Forschungsgemeinschaft (DFG). In this interdisciplinary project, research groups from computer sciences, information systems and management, finance, and economics at the University of Augsburg and the Friedrich-Alexander-University Erlangen-Nürnberg collaborated to examine efficiencies for the cooperative production and marketing of individualized services. The sub-project I have been working on concentrates on the development of methods to efficiently generate individualized financial services based on customer data and customer behavior. The funding is greatly acknowledged! This book is written in the context of a number of my colleagues' publications on several aspects of improving relationships between a financial services provider and an end-customer.

Writing this book has been a painstaking yet enjoyable process, and there are a number of people I would like to thank. I am especially grateful to my doctoral thesis supervisor Prof. Dr. Hans Ulrich Buhl for being a very constructive "sparring partner" for my ideas. He gave me guidance at the necessary crossroads, and at the same time left me the freedom to pursue research ideas with my colleagues. I am also indebted to Prof. Dr. Günter Bamberg for being the second referee in the process of the dissertation. He provided me with excellently helpful suggestions particularly concerning the more formal parts of the text. I also want to thank Prof. Dr. Manfred Steiner who took the chair of the oral examination.

My thanks also go to my colleagues at the University of Augsburg with whom I could constructively discuss ideas and collaborate in a very friendly environment. I greatly benefited from their input, the discussions and the collaboration. Apart from the technical contents, I would personally like to thank Dr. Axel J. Schell and Nina Schroeder for their help in finalizing the text. Moreover, I also thank my family, especially my parents without whom this project would not have been possible. They have been a continual source of encouragement to me as this project progressed. Finally, I wish to express my sincere thanks to Georg Post – my former English teacher at secondary school in my hometown Schwenningen – for carefully reading and correcting the text and for helping me with the orthographical pitfalls in American English. Any remaining errors – either technical or orthographical – are of course mine!

I welcome comments on the book from any readers. My e-mail address is

dennis.kundisch@wiwi.uni-augsburg.de

Enjoy!

Dennis Kundisch
University of Augsburg
2003

Table of Contents

1 Introduction

Money is better than poverty, if only for financial reasons.
WOODY ALLEN

1.1 Motivation

Big German financial services providers all seem to share the same problem: They have hundreds of thousands of private customers but they are not able to leverage that customer base and make money with them. This problem is not new, though. (Rolfes et al. 1997) titled back in 1997 "The business with the private customer – The Achilles' heel of German credit institutions", emphasizing the problems that would arise due to foreseeable fundamental structural changes in that business. And in fact these structural changes took place and overall the profit contribution of the business with private customers in the financial services market has suffered heavily in recent years. Fig. 1 exemplarily shows the cost-income-ratio for different group divisions and for the corporate divisions within the group division "Private Clients and Asset Management" for Deutsche Bank AG between 1999 and 2001.

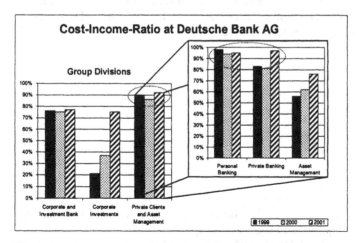

Fig. 1. Cost-Income-Ratio at Deutsche Bank AG 1999 - 2001[1]

---

[1]   Data taken from Annual Report 2001 available at http://www.deutsche-bank.de.

Deutsche Bank is not alone, though. For 2001, Commerzbank AG, Dresdner Bank AG, and Bayerische HypoVereinsbank AG report a cost-income-ratio of 102.0%, 86.4% and 91.3%, respectively.[2] These figures translate into unsatisfactory profit contributions at the respective firms.

The net income before taxes was -299 million Euro for HypoVereinsbank's "Private Customers and Professionals" division (Group: 1,549 million Euro) in 2001. At the same time Deutsche Bank's "Private Clients and Asset Management" division generated a mere 12% (397 million Euro) of the groups total net income before taxes of 3,340 million Euro. Of these 397 million Euro, the "Personal Banking" division contributed 156 million Euro and the "Private Banking" division even lost 52 million Euro. Analogously, Commerzbank's "Retail Banking" business line had a net income before taxes of -185 million Euro and Dresdner Bank's "Private Clients" contributed just 92 million Euro to the groups total net income before taxes of 773 million Euro.[3] One explanation surely lies in the fact of the bad year in terms of stock market performance. This resulted in cautious customers and thus less commission from buying and selling securities. But the trend towards a difficult market environment in the retail and private banking market has more profound roots.

In recent years the competitive situation has intensified dramatically. Due to new means of communication, such as the Internet as well as regulatory changes, markets have become more transparent and more contestable, and this trend is supposed to hold on for another couple of years.[4] At the same time customers being empowered with these new means of communication, have become better-informed as well as more demanding on the one hand and less loyal to their financial services provider on the other hand.[5] The time when customers maintained a relationship with their financial services provider for a lifetime seems to belong to the past while margins have become razor thin. Fig. 2 exemplarily shows the historical development of interest margins for German credit institutions. Within the category of the commercial banks the development for the big banks has even been worse in the last years, as the dotted line shows.[6]

---

[2]   All data are taken from the respective Annual Reports 2001 available at http://www. commerzbank.de, http://dresdner-bank.de, and http://www.hvb.de.

[3]   Data taken from the Annual Reports 2001. See footnote 1 and footnote 2.

[4]   See e.g. (Kopper 1998).

[5]   See e.g. (Institut für Demoskopie Allensbach 2002), (Krämer 2002), (Schüller 2001).

[6]   See (Deutsche Bundesbank 2001).

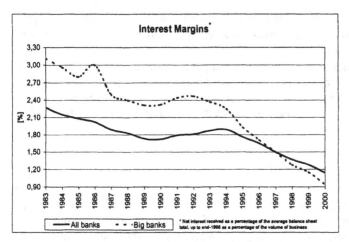

Fig. 2. Interest Margins for All Categories of Banks and Big Banks in Germany[7]

Apparently, this had its effects on the stock prices of financial services firms. Fig. 3 shows the stock price development relative to the market between 1995 and 2000. Obviously, shareholder value has been destroyed instead of being created since 1998.

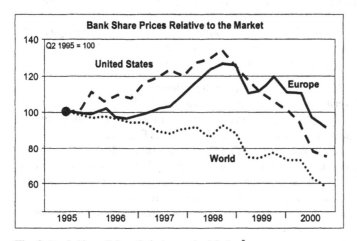

Fig. 3. Bank Share Prices Relative to the Market[8]

---

[7]   Data taken from (Deutsche Bundesbank 2001). For a discussion about the performance of German credit institutions see (Deutsche Bundesbank 2001). For a short discussion also see (Rolfes 2001), who deduces strategic consequences based on the structural changes in the European financial services market.

[8]   See (Anonymous 2000e).

Concerning the German financial services market in particular, the firms operating in this market even performed worse compared to their European peers in terms of return on equity.[9]

And making things worse, although banks put a substantial share of their workforce at the provision of superior services to their customers[10], the quality of consultancy at banks has been consistently disappointing over the last years.[11]

Not an attractive market to operate in? Well, as most of the times: It depends!

1.2   Problem Statement

Given these insufficient financial results sketched above and potentially enough room for service improvements, a new way of dealing with private customers has to be found. Therefore, the following three questions are the center of interest in this contribution:

- What are the shaping trends of the years to come in the financial services market that have to be taken into account to formulate an adequate strategy?
- What strategy should a financial services provider operating in the European and especially in the German financial services market pursue to generate a sustainable competitive advantage and, thus an adequate return for the shareholders?
- Where is it an economically sound decision to use information technology (IT)? And what concepts should be implemented to generate profitable relationships between a financial services provider and its customers?

Particularly the role of IT as an enabler in the strategy, and concepts to support the process of delivering a superior service to customers will play an important role in this book. Due to the fact that bank business is information business, financial services firms have been early adopters of IT and the financial services industry was one of the first big industries embracing the Internet with electronic banking strategies. However, one has to decide between IT investments that are a necessity to stay in business and IT investments that shape the quality of the service of a financial services provider. The first group of investments cannot be circumvented if one wants to stay in the game. The latter group leaves a lot of space

---

[9]   See (Fischer and Rolfes 2001).

[10]   Even though the new means of communication were assumed to allow for huge cost-cutting effects on the side of the financial services providers, retail and private banking services are still activities intense in human resource. For instance in 2001 45% of HypoVereinsbank's and 42% of Deutsche Bank's employees worked in this area. Data taken from the Annual Reports 2001; see footnote 1 and footnote 2. The figure for HypoVereinsbank refers to the division "Private Customers and Professionals", the figure for Deutsche Bank refers to the division "Private Clients and Asset Management".

[11]   See (Rehkugler et al. 1992), (Anonymous 1995, 1997a, 2000b, 2000c, 2001e). This seems not only to be true for the German financial services market but also for European neighbors such as Austria; see e.g. (Lucius 2002).

for strategic considerations. In the last couple of years a lot of money has been "burned" by implementing applications that will not even recover the costs in the long run. Thus based on a rigorous strategy, the deployment of IT has to be a sound *business* decision contributing to an increase of the shareholder value of the company.[12]

1.3 Delimitation

In this contribution the focus will be the market for financial services for the private customer, i.e. the business-to-customer market (B2C). All other areas of financial services – such as corporate finance, investment banking, securitization and other business-to-business services (B2B) – and respective strategies for these products and markets will not be covered.

Talking about the B2C market, the decision to operate in that market will not be challenged but will be taken as given.[13] Market entry or departure strategies will not be covered. Thus the focus will be on developing a sustainable strategy for financial services providers that already operate in that market and have a substantial customer base, i.e. more than 1 million private customers.[14] Special attention will be devoted to the German financial services market.

In the analysis, which is based on the private customer's needs, objectives and preferences, the design and management of the interface between a financial services firm and a customer as well as the products and services that are marketed via this interface will be the focus. The identification and conceptualization of tasks that can and should be supported by IT from an economic point of view is the guiding underlying research question in this context. In contrast, the internal processes, such as production processes and organizational issues[15] of a financial services provider will be of no particular interest.

---

[12] These are the issues "Wirtschaftsinformatik" deals with as a science. The German term „Wirtschaftsinformatik" has no real equivalent in English. Very briefly, the science of "Wirtschaftsinformatik" deals with the development of information systems as interrelated socio-technical systems – thus explicitly integrating human beings – and their economically sound deployment; see e.g. (Mertens et al. 2001).

[13] According to (Straub 1990) the decision to operate in the mass market can hardly be cancelled. And efforts to sell the business with private – especially retail customers – has not been fruitful so far.

[14] Currently, all big German commercial banks would satisfy this constraint. The opportunity for savings banks and regional institutions of credit cooperatives to outsource high net worth individuals for reasons of scale effects discussed in (Popp 1998) will not be covered.

[15] On network organizations for one-stop-shopping financial services providers see (Bülow 1995). More general on information, organization, and management see (Wigand et al. 1997). (Straub 1990) discusses organizational issues with respect to an integration of electronic banking in a banking organization.

1.4 Outline

The book is organized as follows.

After these introductory remarks, the problem statement and the delimitation, the basic technical terms that are widely used throughout the book are defined in *Chap. 2* to give a consistent understanding of their meaning.

Chap. 3 covers the mega trends in the financial services industry in order to formulate and describe an adequate strategy and associated concepts in subsequent chapters. Though there is an enormous number of foreseeable trends that will shape the market environment, the four trends with the most impact (therefore denoted as *mega trends*) – namely regulation, society changes, changes in working life conditions, and new means of communication – are discussed in detail. Comparatively much attention is dedicated to the issue of increased market efficiency in the financial services market with the help of a search cost model.

Consequently, strategic options are presented in *Chap. 4*. Here, Porter's generic competitive strategies – cost leadership, differentiation, and focus – are discussed and evaluated with respect to the special characteristics of the financial services market.

Chap. 5 outlines the proposed life-cycle solution provision strategy. After the discussion of the vision, the strategy is laid out. The focus is set on the design and the management of customer interaction with the financial services provider and the role of IT in this setting.

Chap. 6 covers two important concepts – a content and a product model – to implement a life-cycle solution provision strategy. The two concepts are embedded in a research framework that has been developed at the Competence Center IT & Financial Services at the University of Augsburg. The content model facilitates the provision of relevant finance-related information to a specific customer using the appropriate communication channel at the right time. While the content model may help to satisfy informational needs of the customer, the product model facilitates the consultation process in terms of finding good solutions to a customer's financial problems. Apparently, these concepts are just two among a number of different building blocks for a profound strategy. Thus it is not the objective here to provide a complete set of concepts to implement the life-cycle solution provision strategy. Instead two contributions that may help to generate a more profitable relationship between customers and their financial services provider shall exemplarily illustrate how the proposed strategy might be turned into reality.[16]

---

[16]   This book has to be seen as one building block among a number of contributions by the author's colleagues at the Competence Center IT & Financial Services at the University of Augsburg, who also work on appropriate IT concepts to turn the vision into reality. At the Competence Center topical focal points comprise (1) customer-centric information systems in the financial services industry, (2) multi-channel CRM in the financial services industry, (3) chance and risk management technology, and (4) financial planning. The author belongs to the financial planning research group. Forthcoming dissertations include the following: Michael Fridgen focuses on customer-centric information systems; see (Fridgen 2003). Jürgen Schackmann deals with the concept of individuali-

A long-term perspective is taken in *Chap. 7* to challenge the presented business model and sensitize the decision makers when implementing the strategy. It turns out that due to decreasing switching costs, the issue of trust that is already an important concept in any business transaction will become even more important in the years to come.

Chap. 8 is the conclusion. A brief summary of the contributions in this book as well as prospects for further research are provided there.

Fig. 4 schematically illustrates the organization of the book.

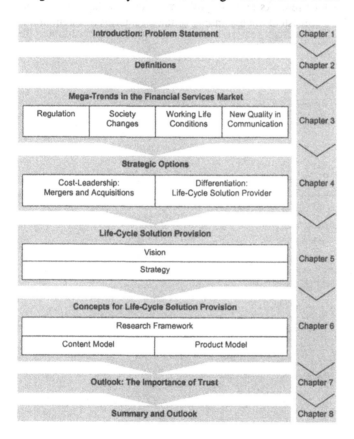

Fig. 4. Outline of the Book

For the most part, this book is based on research that has been conducted in the course of a multi-year project *efficient coordination in the services sector* funded by the German National Science Foundation (Deutsche Forschungsgemeinschaft).

zation and personalization from an economic point of view; see (Schackmann 2002). Werner Steck works on the effective and efficient design of customer relations in the financial services industry; see (Steck 2003). Stefan Volkert works on knowledge management and software architectures for CRM; see (Volkert 2003).

In this interdisciplinary project, research groups from computer science, information systems and management, finance, and economics of the University of Augsburg and the Friedrich-Alexander-University Erlangen-Nuremberg[17] collaborate to deduce efficiency conditions for the cooperative production and marketing of individualized services. The sub-project the author has been working on aims at the development of concepts to efficiently generate individualized financial services based on customer data and customer behavior. The funding is greatly acknowledged.[18]

After these introductory remarks and the problem statement, the next section will lay the ground for a consistent understanding of the used terms throughout the book.

---

[17]   So, the research group is referred to as *Forschergruppe Augsburg Nürnberg* FAN (research group Augsburg Nuremberg).

[18]   For more information on the broader scope of this interdisciplinary research group see http://www.wiso.uni-erlangen.de/WiSo/BWI/BuB/fan/.

2 Definitions

Name is sound and smoke.
JOHANN WOLFGANG VON GEOTHE, Faust I, 1808

It is a sad truth, but we have lost the faculty of giving lovely names to things.
Names are everything.
OSCAR WILDE, The Picture of Dorian Gray, 1891

In this chapter, the basic technical terms that will be widely used throughout the book will be defined.[19] As was already made clear in the introduction, this book is about the B2C financial services market. Therefore, products and services that are produced and marketed in this industry first have to be described in more detail. Next, the organizational settings for production and marketing of these products and services have to be defined. Finally, a customer problem is the issue of interest.

2.1 Financial Services and Financial Products

From an enumerative perspective financial services comprise all marketable services that are provided by banks, insurance companies, credit card organizations, savings and loan associations, investment organizations, and other special institutions.[20] This definition is illustrative and practical on the one hand, unsatisfactory, however, from a scientific point of view, since it is not constant in time. There may evolve new businesses that offer products or services that should be included in the definition but that do not fall in any of the enumerated categories.

---

[19] On definitions in general see e.g. (Straub 1990) or (Gutenberg 1953). Following Gutenberg, who states that each one is free to define technical terms as one needs them for the purpose of the analysis, in this chapter there will be no comprehensive argument about different definitions. The definitions provided here mostly follow those of (Will 1999).

[20] In (Brunner and Vollath 1993) several contributions on each category of financial services can be found. On different financial services also see (Büschgen 1991). A nice introduction to financial services can also be found in (Stracke and Geitner 1992).

A lot of space in literature is devoted to the definition of services in general.[21] In case of financial services a definition based on constituting characteristics seems reasonable.[22] Excluding any transactional or informational services, one constituting characteristic of financial services in their fundamental function is the transformation of liquidity over time, i.e. intertemporal distribution of liquidity.[23]

> *Financial services in the narrower sense* are legally binding, mutual payment promises between one or several suppliers and one customer, which represent legally and economically marketable services. The level as well as the point in time of a payment may be subject to uncertainty. Financial services in the narrower sense are referred to as *financial products*.[24]

Financial products can be roughly divided into savings services, insurance and protection services, and borrowing. However, there are a number of other financial services such as transaction services, investment services, and information services that are not included in the definition above.[25] All these functions have in common that the object of the service is a financial product.[26]

> *Financial services in the broader sense* are financial products or services that have a financial product as the object of the service.[27]

Financial services have to be produced by someone and marketed somewhere. This will be the issue of the next section.

2.2 Financial Services Providers, Markets and Organizations

Financial services are produced and marketed by a number of different institutions such as banks, insurance companies, credit card organizations, savings and loan associations, investment organizations, and other special institutions. However, there are numerous new entrants in the financial services market often denoted as non- or near-banks[28]. Generally speaking, it is not important to distinguish be-

---

[21] See e.g (Corsten 2001), (Roemer 1998), (Schneider 1999b), (Hardt 1996), (Thede 1992) and respective references therein.

[22] For a discussion see e.g (Roemer 1998). (Corsten 2001) distinguishes services definitions that are *enumerative, negative* or *constituting*.

[23] See (Will 1999), (Roemer 1998), (Niehans 1983).

[24] (Spremann 1996) refers to them as financial contracts.

[25] See e.g. (Lipstein 1984), (Wagner 1991).

[26] See e.g. (Roemer 1998).

[27] In the following, if the expression *financial services* is used, it refers to *financial services in the broader sense* if not stated otherwise.

[28] On current trends with respect to non-banks in Europe see e.g. (Bürkner and Grebe 2001).

tween these different institutions for the purpose of this book and they could all be called *financial services providers*. However, since pure information providers such as publishers of finance-related periodicals are not able to directly satisfy any customer problem that stems from an intertemporal liquidity distribution, the scope of this definition would be too broad. The same applies for firms offering pure transaction services. Thus the constituting characteristic of financial services providers in this book is the provision of financial products.[29]

> *Financial services providers* are firms that market financial products to consumers.[30]

Certainly, this does not mean that a financial services provider necessarily offers all different kinds of financial products. But of course, a financial services provider may offer the whole range of financial services.

> A *one-stop shop in the financial services industry (one-stop shop)* is a financial services provider that offers the whole range of financial services that may be used to satisfy customer needs.

Accordingly the action of satisfying all needs of a customer with respect to his financial problems at one financial services provider, i.e. at the one-stop shop is referred to as *one-stop shopping*. Where does this shopping take place?

The abstract place where financial services are sold is called a *market*. Most financial services are not openly traded at an exchange like a stock market. For instance, the rates of a mortgage loan or the details of a leasing contract are often bilaterally agreed on between a customer and his personal financial advisor as representative of a financial services provider. Therefore, a market is defined as follows:

> A *market* is the abstract place for the spontaneous, voluntary and price mediated exchange of goods and services.[31]

A market is a *coordination form* where unilateral, autonomous adjustment processes (price or volume adjustments) lead to autonomous buy or sell decisions of the exchange partners.[32] Markets as well as firms are *organizations*.

> *Organizations* are specific institutional mechanisms that aim at aligning the activities of associated members. Members subordinate the resources they introduce to the organization to a uniform leadership.

---

[29] See e.g. (Büschgen 1991), (Bitz 1995), (Süchting and Paul 1998), (Barton 2001) for a categorization of financial services providers in the German market.
[30] The term *firm* and *provider* are used interchangeably in this book.
[31] On markets, hierarchy, and organizations see e.g. (Laux and Liermann 1997).
[32] See (Will 1999).

Obviously, members of an organization may be either persons or machine play-ers[33] also comprising *software agents*[34]. A special form of an organization is a firm which generally has various and demanding coordination problems. Organizations not only have a coordination task but also an institutional semantic. Organizations that support the market-based exchange of goods and services are commonly re-ferred to as *markets*. Thus a weekly market as well as a futures market are *organi-zations*.

In recent years, single, several or all market transaction phases[35] have increas-ingly been supported by new means of communication. This is generally referred to as *electronic commerce*.[36] Particularly in the financial services industry – often denoted as one of the most important electronic services industries – most market transactions can already be performed using, for instance, a call center or the WWW, since the primary product that is offered in this industry just consists of information.

> An *electronic market in the broader sense*[37] is an IT[38]-enabled organization that supports at least one market transaction phase.

A special form of *electronic markets in the broader sense* are *net markets*.

> A *net market* is an electronic market in the broader sense that is based on open and integrated computer networks such as the Internet.[39]

Due to the immateriality of financial services they can be exchanged preemi-nently via net markets. The sales and marketing of financial services via net mar-kets is assigned to electronic commerce. However, other terms such as *online banking, Internet banking*[40] or *electronic finance*[41] are usually used to denote this activity. Some firms exclusively rely on electronic communication channels to in-teract with customers.

> Financial services providers that exclusively rely on electronic communica-tion channels to interact with their customers are called *direct financial services providers*. If the offered services are primarily banking services, they are called *direct banks*.

---

[33] See e.g. (Ferstl and Sinz 2001).
[34] On *software agents* see e.g. (Mainzer 1999) or (Rahman and Bignall 2001).
[35] On *market transaction phases* see e.g. (Merz 1999). Usually, *information, agreement*, and *transaction/settlement* phase are distinguished.
[36] See e.g. (Merz 1999).
[37] In contrast, an *electronic market in the narrower sense* is an IT-enabled and market co-ordinated organization that supports *all* market transaction phases.
[38] IT refers to information and communication systems in this context. On information and communication systems see e.g. (WKWI 1994).
[39] See (Will 1999).
[40] See.g. (Straub 1990).
[41] See e.g. (Bank for International Settlements 2001).

Note that there is a difference between *virtual organizations* and *direct financial services providers*. A virtual organization is an organizational form of legally and economically autonomous actors collaborating to accomplish a task and act as one firm from the perspective of the customer. In the extreme, institutional centralized management functions may be abandoned and necessary coordination is performed using appropriate IT.[42] Thus a direct bank may but need not be a virtual organization.[43]

2.3 Financial Problem, Individualization, and Customer Relationship Management

Having talked about financial products and services, the places where they are marketed and the organizations which produce and market these products and services, the question remains why financial services are needed. Generally speaking, customers do not need financial services since they cannot derive any direct utility from them. However, financial services can indirectly help to satisfy a customer's needs.

A customer has many and various consumption needs, most of which are connected with cash inflows or outflows. For instance, the need to consume a house[44] generally leads to a large cash outflow, if the house is purchased. The corresponding problems are denoted as financial problems. Financial products are means to solve financial problems, since they provide for a way to transform liquidity over time. However, having in mind a solution to a financial problem, some kind of decision rule or objective function has to be identified in order to be able to determine an appropriate solution for the customer.

> A *financial problem in the narrower sense* is sufficiently described by an objective function subject to constraints.[45]

These constraints will generally comprise the transformation of an expected cash flow stream based on the status quo into a desired cash flow stream.

Due to the complexity of financial products a customer will not only have a plain financial problem in the narrower sense but also related informational problems that have to be satisfied as well. A customer will often not agree to purchasing financial products if he does not understand them. Thus information consti-

---

[42] See e.g. (Will 1999), (Mertens et al. 1998), (Arnold et al. 1995). On *virtual organizations* also see (Mertens and Faisst 1995).

[43] One example of a virtual organization is the Advance Bank; see e.g. (Buhl et al. 1999c). Advance Bank used to be a direct bank as well as a virtual organization. With the recent opening of several branch outlets, it is no traditional direct bank anymore.

[44] It sounds a bit odd to talk about „consuming a house". However, abstracting from psychological effects, the utility is (mainly) derived by the use or consumption and not by the ownership of a good.

[45] See e.g. (Roemer 1998).

tutes a vital part of a solution to a customer's financial problem. In addition, if an offered solution is to be realized – solving the financial problem in the narrower sense and thus satisfying the needs – transactional services are required.

> A *financial problem in the broader sense* comprises financial problems in the narrower sense and the need for related informational and transactional services.

How to solve financial problems in the narrower sense as well as financial problems in the broader sense with respect to informational needs is one of the focal points in this book.[46]

Financial services providers may either sell standardized financial services to their customers without answering their exact needs or they can individually bundle and tailor financial services to optimally solve a customer's financial problem.

> The active process of individually tailoring products and services according to specific customer needs, preferences and problems is called *individualization*.[47]

Note that individualization does not refer to financial services providers that passively offer their customers a great choice of products or product and service bundles, which indeed may or may not solve a specific customer problem. The customer is thus asked to select himself a financial service or bundles of products and services that satisfy his needs. Unlike this activity of *self-selection*, the process of individualization comprises the evaluation of the customer's needs, preferences, and financial problem by the financial services provider, i.e. the integration of the customer into the service process and the tailoring of the financial services according to these needs, preferences and the financial problem. This process of tailoring may comprise e.g. the following methods:[48]

- *Selection*: Selecting the appropriate financial services and eventually the appropriate mix of these services.
- *Configuration*: Intelligently choosing product parameters, such as the debt discount of a mortgage loan.
- *Classification*: Classifying solutions as feasible judging from a solution set based on problem characteristics, e.g. design of a loan contract based on a creditworthiness analysis.

Individualization is not a binary concept in the sense that a solution to a customer's problem is either individualized or not. Instead, individualization is a continuous characteristic of a solution. Thus the degree of individualization lies between 100% and 0%, with 100% being a perfectly individualized solution based on the customer's needs, preferences and financial problem and 0% being a stan-

---

[46]   See the *content model* and the *product model* in Chap. 6.

[47]   A much more comprehensive definition of individualization can be found in (Schackmann 2002). In the context of this book, this rather superficial definition shall suffice.

[48]   See (Roemer 1998).

dardized (or randomly) chosen solution. This does not mean that this standardized solution may not happen to fit the needs, preferences and financial problem of a specific customer. However, coincidental fitting has nothing in common with the active process of tailoring a solution and therefore has nothing to do with individualization.

The process of individualization is more and more supported using IT.

> *Personalization* is the individualization of products and services as well as the communication with a customer using IT.[49]

Individualization has become an important concept in the way businesses service and communicate with their customers. Individualization strongly relates to the concepts of *One-to-One Marketing*[50] and *Customer Relationship Management* (CRM)[51,52]. In Chap. 5 and Chap. 6 it will become clear how individualization ties in with these concepts. Whereas individualization has a strong focus on customer *integration*, CRM has its focus on customer *interaction*.

> *Customer Relationship Management* comprises the establishment, continuous optimization as well as the maintenance of sustainable and profitable customer relations.

So, CRM is the activity of individually and professionally managing customer accounts by establishing and keeping "economically valuable" customers and repelling and eliminating "economically invaluable" ones. Due to the new means of communication, the term *Electronic Customer Relationship Management* (eCRM) has evolved in recent years, emphasizing the use of modern information and communication technology to facilitate the management of a customer account. In the financial services industry, CRM is not imaginable without leveraging appropriate IT due to the terabytes of data and the high number of customer accounts that have to be handled and serviced. When talking about CRM methods in the financial services market in the following, eCRM is primarily referred to or at least included.

Having defined all basic technical terms, in the following chapter the shaping trends with the strongest impact on the development of the financial services market for the private customers – so-called *mega trends* – will be described in detail.

---

[49] This definition relates to the understanding of personalization in (Piller and Zanner 2001) or (Schackmann 2002).

[50] On *One-to-One Marketing* see (Peppers and Rogers 1997), (Pine et al. 1995), (Gilmore and Pine 2000). On one-to-one approaches with respect to information systems see e.g. (Hansen 1995).

[51] On *management information systems research in CRM* see (Romano 2001). A comprehensive and valuable list of CRM articles is available on request from Nicolas Romano.

[52] Although in their details these concepts may be different, both terms will be used equivalently in this book.

3 Mega Trends in the Financial Services Industry[53]

Even after the dramatic fallback of the worldwide stock markets – particularly in the high-tech sector – the fast evolving IT-development remains the most important driver of structural change in the financial services industry. Fig. 5 provides a quick overview of the development of important German and international stock markets in the last two years. Particularly shares of high-tech companies – listed at the Neuer Markt in Germany (NEMAX Index) or at the Nasdaq in the U.S. – have suffered severely as the dotted circles illustrate.

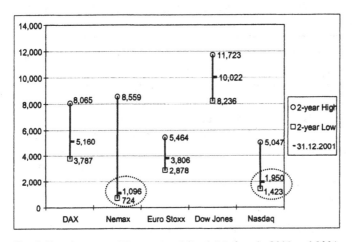

Fig. 5. Development of International Stock Markets in 2000 and 2001

Besides more uniform regulation on an international scope (Sec. 3.1) and dramatic changes in the population pyramids (Sec. 3.2), changes in working life conditions (Sec. 3.3) and the new quality in communication in all its aspects (Sec. 3.4) are the shaping mega-trends for the years to come. Particularly the latter two are

[53] Some parts of this chapter – except Sec. 3.2 and Sec. 3.4.2 – are based on joint research efforts with Hans Ulrich Buhl, Werner Steck, and Andreas Leinfelder. See (Buhl et al. 2000a) for the fundamental paper. For extended versions see (Buhl et al. 2001) and (Buhl et al. 2002). For a discussion of mega-trends in the financial services market with special emphasis on technological developments and an analysis of the financial services market using the concept of Porter's five forces see (Wolfersberger 2002).

fostered by the fast development of IT. In the following sections, these mega-trends will be discussed in more detail to lay the ground for the deduction of a promising strategy for sustainable profitability of a financial services provider in the (Post) Information Age[54]. The main findings are briefly summarized in Sec. 3.5.

3.1 Regulation

> But who would guard the guards themselves?
> JUVENAL

> One of the greatest delusions in the world is the hope
> that the evils in this world are to be cured by legislation.
> THOMAS B. REED

One important development that is not influenced by IT but has also great impact on the financial services sector is (de)regulation. The last couple of years have been characterized by attempts to foster competition in the financial services markets either by breaking up monopolistic structures[55] with deregulation or by harmonizing national laws while setting common standards on a supranational level, particularly in the EU.

The country with the biggest market for financial services, the United States, has seen a major change with the repeal of the *Glass-Steagall Act* in 1999.[56] In fact the passage of the *Gramm-Leach-Bliley Financial Modernization Act* has knocked down walls that divided financial services industries. Thus banks, insurance companies, and Wall Street firms are now able to enter the others' businesses, which was prohibited by the 66-year-old Glass-Steagall Act.[57] The Gramm-Leach-Bliley Act is anticipated to allow for more rational regulation of financial products providers and distributors due to the introduction of a framework for functional regu-

---

[54] Nicloas Negroponte, a researcher with MIT, was one of the shaping authors writing about and describing the move towards an information economy in his seminal book "Being Digital"; see (Negroponte 1995). However, in his book he already talks about the Post Information Age where information is extremely personalized and everything is made to order. The themes of *individualization* and *personalization* will also be a major issue in this contribution.

[55] Deregulation has also been a mega trend in other – formerly monopolistic – sectors such as utilities, aviation, telecommunication. Also see Chap. 21 in (Carlton and Perloff 1994) on partially or totally deregulated industries such as airlines, interstate trucking, and railroads.

[56] Concerning the *geographical expansion* of banks, there has already been a series of removals of restrictions on *intra*state and *inter*state banking in the 1980s and 1990s. See (Berger et al. 1995).

[57] An executive summary of the Gramm-Leach-Bliley Act can be found in (Anonymous 2000a). For a brief history why Glass-Steagall was enacted see (Bennett 2001).

lation of the issuers and distributors of banking, securities, and insurance products. This will not necessarily mean less regulation but it will make the financial services market a level playing field for all firms participating in the market on the one hand and a market with consistent consumer protection on the other hand.[58]

With this development the conditions for American financial services providers are not only the same for firms operating in the U.S. market but also similar to the conditions in the rest of the (relevant) world.[59] By this the entry in foreign markets for U.S.-based companies as well as for firms from the rest of the world in the U.S. is relieved most likely resulting in increased competition.[60]

Turning to German and European legislation[61], particularly in the area of electronic commerce and distance contracts a lot has been done to stimulate competition, protect consumer rights, and to align national laws in order to achieve a single market.

Basically, the *Directive on electronic commerce*[62] lays down the legal framework for free movement and provision of so-called *information society services*[63] throughout the European Union. Especially Article 9 (1) of this directive is to foster consumer confidence in the use of electronic means in order to sign (distance) contracts and allow companies to operate in the whole EU without maintaining a large set of branches. It says "Member States shall ensure that their legal system allows contracts to be concluded by electronic means. Member States shall in particular ensure that the legal requirements applicable to the contractual process nei-

---

[58]   See e.g. (Cain and Fahey 2000).

[59]   "Relevant" in terms of market size, trade volume and GDP. This especially includes countries in the EU, as well as Canada and Japan.

[60]   One of the first deals after the passage of the new legislation was the merger between Charles Schwab Corp. and U.S. Trust Corp., announced on Jan. 13, 2000 and approved by the Federal Reserve Board on May 1, creating a company with client assets totaling $913 billion and net revenues of $4.5 billion.

[61]   Information about European legislation in the area of financial services can be accessed at http://europa.eu.int/comm/internal_market/en/finances/index.htm. In the following, the focus will be on European instead of German legislation, since nowadays (most) German legislation with respect to financial services is just an implementation of EU directives. Due to the fact that the focus of this book is on the private end-customer, legislation such as the "German Control and Transparency in Business Act" ("Gesetz zur Kontrolle und Transparenz in Unternehmen" (KonTraG)) will not be discussed although it will most likely have a great impact on the financial services industry. KonTraG forces corporations to introduce risk controlling on a broad scale in their organizations independent of the market they are operating in. See e.g. (Reitwiesner 2001) and the forthcoming dissertation by (Huther 2003) on innovative integrated performance und risk management concepts. In addition, Basel II, the new capital regime for banks worked on by the Basel committee on Banking Supervision, will not start before 2006; see (Anonymous 2002c).

[62]   Directive 2000/31/EC of the European Parliament and the Council of 8 June 2000.

[63]   Any service normally provided for remuneration, at a distance, by electronic means and at the individual request of a recipient of services. See Directive 98/48/EC of the European Parliament and of the Council of 20 July 1998.

ther create obstacles for the use of electronic contracts nor result in such contracts being deprived of legal effectiveness and validity on account of their having been made by electronic means." The *Directive on electronic commerce* is complemented by the *Directive on the protection of consumers in respect of distance contracts*[64] and the *Directive on injunctions for the protection of consumer interests*[65] passed in 1997 and 1998, respectively.

Along with this framework for online services, the *Directive on a Community framework for electronic signatures*[66] provides a legal recognition of electronically signed documents. In fact, in Germany a *signature law* was passed already back in 1997 to facilitate online trade, at that time being a worldwide pioneer in the field.[67]

Due to the very nature of financial services and their quite diverse regulatory framework in the Member States, financial services have been excluded in the *Directive on the protection on consumers in respect to distance contracts.*[68] Although the *Directive on electronic commerce* is broad in scope it does not take a closer sectoral look into the financial services market. Therefore, the EU has been working for a couple of years to ensure high standards of consumer protection while creating an appropriate framework for the development of electronic commerce in the area of financial services. In 1998 a Directive to establish a clear regulatory framework for the marketing of financial services at a distance within the Single Market was proposed by the European Commission.[69] This proposal was amended in 1999[70] and in late September 2001 found political agreement in the Council of Ministers. Currently, the Council is to adopt its common position on the proposed directive, and will proceed with its final adoption once the European Parliament will have concluded its second reading on the proposal. Thus the deadline 2005 for the creation of an integrated European market in financial services still seems achievable.

Apparently, consumer protection is one of the main issues as the following main features of the proposal reveal:[71]

---

[64]   Directive 1997/7/EC of the European Parliament and the Council of 20 May 1997.

[65]   Directive 1998/27/EC of the European Parliament and the Council of 19 May 1998.

[66]   Directive 1999/93/EC of the European Parliament and the Council of 13 December 1999.

[67]   See e.g. (Engel-Flechsig et al. 2001).

[68]   For instance the right of withdrawal obviously poses some severe problems due to the immaterial or in some cases speculative nature of financial services. For the full four major problems with respect to the inclusion of financial services in Directive 1997/7/EC see the proposal for the distance marketing of consumer financial services from 14.10.1998, COM/98/0468 final – COD 98/0245.

[69]   Proposal for a Directive of the European Parliament and the Council concerning the distance marketing of consumer financial services COM/98/0468 final – COD 98/0245.

[70]   Amended Proposal for a Directive of the European Parliament and the Council concerning the distance marketing of consumer financial services COM/99/0385 final – COD 98/0245.

[71]   See (Muench et al. 2001).

- The prohibition of abusive marketing practices seeking to oblige consumers to buy a service they have not solicited.
- Rules to restrict other practices such as unsolicited phone calls and emails.
- An obligation to provide consumers with comprehensive information before a contract is concluded.
- A consumer right to withdraw from the contract during a cool-off period – except in cases where there is a risk of speculation.

Also strongly affecting transparency and consumer protection in the EU, the *Directive on consumer credits* set a common standard for the calculation of the annual percentage rate of charge.[72,73]

On the institutional side, there are also a number of Directives that have led to a harmonization of banking supervision legislation in the EU. As a result, the legal conditions have been created for the freedom of banking activities and financial services in the single European market. Throughout the EU the same regulations now apply to the authorization and the ongoing supervision of credit and financial services institutions, to the supervision of branches in other EU countries of credit and financial services institutions having their headquarters in an EU country by the competent home country authorities, to the definition of capital, to the consolidated supervision of groups of institutions and financial holding groups, and to large exposures.[74]

---

[72]   Directive 1998/7/EC of the European Parliament and the Council of 16 February 1998. In German national law, the implementation of the directive on 1 September 2000 led to an adaptation of the *Preisangabenverordnung* (PangV).

[73]   The above enumeration of European legislation concerning the financial services market is by no means exhaustive. Directives 2000/28/EC and 2000/46/EC deal with issues related to electronic money. Directive 1997/5/EC deals with cross-border credit transfers. More generally Directives 1995/46/EC and 1997/66/EC are concerned with the protection of individuals with regard to the processing of personal data and the right to privacy in the context of electronic commerce.

[74]   See (Deutsche Bundesbank 2002). Directives include among others Directive 2000/12/EC of 20 March 2000 relating to the taking up and pursuit of the business of credit institutions; Directive 2000/28/EC of 18 September 2000 amending Directive 2000/12/EC; Council Directive 86/635/EEC of 8 December 1986 on the annual accounts and consolidated accounts of banks and other financial institutions; Council Directive 85/611/EEC of 20 December 1985 on the coordination of laws, regulations and administrative provisions relating to undertakings for collective investment in transferable securities (UCITS); Council Directive 88/220/EEC of 22 March 1988 amending, as regards the investment policies of certain UCITS, Directive 85/611/EEC; Council Directive 93/6/EEC of 15 March 1993 on the capital adequacy of investment firms and credit institutions; Directive 98/26/EC of 19 May 1998 on settlement finality in payment and securities settlement systems (this Directive found its implementation in German law in the sixth amending law of the *Banking Act* (*Gesetz über das Kreditwesen* (KWG))).

This evolving level playing field for all financial services firms is complemented by changes in the population pyramid as well as in working life conditions.

3.2 Society Changes[75]

> A growing nation is the greatest Ponzi game ever contrived.
> PAUL SAMUELSON, 1967

There is little doubt in literature and among politicians that pay-as-you-go (PAYG) pensions systems implemented in many countries in the world make little sense at the best of times, and even less in an ageing world. Pensions in the PAYG schemes do not reflect the contributions (plus interest) a person has made and the length of time he is likely to spend in retirement. Basically, such systems tax the income of today's workers and distribute it to today's pensioners.[76] To make things worse, at least most industrialized countries face the problem of an ageing population. Fig. 6 and Fig. 7 illustrate these problems with figures concerning Germany. Not only due to progress in medical treatment resulting in higher life expectancy but also due to a lower, even negative, population growth rate are these problems with ill-designed pension schemes toughened.

---

[75] This section is for the most part based on (Anonymous 2002a) providing an excellent overview of the global challenges and solution approaches with respect to pension schemes. A valuable list of sources used in that survey can be accessed on The Economist's website at http://www.economist.com. For a contribution on the ageing society in Germany and its impact on the financial markets see (Schmidt 2002) and (Heigl 2001).

[76] This unenforceable contract between the workers and the pensioners is often referred to as the *Generation Contract*.

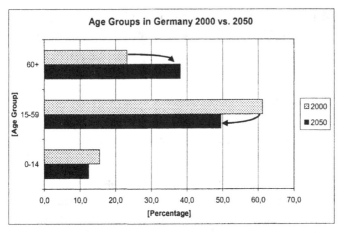

Fig. 6. Age Groups in Germany, Changes between 2000 and 2050[77]

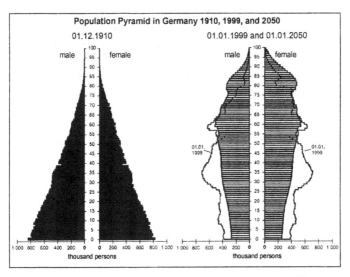

Fig. 7. Population Pyramid in Germany 1910, 1999, and 2050[78]

Taking the figures from Fig. 6, the ratio of those aged over 60 to those aged 15-59 will halve over the next 50 years from 2.6 to 1.3. In result to keep pensions in real terms on the same level as today, this would require either a strong cut in benefits or contribution rates – which are currently already quite high at 19.1% in Germany – must significantly go up. Finally, retirement age could go up extending the phase of contributions in the system for each individual while cutting the phase of pension payments.

---

[77] Figures taken from the United Nations Population Division, Department of Economic and Social Affairs (DESA) accessible at http://www.un.org/popin/wdtrends.htm.

[78] The graphs are taken from (Statistisches Bundesamt 2000).

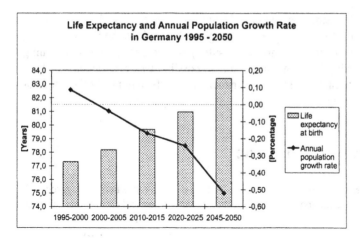

Fig. 8. Life Expectancy at Birth and Annual Population Growth Rate in Germany between 1995 and 2050[79]

Further focusing on Germany, a trend to escape this system has been observable in the last decades. For instance the self-employed are not forced to pay into the PAYG system and in fact the proportion of self-employed people making discretionary contributions fell from 60% in the mid-1980s to 20% in the mid-1990s.

Though many countries, including Germany, have recognized the strong need for reforms in this area, these reforms generally may not be able to accomplish a rapid switch from PAYG schemes to funded-only systems, i.e. so-called *defined contribution* (DC) schemes. There a link between what people put in and what they get out is made explicit. In a possible transition phase the trade-off is not to put too much burden on the younger generation, which has to pay for today's pensioners and accumulate assets for their own retirement. But it is not to cut too much into the pensions of today's and tomorrow's pensioners either, who have contributed to the system during their whole working life and who should receive at least something adequate in return during their retirement. Neither can public borrowing in order to bridge and smooth that gap be a solution in the long run.[80]

It is not the objective here to propose new reforms or adjustments to reforms already in place but to deduce the need for careful retirement planning for most customers of financial services providers. Even with the German reform efforts there will still remain a high proportion of workers, employees and self-employed persons that may not be able to cover their expenses after their retirement by solely relying on public pensions and the newly introduced state-supported private pension scheme (the so-called *Riester-Rente*, named after the current minister of labor and social affairs Walter Riester). The reform also offers opportunities for finan-

---

[79] Figures taken from the United Nations Population Division, Department of Economic and Social Affairs (DESA). Accessible at http://www.un.org/popin/wdtrends.htm

[80] Without a reform, by 2020 a majority of the current 15 EU states would be downgraded drastically to BBB due to an enormous debt build-up.

cial services providers since people have been more sensitized with respect to retirement planning due to the vast press coverage of this topic in the last months.

Not only is there a need for financial consulting in terms of retirement planning but changes in working life conditions – made possible by developments in IT – also contribute to the fact that standard financial products may not fit the needs of current and forthcoming generations.

3.3 Working Life Conditions

> The new economy is a molecular economy. The old corporation is being disaggregated, and replaced by dynamic molecules and clusters of individuals and entities that form the basis of new economic activity.
> DON TAPSCOTT

After the defeat of the traditional economics of information[81] temporary organizations formed by specialized units that are connected by standardized (Internet) communication channels have become possible. These virtual organizations are set together as parts of the former value chain creating new *value networks* by heavy use of (traditionally prohibitively expensive) communication systems and by this become able to better match the demand of the markets. The breakup of the hierarchical organizations brings firms both opportunities and threats. It "foster(s) entrepreneurship and encourage(s) firms and individuals to exploit new opportunities and move into high value-added activities."[82]

Since the beginning of the 90s, there has been a lot of research on this issue. (Rockart and Short 1991) describe the networked organization where all participants are linked. In result, this allows firms in such an organization to flexibly reorganize itself around each new task (Baker 1992).[83] A very interesting feature of this new form of organization is the fact that it extends beyond the boundaries of individual firms to form a wider network of multiple organizations.[84] At the extreme, the network model can be applied to a market of networked "organizations of one"[85], a virtual organization[86,87]. The virtual organization is a set of loosely

---

81   See (Evans and Wurster 1997).

82   See (OECD 1998).

83   Also see (Ancona et al. 1999) who describe the "new" model of the organization with five complex, interacting features: networked, flat, flexible, diverse, and global. (Drucker 1990) talks in this context of modular, highly flexible "flotilla" organizations.

84   See (Malone and Laubacher 1998). Also see (Wigand et al. 1997) give a very nice overview of the organizational changes due to new means of communication with respect to management issues.

85   (Malone and Laubacher 1998).

86   See (Davidow and Malone 1992). On *virtual organizations* also see (Mertens et al. 1998), (Arnold et al. 1995), (Mertens and Faisst 1995).

87   (Laubacher and Malone 1997) describe their vision of two alternative scenarios for the future: "Small Companies, Large Networks" and "Virtual Countries".

coupled, self-organizing networked individuals in geographically dispersed locations. Individuals come together pooling their resources to accomplish a specific task or project and may dissolve the group upon task completion. Thus virtual organizations are considered to be more "spider webs" rather than networks.[88,89]

In result, on the one hand the creation of virtual organizations or "hyperarchies"[90] allows firms to react faster to market changes by recreating virtual value networks. On the other hand – and this is the more important issue in the context of this book – there are impacts of this new organizational form on the ways of working and employment. There is a visible trend that a lot of the members of these virtual companies are freelancers[91] who are specialist in one or more parts of the value network. (Malone and Laubacher 1998) propose the emergence of an "e-lance" economy.[92]

The use of IT offers the opportunity to coordinate these specialized parts and form a "best-of-everything" value network and by this enables companies to provide an improved solution for customers. The possibility of the fast exchange of the players in this network also allows for a more flexible adaptation to changing market and customer needs. However, the income of this group might vary in a wide range. On the low-end there might be a group that is not even able to afford health insurance.[93] On the high-end people will earn so much money that they are interested in large financial investments and possible tax savings. Still there is one thing that all of these freelancers have in common: They are not living in the world of regular income and constant cash flows any longer. In combination this means that in the future there will be an increasing number of customers that do

---

[88] See (Wigand et al. 1997). Also see (Salmons and Babitsky 2002) for a more radical argument for what they call "Small Is Good Business Webs".

[89] On *virtual organizations* also see Sec. 2.2.

[90] See (Evans and Wurster 1997).

[91] See (Abby 1999). This generation of freelancers is often referred to as *Generation Y*. See e.g. (Daum 2000).

[92] (Malone and Laubacher 1998) focus in their HBR case study on this new kind of organization and people working in such organizations. "In the future, as communication technologies advance and networks become more efficient, the shift to e-lancers promises to accelerate. Should that indeed take place, the dominant business organization of the future may not be a permanent corporation but rather an elastic network that may sometimes exist for no more than a day or two." Also see (Tapscott et al. 2000) who focus on the emergence of *business webs*, or *b-webs*. These are fluid collaborations of businesses that come together loosely or in highly structured networks to accomplish shared agendas. The Economist titled in this context "The end of jobs for life?"; see (Anonymous 1998c).

[93] See (Abby 1999).

not fit the standardized financial products and services of today, which are usually designed to fit to constant monthly income streams.[94]

This trend towards an *income lifecycle* that does not correspond to the income and asset growth of a lifetime typical after World War II is reinforced by another foreseeable development. The number of people who will inherit a lot of money from their ancestors is growing tremendously. For example in Germany the value of money that will be shifted from one generation to the next will rise from 52 billion Euros in 1987 to 212 billion Euros in 2002. The average amount of money being shifted will increase from 102,000 Euro in 1990 to 241,000 Euro in 2002.[95] Fig. 9 shows the estimated development of the total value of inheritances per year in Germany from 1990 until 2002. According to BBE consulting, in the next 5 years roughly 0.8 trillion Euro will be bequeathed. Along with this change of generation comes a change in investment mentality. The younger inheritance generation consumes more and is less risk-averse compared to the postwar generation.[96]

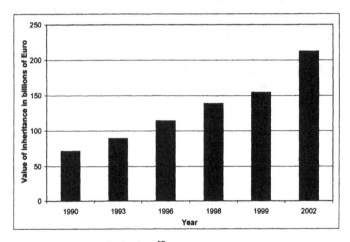

Fig. 9. Generation of Inheritors[97]

In addition 320.000 owners of privately held companies looked and will look, respectively, for a successor between 1999 and 2004. In roughly a quarter of these cases, the succession will be managed by sale.[98] In result, the successor may need an unusual amount of money at a specific point in time (*financing problem*), whereas the seller receives an unusual amount of money at a specific point in

---

[94] (Laubacher and Malone 1997) also come to the conclusion in their visionary contribution that regardless of the scenario that turns out to become reality, both scenarios potentially might work to "exaggerate already existing tendencies toward polarization of income and wealth in society as a whole and winner-take-all outcomes in particular industries and professions".

[95] (Anonymous 1998a).

[96] (Anonymous 2001b).

[97] Figures taken from (BBE Unternehmensberatung 2001).

[98] See (BBE Unternehmensberatung 2001).

time, with which he often has to manage retirement planning for his family and himself (*asset allocation problem*).

This means that there will be a lot of people facing the "problem" to decide at one time what to do with an amount of money they normally would have to work a long part of their life for. This also seems to indicate that there is a growing number of people who have a demand for financial services, that do not require constant income streams. Instead these people need sophisticated solutions that allow them to handle "unusual" amounts of money at one point in time.

But IT is not only an enabler for these new organizational forms and the possible emergence of an "e-lance" economy but has also more fundamental impacts on markets particularly in terms of efficiency.

3.4 New Quality in Communication

> It is a power that is revolutionizing equities trading, a power likely to
> spread into core investment banking, in the process stripping away
> the inefficiencies previously integral to the financial system.
> EUROMONEY 1991

A lot has been written about new means of communication along with fast evolving technologies[99]. In the following, firstly, a brief recap of these new opportunities is provided. Secondly, to grasp the impacts of these developments on consumer behavior and (electronic) market outcomes a formal search cost model is presented. The model is supported by empirical evidence.

3.4.1 Overview

> The person who succeeds will be the person with the best information.
> DISRAELI

To begin with the technical or hardware side of this development, the miniaturization of devices on all levels, especially of transistors in microelectronics has led to a dramatic decline in prices on the one hand for computers and mobile devices and on the other hand to a distribution and interconnection of these devices on a tremendous scale. When talking about trends, it is certainly worthwhile looking back and examining developments in the past. However, the interesting question is what the future will look like.[100] Has the miniaturization of devices come to a natural end or is there still enough potential for significant improvements? Indeed, it seems that even the last years have brought such tremendous improvements in the price/performance ratio, this trend is very likely to continue.

---

[99] See e.g. (Evans and Wurster 1997), (Wolfersberger 2002) and references therein.

[100] Sometimes the past may be a good proxy for developments in the future. Often past data is extrapolated to predict the future.

According to *Moore's Law*, computing power doubles every 18 months with cost of production staying constant. In 1965 Gordon Moore, co-founder of Intel Corp., predicted that the density of transistors in an integrated circuit would double each year (later changed to 18 months). Moore's Law has proven remarkably accurate for over three decades not only for transistor density but also for microprocessor performance.[101] The International Technology Roadmap for Semiconductors of the Semiconductor Industry Association predicts this trend to continue for at least another 15 to 18 years.[102]

Along with this predicted miniaturization, a doubling of the number of PCs from 521 million in 2000 to 1008 million in 2005 is estimated.[103] Not only the number of PCs will increase considerably in the forthcoming years but also the number of interconnections between these PCs.[104]

Unsurprisingly, also the number of Internet users is predicted to still rise in the future (Fig. 10 and Fig. 11 show some historical data). Researches with eMarketer come to the conclusion in their recent eGlobal Report[105] that though the U.S. and Scandinavian countries are maturing in terms of Internet users, other regions, previously a little bit behind, will catch up sharply. They conclude that there are 446 million Internet users as of January 2002 and predict this number to rise to 709 million in 2004.

---

[101]   See e.g. (Stam 1999).

[102]   Access ITRS-website for up-to-date information on trends in the semiconductor industry at http://public.itrs.net/Home.htm. For the two main problems – the so-called *cooking problem* and *spaghetti problem* – concerning the ongoing miniaturization see (Vitányi 2001).

[103]   See (NFO Infratest 2001a). For Germany an increase from 40 PCs per 100 citizens in 2002 to 61 PCs per 100 citizens is predicted.

[104]   Between July 1999 and November 2000 the number of Internet users more than doubled. See (Robben 2001) and (NFO Infratest 2001b) for more detailed information. On February 5, 2002, the U.S. Commerce Department reported that 54% of the national population (143 million) had been using the Internet as of September 2001; see (U.S. Department of Commerce 2002).

[105]   See (eMarketer 2002).

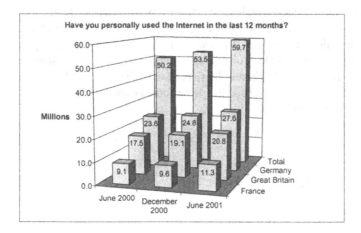

Fig. 10. Internet Users in Germany, Great Britain, and France[106]

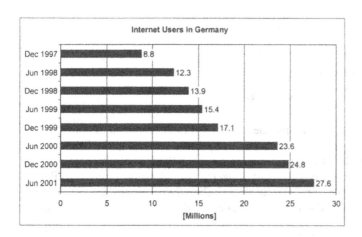

Fig. 11. Internet Users in Germany

Standardized protocols on higher layers of the ISO/OSI model such as SMTP for email or HTTP for the websites allow to perform a wide range of communication tasks. Thus turning to the financial services market, the Internet enables non-face-to-face communication not only adequate for "basic" financial services like managing a current account or a stock order. It also supports complex consultations in order to generate high-level solutions for financial problems like real estate financing. At the same time a huge number of people can be reached at nearly no cost. "The rapid emergence of universal standards for communication (is) allowing everybody to communicate with everybody else at essentially zero cost."[107]

---

[106]   See (NFO Infratest 2001b).
[107]   (Evans and Wurster 1997).

Particularly evolving common standards of data exchange such as XML and rich Internet services such as SMTP or HTTP enable a cost-efficient way of information search, selection, and transport as well as high level communication.[108] So with the Internet the former trade-off between richness and reach of communication has vanished (see Fig. 12)[109] Former barriers of entry like a set of branches or a big sales force that took years to establish were forced down by this to a few months and to much less investment.

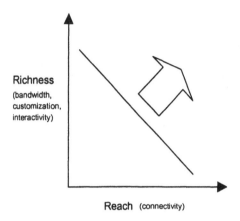

Reach (connectivity)

Fig. 12. Trade-off between Richness and Reach[110]

Consequently a lot of new intermediaries used their chance to establish purely web-based and thus relatively cheap and competitive services in the financial service business. On the one hand firms highly specialized in certain products and services like the so-called *discount brokers*, e.g. globally acting E*TRADE (http://www.etrade.com) or DAB bank AG (http://www.diraba.de), and on the other hand direct banks, e.g. the United States NetBank (http://www.netbank.com)

---

[108] The means of communication already enable universities to offer complete virtual bachelor and master degrees (Greco 1999). A prominent example of a for-profit Internet education provider is the University of Phoenix Online with 25,700 students enrolled in degree programs at the end of May 2001. Also top universities such as Harvard, MIT, and Stanford extend their offerings in the online education market. Moreover, corporations have begun to embrace technology for learning. It is estimated that in 2000 10% of all corporate learning took place on computers. This figure is predicted to reach 50% in 2003 (Bylinsky 2000). For the German e-learning market, especially in the IS online education area, prominent examples include the "Virtual Global University , School of Business Informatics" (http://www.vg-u.de, founded 2001) and "Virtuelle Aus- & Weiterbildung Wirtschaftsinformatik" (http://www.vawi.de, founded 2001). Moreover, the offerings of the Bavarian initative "Virtuelle Hochschule Bayern" (http://www.vhb.org, founded 2000) are one important step in the direction of e-learning.

[109] (Evans and Wurster 1997).

[110] See (Evans and Wurster 1997).

or the German Advance Bank (http://www.advance-bank.de)[111], have been founded. A sharp rise in competition,[112] especially in the field of online-brokerage where costs were cut dramatically is the impressive result of the new possibilities described above. Not only in this area but in many fields of banking and insurance, have web-based solutions been established and turn past investments of traditional financial services providers into expensive liabilities and by this into competitive disadvantages. In addition these web-based companies reduce returns for traditional banks by only targeting special and interesting customer segments. This switching of customers to the web-based companies is supported by an astonishing lack of quality in consultation by the established players.[113]

Along with the ongoing pervasiveness of the Internet and the ongoing virtualization and digitization, markets are undergoing a fundamental shift. Enabled by advances in technology and means of communication, electronic market or electronic marketplaces have been emerging very fast. A high market efficiency on the one hand has a positive impact on consumer surplus and on the other hand a negative effect on suppliers' profits due to shrinking margins, thus increasing social welfare.[114] Therefore the impact of emerging electronic markets on market efficiency has been a major research issue in recent years.[115] This will be discussed in the next section.

---

[111] In fact, launched on March 1996 as a pure Internet player, Advance Bank has started to open so-called *Investment Centers* in major German cities since mid 2001 and cannot be called a pure direct bank anymore.

[112] See e.g. (Rhodes et al. 1999) who emphasize that even though the market shares of these newcomers are still comparably small, "the impact of these newcomers on margins has been significant." The ECB reports a downward trend – particularly for Germany – in banks' lending margins and attributes this trend – among other reasons – to new entries into banking; see (European Central Bank 2000a).

[113] In fact, the quality of financial advice has been poor for a number of years as several studies regularly reveal. See e.g. (Rehkugler et al. 1992), (Anonymous 1995, 1997a, 2000b, 2000c, 2001e). Tenhagen, editor-in-chief FINANZtest, comes to the distressing conclusion that the quality of advice has even diminished since 1997; see (Tenhagen 2000). On *self assessment techniques* to increase service quality see e.g. (Barton 2001).

[114] On the concept of *social welfare* see e.g. (Train 1991), (Samuelson and Nordhaus 1998).

[115] See e.g. (Bakos 1991, 1998).

3.4.2 Increasing Market Efficiency

> The web costs you nothing, and that price may sometimes overstate its value.
> But there are many diamonds buried in the mountains of bits.
> PAUL A. SAMUELSON, WILLIAM D. NORDHAUS

One of the most cited reasons why *electronic* markets are expected to be more efficient than *conventional* markets is a reduction in information asymmetries between a seller and a potential buyer due to lower search cost.[116,117] Economic theory predicts that (high) consumer search cost will lead to prices above marginal cost in equilibrium.[118] If electronic markets allow consumers to more easily determine retailers' prices and product offerings, these lower search cost will lead to lower prices for both homogeneous and differentiated goods.[119] There are four dimensions of Internet market efficiency that can be distinguished:[120]

- *Price level*: Are the prices charged on the Internet lower?
- *Price elasticity*: Are consumers more sensitive to small price changes on the Internet?
- *Menu costs*: Do retailers adjust their prices more finely and more frequently on the Internet?
- *Price dispersion*: Is there a smaller spread between the highest and lowest price on the Internet?

Early research suggests that electronic markets are more efficient than conventional markets with respect to price levels[121], menu costs, and price elasticity. At the same time, several studies find significant price dispersion in Internet markets. This price dispersion may be explained by heterogeneity in retailer-specific factors

---

[116] The standard definition of buyer search cost in the economic literature as the cost incurred by the buyer to locate an appropriate seller and purchase a product is adopted here. This includes the opportunity cost of time spent surfing as well as associated expenditures such as telephone fees, online fees, etc.

[117] Note that there is a significant difference in distances between stores and the consumer in physical markets and electronic markets. While point of sales in physical markets may be at different distances, two online stores seem to be / are level for a specific user. Physical distances will not be an issue in this text. Interested readers are referred to (Domschke and Drexl 1996) for warehouse location problems in physical markets. For a transfer of warehouse location problems in the virtual world see e.g. (Frank et al. 2000).

[118] See e.g. (Stigler 1961), (Diamond 1971) and references later in this section.

[119] (Bakos 1997).

[120] See e.g. (Smith et al. 2000).

[121] In contrast e.g. (Lee 1998) presents empirical evidence that the prices of goods traded through electronic marketplaces may be actually higher than those of products sold in traditional markets.

such as branding and trust, retailer efforts to build consumer lock-in, and various retailer price discrimination strategies.

For instance (Brynjolfsson and Smith 2000) find that prices on the Internet for the commodity products like books and CDs are 9 to 16% lower than prices in conventional outlets. They "conclude that while there is lower friction in many dimensions of Internet competition, branding, awareness, and trust remain important sources of heterogeneity among Internet retailers." (Brown and Goolsbee 2000) seem to be the only ones to have analyzed the efficiency effects of emerging electronic commodity markets with respect to financial services. They provide empirical evidence that Internet comparison shopping in the life insurance industry had reduced term life prices by 8 to 15% from 1995 - 1997. Interestingly, they also find that the initial introduction of Internet search sites is initially associated with an increase in price dispersion whereas dispersion falls with the share of people using the technology rising.

Before getting into more detail it is important to be very precise about the products in focus. Products and services can usually be described by three different attributes:[122]

- *Search qualities* are attributes that potential buyers can determine prior to purchase such as price and quality.
- *Experience qualities* are attributes determined only after or during consumption.
- *Credence qualities* are intangible attributes that a potential buyer may be unable to determine even after purchase and consumption.

Hardly any financial service can be found that does not possess some characteristics of all of the above attributes. However, in most cases, either the search or the credence qualities prevail considering a specific financial service. Examples for financial services with search qualities include all kinds of (highly) standardized products, such as home mortgage loans, stock orders, time or fixed-term deposits, life insurance. Many of these standardized products also contain experience qualities. For instance a mortgage loan may be purchased based on search qualities such as the internal rate of return. The customer experiences the product after the purchase in so far that he can see the loan payout on his statement of bank account. Financial services possess credence qualities whenever it comes to consulting services, such as retirement planning or – in a broader context – financial planning.

Generally, some sort of consulting service has to be called on before financial products are bought. Particularly in the domain of standardized financial services, dramatically shrinking margins have been observed in recent years. In the following a search cost model is presented that may be used to explain some of the ob-

---

[122] See e.g. (Kulkarni 2000), (Lehmann 1998). Nice examples for the different qualities with respect to financial services can be found in (Roemer 1998). The categorization in *search* and *experience qualities* is originally due to (Nelson 1970), *credence qualities* were added by (Darby and Karni 1973).

servable tendencies in the financial services markets with respect to shrinking margins. It all has to do with information.

3.4.2.1 Literature Review

Prior to the seminal paper by (Stigler 1961) on the economics of information, economic models assumed perfectly informed customers or implicitly a costless information process for both the supplier and for the potential consumer.[123] In such a setting without capacity constraints on commodity markets, the standard economic *Bertrand model* suggests that the price will be driven down to marginal cost independent of the number of firms.[124] This market outcome is generally referred to as the *Bertrand Paradox*.[125] In the context of traditional theory this setting includes the predictions that a given commodity is sold at the same price by all stores (*Law of the Single Price*) and that differences in price just reflect differences in the quality of a product.[126] Introducing a costly search process to this scenario yields the so-called *Diamond Paradox*, where firms paradoxically will set monopoly prices in equilibrium independent of the number of firms, and consumers will not search.[127] This shows impressively how sensitive the conclusions of the traditional paradigm are to its assumptions concerning information.[128]

In contrast, Stigler (initially) takes price dispersion as given and analyzes the behavior of an imperfectly informed consumer interested in buying a homogeneous product, i.e. a product sufficiently described by its price and therefore just having search qualities. Based on this model, Stigler derives a number of interesting hypotheses suggesting that search activity is driven by both cost and benefit factors.[129]

- There is an inverse relationship between the optimal amount of search and the cost of search in terms of the consumer's opportunity cost of time, the cost to the individual of processing new market information, and other direct search related costs such as transportation.

---

[123] This is quite a noteworthy point, since it is not only the buyer who bears uncertainty about price and quality of products and services but also the seller who does not know whether the buyer will be able to pay the bill or exhibit other opportunistic behavior. Most models do not account for this information asymmetry on the side of the seller.

[124] See (Bertrand 1883). (Anderson and Renault 1999) point out that the credits for this finding on equilibrium prices should go to Fauveau since he published a paper on that topic some 16 years earlier.

[125] See e.g. (Tirole 1988).

[126] See e.g. (Stiglitz 1989).

[127] See (Diamond 1971). (Anderson and Renault 1999) bridge the gap between the two limit cases *Bertrand Paradox* and *Diamond Paradox* with a search cost model.

[128] See (Stiglitz 1989). Stiglitz discusses three paradoxes. The double paradox due to (Diamond 1971) and the paradox that no equilibrium exists if all individuals face strict positive search costs for all searches. This paradox is due to (Salop and Stiglitz 1977, 1982).

[129] Also see (Wilde 1980), (Avery 1996).

- Either greater dispersion of prices or greater expenditure on the commodity will lead to more search.

Based on and extending Stigler's model a wide range of research on consumer search behavior has been conducted.[130] (Anderson and Renault 1999), (Will 1999), (Burdett and Coles 1995), (Stahl 1989), and (Salop and Stiglitz 1982) all deal with price dispersion as an equilibrium outcome that can be explained by the costly search of information. (Davis and Holt 1996) test the conclusions of Diamond's Paradox and (Bakos 1997) examines the role of buyer search costs in markets with differentiated product offerings. (Steck and Will 1998) identify action consequences for suppliers in electronic markets due to changing consumer behavior that is attributable to a change in search costs. (Salop and Stiglitz 1977) address the problem of heterogeneity of consumer rationality in the context of a costly information gathering. One of the few works dealing with financial services and search costs include (Calomiris 1995) who qualitatively uses search cost theory to explain above marginal cost pricing in the retail banking market and proposes a decline in margins with the introduction of new services such as home banking.

In the context of the financial services market, it is assumed in the following that a potential consumer has already identified the product he likes – for instance by getting advice from a financial consultant or by self-consulting with tools provided on the Internet – and is now looking for the lowest price. Thus along with Diamond's model, the search process to find a *product* he likes is excluded here.

In some instances, this might be a quite realistic assumption. In the mortgage loan market, many people already know that they are looking for the least expensive standard annuity loan, hence they already know the product they are looking for in order to finance the purchase of a house.[131]

3.4.2.2 Search Cost Model[132]

Similar to searches in traditional markets, online searches can be carried out either sequentially or simultaneously. Surfing through different web stores evaluating products and prices is a sequential search; a price search based on a price database is an example of a simultaneous search.[133] Ideally a search result of a simultaneous search looks like a table where all the relevant information is gathered, compressed and structured, and the consumer may directly decide to buy the least expensive product upon the search result by a single mouse click. As the Internet be-

---

[130] For excellent general overviews on search theory see e.g. (Diamond 1989), (Hey 1981), and (Stiglitz 1989). For an overview on consumer's search for information with special respect to electronic commerce and search market efficiency see Chap. 7 of (Whinston et al. 1997).

[131] In fact, (Kundisch 2001c, 2002a) could show that in most instances, the decision for the mortgage loan with the lowest internal rate of return will be optimal for the private customer with respect to the net present value after tax, if he does not want to rent out the house or apartment.

[132] This section is based on the model developed in (Kundisch 2000).

[133] See e.g. (Whinston et al. 1997).

comes more and more pervasive, search costs studies have recently experienced a renaissance. Search costs have been dropping dramatically since physical distances have become much less relevant in net markets. A number of reasons contribute to decreasing search costs:[134]

- Traditional regional markets often contained products that were untraceable for the customer. These products can now be found in the electronic market.
- New suppliers of already known products can be found.[135]
- The data provided by online stores and intermediaries are generally accessible more quickly, richer in content, and more up-to-date.

Hence, more products can be found much faster compared to physical markets. The shift from a traditional market to an electronic market is not only complemented by a sharp drop in search costs, but also a trend towards declining search costs in electronic markets is observable.

- The telecommunication markets in many countries have become more liberalized (e.g. in the EU) resulting in decreasing prices. Moreover there is high competition for online users among the ISPs leading to declining access fees[136] (see Fig. 13 and Fig. 14).
- Prices for computers and processing power, respectively, have fallen dramatically in the last decades.[137]
- Fast and dynamically emerging Internet-based technologies facilitate the decrease of search costs. On the one hand search engines, either generic (like Google), hierarchical directories (like Yahoo!), or domain-specific tools (like PlanetHome for the mortgage loan market) and on the other hand intelligent agents keep lowering buyers' search costs.[138]

---

[134] See e.g. (Bakos 1997, 1998), (Steck and Will 1999).

[135] See especially (Steck and Will 1998) for a nice graphical illustration of this fact.

[136] On 09/01/2002 a number of ISPs in the U.S. offering free access to the Internet, such as Address.com, DotNow, Juno, and NetZero could be found. In Germany, prices for online connections have also fallen significantly in the last years. Currently there are (regional) suppliers of flat rates (such as M''net) in the market offering access to the Internet for 12.90 Euro/month. Call-by-call rates are well below 1Ct./minute. See e.g. http://www. preisauskunft.de or http://www.onlinekosten.de for up-to-date prices.

[137] See Sec. 3.4.1.

[138] Popular examples for already existing search agents include comparison shopping sites with respect to various product categories such as Dealtime (http://www.dealtime.com), mySimon (http://www.mysimon.com) PriceSCAN.com (http://www.pricescan.com), smartshop.com (http://www.smartshop.com). With regard to the financial services market popular examples in Germany include planethome (http://www.planethome.de; home mortgage lending), Discountbroker (http://www.discountbroker.de; brokerage) and einsurance (http://www.einsurance.de; insurance). See (Kundisch et al. 2001d) for more comparison shopping sites in the financial services industry. For different examples also see (Bakos 1998).

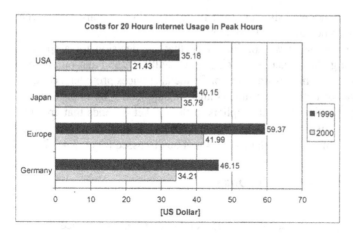

Fig. 13. Decline in Costs of Internet Usage[139]

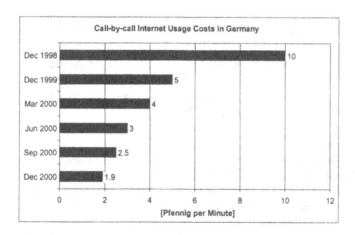

Fig. 14. Development Call-by-Call Costs in Germany[140]

According to (Drucker 1999) the financial services industry's products have become commodities during the last three decades. Thus a simple search cost model shall suffice here to analyze consumer behavior and its implications on market outcomes in the financial services market. (Shy 1997) examined the strategy of consumers searching sequentially in such a commodity market[141] and determined the expected number of store visits until a customer will buy a product. Here, while allowing for more flexibility, a model is developed building upon and extending the work of (Shy 1997) by combining the sequential search model with

---

[139] Figures taken from (NFO Infratest 2001a).

[140] Own graph, figures are taken from (NFO Infratest 2001a).

[141] In the following, such a market will be referred to as a *sequential search market*. Accordingly, a market where consumers search simultaneously will be referred to as a *simultaneous search market*.

a simultaneous search model[142] allowing for a full examination of consumer search behavior in an (electronic) commodity market.

In the following section, it will be illustrated that the decision for a specific search method has a great impact on which product will be found and purchased. As this is certainly interesting information for financial services providers, conclusions will be drawn for both the consumers and the suppliers. The impact of decreasing search costs and additional suppliers in the market – trends that are currently observable on the Internet – on search behavior will also be identified. Consequently, some limitations of the analysis will be discussed (Sect. 3.4.2.7).

3.4.2.3   Model and Its Assumptions

(AP) *Product*
The offered product is homogeneous and sufficiently described by its price.

(AM) *Market*
In an electronic market there are n financial services providers selling a homogeneous product. With no loss of generality[143], it is assumed that the price charged by each financial services provider of type i, $i = c, c+1, ..., e$ with $0 \leq c \leq e < \infty$ and $n = (e - c + 1)$, is $p_i = i$. That is for example a financial services provider of type 3 charges $p_3 = 3$. Note that for the case when $c = 0$ there is also a financial services provider of type 0 that charges $p_0 = 0$. Prices are exogenously given, and financial services providers do not change prices.[144]

(AC) *Consumer*
The risk-neutral consumer knows the range and the probability distribution of the prices but does not know which price is charged by a particular financial services provider.[145] That is, the consumer knows that in the market there are n prices in the range of $p = c, c+1, ..., e$ and the probability to find a store i is $1/n$ but he does not know the exact price offered by each individual financial services provider. The consumer can decide to search simultaneously or sequentially. If he decides to

---

[142] Thus addressing the identified limitation of pure sequential search model by e.g. (Weitzman 1979).

[143] A known range and probability distribution of the prices is assumed to simplify the analysis. (Rothschild 1975) has shown that in many cases the qualitative characteristics of optimal search strategies with known distribution of prices are equal to those where the customer at first knows nothing about the distribution of prices but learns during his search about it. Note that the observations in a sampling process with known distribution are uninformative (Telser 1973). For models with unknown probability distribution see e.g. (Telser 1973), (Kohn and Shavell 1974).

[144] The price determination process of online stores is not analyzed; store prices are taken to be given. Thus the source of noise is exogenous.

[145] Thus the model represents the static case, where the sampling takes place from a mutually independent and identically distributed population with known distribution. Any search problem not of this type is called adaptive. See e.g. (Kohn and Shavell 1974).

search simultaneously he will bear a constant search cost (including possible fees from the search agent) of $\alpha_{si} > 0$ per search. If he decides to search sequentially he will bear a constant search cost of $\alpha_{se} > 0$ for each time he visits a financial services provider.[146]

(AD) *Decision Rule*
The consumer will opt for the search method with the lowest expected total cost, that is the expected costs for the search and the expected product price.

(AE) *New Market Entrants*
New market entrants can either charge a lower price than financial services provider c or a higher price than financial services provider e.

The range of the prices can be graphically illustrated in Fig. 15. In this example the lowest price is $p_c = 0$.

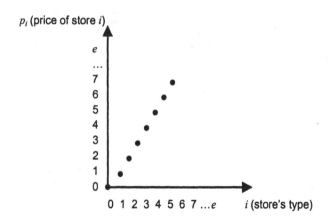

Fig. 15. Supplier Prices and Store Distribution[147]

Zero prices are a phenomenon that can often be observed on electronic markets concerning *digital products*. Some rational reasons for this pricing behavior are listed below.

- First, a supplier can decide to generate his revenues from online advertisements (paid banners or paid links) rather than charging the consumer himself.[148]
- Second, a supplier aims to utilize the lock-in effect, hence providing his digital product for free. Besides domain independent products such as the freely distributed Acrobat Reader, one example in the domain of financial services is the free distribution of HBCI home banking software by LBBW for a limited time.

---

[146] The opportunity for *recall* is not provided for in the model (see Fig. 16).
[147] See (Shy 1997), modified.
[148] See (Skiera and Lambrecht 2000) for generic business models on the Internet.

- Third, in order to become well-known a new supplier in the market might provide his digital product for a limited period for free.
- Fourth and in the context of financial services most important, marginal cost of digital products approach zero, excluding any copyright duties. Hence, suppliers may charge some kind of subscription or other fixed fee to cover their high fixed costs but nothing for the product or service.

To summarize, the consumer knows the range and probability distribution of the prices and will calculate the expected total costs before starting to search. He will opt for that search method that leads to the lowest possible total cost. This scenario can be visualized in Fig. 16.

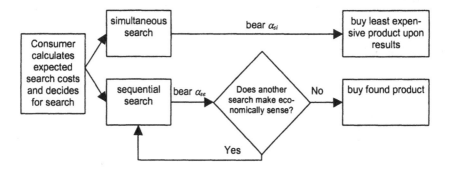

Fig. 16. Consumer Search for Homogeneous Products

In a first step the sequential search will be examined in more detail (Sect. 3.4.2.4). In a second step the expected costs for a simultaneous search will be the center of interest (Sect. 3.4.2.5). Consequently both approaches will be combined in Sect. 3.4.2.6.

3.4.2.4 Sequential Search

Suppose a consumer has decided to search sequentially, how can he determine when to stop the search process with a price offer p_i in hand? In a sequential search the consumer has a strict *sunk cost perspective*. This means a consumer will never look back and stop his search because of the loss caused by several searches in the past. Each time he visits a financial services provider and gets the price information p_i, he calculates the expected price reduction from visiting one additional financial services provider and compares this with his search cost α_{se}.

Since by assumption the consumer knows the prices (Assumption (AC)) and each price is realized with probability $1/n$[149], the expected reduction epr is

$$epr(p_i) = \frac{(p_i - p_c) \cdot ((p_i - p_c) + 1)}{2 \cdot n}. \tag{3.1}$$

If the consumer concludes the search by buying the product, then his "loss" is p_i. In contrast, if he rejects the price offer and searches one more time, then the expected loss is the sum of an additional search cost α_{se}, plus the current price offer, minus his expected gain from searching one more time. Formally, the consumer with an offer p_i in hand minimizes

$$L(p_i) = \begin{cases} p_i & \text{if he buys and pays } p_i \\ \alpha_{se} + p_i - epr(p_i) & \text{if he searches one more time .} \end{cases} \tag{3.2}$$

Thus a consumer continues searching if and only if the price in hand p_i satisfies $epr(p_i) > \alpha_{se}$. This is called a *reservation-price strategy*[150,151].

The reservation price $\bar{p}$ represents that price when the consumer is indifferent whether to afford another search or just buy the product with the price offer p_i in hand. Formally, by solving the equation $\alpha_{se} = epr(p_i)$ for p_i, the reservation price is

$$\bar{p} = p_c + \frac{-1 + \sqrt{1 + 8 \cdot \alpha_{se} \cdot n}}{2}. \tag{3.3}$$

Proposition 1: In a sequential search market both new less expensive suppliers and declining search costs will increasingly drive more expensive established suppliers out of the market.

---

[149] If the consumer keeps track of the stores he has already visited, this probability will change as the search progresses. The probability would be $1/(n-k)$ where k is the number of stores already visited. For the sake of simplicity in the presented model, it is assumed that the customer does not keep track of his store visits. In fact, on the Internet, this assumption is not far from reality, since there may be different domain names all belonging to the same financial services provider. Hence, even if the consumer kept track of his store visits he might find the same store again using a different domain.

[150] Also see e.g. (McCall 1965).

[151] This relates to the *reservation utility* and concept of the *reservation frontier* if not only the price but also the quality features of the product or service are accounted for in the search process (Nelson 1970). (Kohn and Shavell 1972) call it the *switchpoint level of utility*.

In most cases, new less expensive suppliers ($p < p_c$) entering the market[152] and declining search costs will cause a decrease in the reservation price[153], making a consumer reject more offered products before he is willing to buy it. New more expensive suppliers[154] will cause an increase in the reservation price. If the search costs become negligible, thus $\alpha_{se} = 0$, the consumer will search till he finds p_c. Storekeepers have to acknowledge the fact that due to the *reservation price strategy* a buyer that once decided not to buy at a found financial services provider will never buy there during the ongoing search process, even if by chance he comes back to this financial services provider.[155] Interestingly, if a storekeeper knew the buyer's search cost (and the price distribution[156]) he could guarantee the customer – if appropriate – that another search makes no sense economically.

Example 3.1: Suppose the consumer wants to perform a stock order on the Internet and knows that there are 25 suppliers offering this service between $30 and $54 ($p_c = 30$, $p_e = 54$). A search agent is not available, and so the consumer may only search sequentially. He calculates his reservation prices for several scenarios that are presented in Table 1.

Table 1. Reservation Prices for Sequential Search

Search costs [$]	# of Suppliers (Price range)		
	25 ($30 – $54) Initial situation [$]	30 ($25 – $54) 5 new cheaper suppliers [$]	30 ($30 – $59) 5 new more expensive suppliers [$]
10	51.90	49.00	54.00
5	45.30	41.80	46.80
2	39.50	35.50	40.50
1	36.60	32.30	37.30

To determine the expected total costs of a sequential search, the chronological order of how costs are incurred is evaluated. The consumer visits the first financial services provider i, looks at the price p_i, compares the price with his reservation price and decides either to buy the product, thus incurring the total cost of one search and the product price p_i or to go on searching. If he goes on searching, in the next shop it is just the same except for the total cost consisting now of two

---

[152] In the following it is assumed that the first new entrant entering the market charges a price p_{c-1}, the second one p_{c-2}, and so on.

[153] This holds only true for $\alpha_{se} < (2n + 1)$ which under realistic circumstances is most often the case.

[154] Analogously to the case of new less expensive suppliers, it is assumed that the first new more expensive entrant will charge a price p_{e+1}, the second one p_{e+2}, and so on.

[155] This result is already well-known in literature. See e.g. Remark 7 in (Kohn and Shavell 1974), Chap. 13 in (De Groot 1970), (Weitzman 1979) and (Telser 1973). The possibility of recall is not provided in the model presented here. In contrast to the *static case*, in the *adaptive case* keeping track of the stores is a superior strategy.

[156] It seems to be reasonable to assume that a supplier knows the offers of his competitors at least as well as his customers.

searches and the "new" product price. Formally speaking, the consumer will calculate the expected number of store visits *esv* to find an appropriate price multiplied by the search cost α_{se} and the expected product price *epp*.

If the price of a found product is below the customer's reservation price, he will buy it without any further searches. Obviously, when the reservation price is above the highest price in the market[157] the consumer will always buy the first found product right away. Hence the expected product price is given by $(p_e + p_c)/2$. If the reservation price is below the most expensive product in the market, the consumer will expect to pay $(\bar{p} + p_c)/2$ since he will only buy a found product that at most costs his reservation price.

$$epp = \begin{cases} \dfrac{\bar{p} + p_c}{2} & \text{if } \bar{p} \leq p_e \\[2mm] \dfrac{p_e + p_c}{2} & \text{if } \bar{p} > p_e \end{cases} \qquad (3.4)$$

The expected total cost of the search process that concludes in buying a product not only comprises the expected product price *epp* but also the expected number of store visits *esv* multiplied by the sequential search cost α_{se}. Denoting the probability that a consumer will not buy at a found financial services provider by σ, the expected number of store visits can be calculated. Bearing in mind that according to the reservation price strategy, the consumer will not buy at a financial services provider *i* where $p_i > \bar{p}$. Thus the probability that he will buy at a single financial services provider is $(\bar{p} - p_c + 1)/n$ since he will reject all price offers higher than his reservation price.

Obviously, the probability that he will buy at the first financial services provider is $(1 - \sigma)$. Accordingly, the probability that he will not buy in the first, but in the second store is $\sigma(1 - \sigma)$ and that he will not buy during his first two store visits but in the third visit is given by $\sigma^2(1 - \sigma)$. Finally, the probability that a consumer will buy at the *t*'s store visit is given by $\sigma^{t-1}(1 - \sigma)$. To find the number of stores to be visited before buying the product, the probabilities of buying at each given visit multiplied by the number of the visit have to be summed.[158] Hence the expected number of store visits *esv* is given by[159]

---

[157] This can occur when there are only a few suppliers in the market and the search costs are relatively high. Formally, if $\alpha_{se} \geq (n - 1)/2$.

[158] See e.g. (Shy 1997).

[159] In the case where the expected number of visits becomes analytically smaller than 1, it is assumed that the consumer searches at least once.

$$esv = \sum_{t=1}^{\infty} \sigma^{t-1} \cdot (1-\sigma) \cdot t \qquad (3.5)$$

$$= \frac{1}{1-\sigma}$$

$$= \begin{cases} \dfrac{2 \cdot n}{1+\sqrt{1+8 \cdot n \cdot \alpha_{se}}} & \text{if } \alpha_{se} < \dfrac{n-1}{2} \\[4mm] 1 & \text{if } \alpha_{se} \geq \dfrac{n-1}{2} \end{cases}$$

Combining Eq. (3.4) and Eq. (3.5) and substituting $\bar{p}$ using Eq. (3.3) yields the expected total costs TC_{se}.

$$TC_{se} = \begin{pmatrix} \text{expected \# of searches} \\ \cdot \text{search cost per search} \end{pmatrix} + (\text{expected product price}) \qquad (3.6)$$

$$= \begin{cases} \dfrac{2 \cdot n}{1+\sqrt{1+8 \cdot n \cdot \alpha_{se}}} \cdot \alpha_{se} + p_c + \dfrac{-1+\sqrt{1+8 \cdot n \cdot \alpha_{se}}}{4} & \text{if } \alpha_{se} < \dfrac{n-1}{2} \\[4mm] 1 \cdot \alpha_{se} + \dfrac{p_c + p_e}{2} & \text{if } \alpha_{se} \geq \dfrac{n-1}{2} \end{cases}$$

Eq. (3.6) can be simplified as follows:

$$TC_{se} = \begin{cases} p_c + \dfrac{-1+\sqrt{1+8 \cdot n \cdot \alpha_{se}}}{2} & \text{if } \alpha_{se} < \dfrac{n-1}{2} \\[4mm] \alpha_{se} + \dfrac{p_c + p_e}{2} & \text{if } \alpha_{se} \geq \dfrac{n-1}{2} \end{cases} \qquad (3.7)$$

Proposition 2: In a sequential search market the expected total cost associated with searching and buying a product equals the reservation price of the customer.

Eq. (3.7) presents a very interesting outcome. Initially, the reservation price was the basis for the customer to decide whether he should search once again or buy the product in hand. Now it has been shown that the reservation price implicitly also represents the expected total costs for finding and buying a commodity in a sequential search market.

The conclusions that can be derived from Eq. (3.7) are generally the same as the ones for Eq. (3.3). A decrease in the consumer search costs decreases the expected total cost. Decreasing search costs favor the less expensive suppliers since the consumer will search more often. If the search costs become negligible, the expected total cost would just be p_c because the consumer searches until he finds the lowest price without bearing any search costs. In such a market all other suppliers would not sell a product anymore. An increase in the number of financial services providers in the market would decrease the expected total cost if cheaper suppliers enter the market and increase the expected total cost if more expensive suppliers enter the market. A market entry in such a market makes sense if and only if $\alpha_{se} \geq (n-1)/2$. Otherwise no revenues can be expected as even slightly less expensive suppliers are not able to sell a product.[160]

Example 3.2: The consumer in Example 3.1 wants to calculate his expected total cost for finding an appropriate supplier and performing the stock order on the Internet. Since he has already calculated his reservation prices for various scenarios (see Table 1) he implicitly has already determined his expected total costs. A new calculation is not necessary.

3.4.2.5 Simultaneous Search

Determining the results of a simultaneous search is much easier compared to the sequential approach. Assume that the information broker or search agent has full information on suppliers, their products and prices, the result of the simultaneous search will be financial services provider c offering the product at price p_c. So – and this is quite noteworthy – the consumer can be sure to get the best offer if he chooses to search with the information broker or search agent. To get the total cost incurred by a simultaneous search, just the least expensive offer and the search cost α_{si} have to summed. Hence,

$$TC_{si} = \alpha_{si} + p_c.$$ (3.8)

> **Proposition 3**: In a simultaneous search market the least expensive supplier will always be found and only this supplier will generate revenues.

A decrease in search costs reduces the total cost for the buyer but does not affect the found supplier. An increase in the number of financial services providers in the market has only an impact on total cost if cheaper suppliers enter the market. In a market where buyers just search simultaneously only the least expensive supplier will survive. It makes no sense economically to enter such a market with more expensive products.

Example 3.3: Suppose the consumer in Example 3.1 discovers that there is a search agent available that allows searching simultaneously for the best broker on the Internet, the total costs can be calculated according to the following different scenarios.

---

[160] Obviously, in the sequential search market, the store with the price offer equaling the reservation price will make the most profit in this market assuming identical cost functions for all suppliers. However, an analysis of the profit function in this model is fruitless since prices are considered to be given.

Table 2. Total Cost for Simultaneous Search

Search costs [$]	# of Suppliers (Price range)		
	25 ($30 – $54) Initial situation [$]	30 ($25 – $54) 5 new cheaper suppliers [$]	30 ($30 – $59) 5 new more expensive suppliers [$]
10	40.00	35.00	40.00
5	35.00	30.00	35.00
2	32.00	27.00	32.00
1	31.00	26.00	31.00

3.4.2.6   Combined Approach

With both approaches in hand, it can now be determined whether the consumer will decide to search simultaneously or sequentially. He simply calculates the expected total costs of the sequential search and compares them with the total costs of the simultaneous search[161]. He will use an information broker or search agent if and only if the total cost of the simultaneous search is lower than the expected total cost of purchasing a product using a sequential search.

$$TC_{si} < TC_{se} \tag{3.9}$$

$$p_c + \alpha_{si} < \begin{cases} p_c + \dfrac{-1+\sqrt{1+8\cdot n\cdot \alpha_{se}}}{2} & \text{if } \alpha_{se} < \dfrac{n-1}{2} \\ \alpha_{se} + \dfrac{p_c + p_e}{2} & \text{if } \alpha_{se} \geq \dfrac{n-1}{2} \end{cases}$$

> **Proposition 4**: A consumer will search sequentially if and only if his reservation price is lower than the least expensive product price plus simultaneous search expense.

Unless information about the differences in the search costs α_{si} and α_{se} is available a particular search method cannot be generally recommended. Obviously, if the search costs become negligible, the consumer is indifferent to the two search methods and will find the least expensive offer without bearing any search costs. An increase in the number of cheaper financial services providers in the market would decrease the expected total costs for both the sequential and the simultaneous search. A financial services provider might be able to charge more than p_c for his product only if the sequential search is the better choice.

---

[161] Since by assumption the consumer is risk-neutral (Assumption (AC)) the *expected* total costs of a sequential search and the *certain* total cost of a simultaneous search may be compared here.

Example 3.4: Suppose the consumer of the Examples 3.1 to 3.3 faces search costs of $10 for a simultaneous search and $2 for each sequential search and still wants to perform the stock order. The results are gathered in Table 3. While the sequential search is the better choice in the initial situation, this changes with 5 new – either less or more expensive – suppliers.

Table 3. Combined Approach - Consumer's Decision

	# of Suppliers (Price range)		
Search Costs	25 ($30 – $54) Initial situation [$]	30 ($25 – $54) 5 new cheaper suppliers [$]	30 ($30 – $59) 5 new more expensive suppliers [$]
Simultaneous Search Cost: $10	40.00	35.00	40.00
Sequential Search Cost:$2	39.50	35.47	40.47
Consumer Decision	Search sequentially	Search simultaneously	Search simultaneously

The search cost on the Internet for both methods will often be approximately the same since most search agents do not charge an extra search fee and the time it needs to search with a search agent is pretty similar to the time it needs to browse the Internet presence of a financial services provider. Hence, on the Internet $\alpha_{si} \approx \alpha_{se}$ will hold in many circumstances. This leads to a general preference for the simultaneous search because the reservation price is always greater or equal to p_c.

> **Proposition 5**: In a market with equal (positive) costs for both search methods, the buyers will search simultaneously to discover the least expensive offer with this supplier being the only one to survive in the market.

Apparently, on the Internet, there is a strong pressure on margins since the search method of choice will generally be the simultaneous method yielding the least expensive supplier in the market. This finding is to be confronted with empirical evidence with respect to comparison shopping from the German financial services market in the following section.

3.4.2.7   Excursus: Simultaneous Search in the German Financial Services Market – Status Quo[162]

Fast evolving search technologies can be observed on net markets, allowing customers to compare (commodity) products increasingly fast and conveniently. In the last sections, a simple search cost model was used to deduce implications for both customers and suppliers in an electronic commodity market.

Due to the immateriality of financial services and products they are the perfectly suited for sale on the WWW. This may be one of the main reasons why the financial services industry has gained a cutting edge on the net with respect to other industries, which is also substantiated by the popularity of finance-related websites. For instance in Germany in November 2000 already more than one third (roughly 4 Mio. persons) of all German Internet users surfing from home regularly accessed finance-related websites.[163]

With respect to a number of product categories – namely broking, current account, real estate financing (mortgages), fixed term deposits, loans, automobile third party insurance, private health insurance, and general third party liability insurance – an empirical study was conducted between November 2000 and January 2001 to assess the status quo of opportunities to compare highly standardized products in the German financial services market.

For all comparison suppliers it became evident that a customer already has to have a good knowledge concerning his needs and preferences. Accordingly he has to have a good knowledge of the financial service he is looking for in order to satisfy his needs[164] due to the fact that all analyzed comparisons are based on a specific financial service in contrast to specific needs of potential customers. Hence, with regard to comparison shopping there is still a product-centric view observable in the market instead of a customer-centric or needs-centric view. For this kind of well-informed customers, the offered comparison services are very helpful and offer valuable opportunities to save substantial amounts of money while optimizing their private financial dispositions. The product comparisons and the information provided with the result set are of particular interest and usefulness if the product or service is a highly standardized commodity (hence a homogeneous product as modeled above) that can just be compared by comparing the price.

Generally speaking, the study revealed that there may be substantial differences in the result sets of suppliers of comparisons, i.e. the top offer based on the price for a specific service varied substantially.[165] Thus consulting several suppliers of

---

[162]   The results of this section are based on joint research efforts with Jochen Dzienziol, Michael Eberhardt, and Marian Pinnow. See (Kundisch et al. 2001d).

[163]   See (Anonymous 2001d).

[164]   In fact, this was one of the basic assumptions in the search cost model. It was assumed that the customer already knew what kind of product or bundle of products he was looking for.

[165]   Due to the relatively small sample, no tests of significance were carried out at that stage of the study.

comparisons before purchasing a financial service or product may be advisable. This point will be addressed in Sec. 3.4.2.8. Some differences in the result sets with respect to the yielded least expensive supplier and the number of the suppliers included in the comparison suppliers are summarized in Table 4.[166]

Table 4. Result Range and Number of Included Suppliers[167]

Product	Range of Least Expensive Offers	# of Suppliers Included
Mortgage Lending	5.51% – 5.57%	74 – 220
Fixed term deposits	4.30% – 4.60%	24 – 49
Auto insurance	550 EUR – 648 EUR	27 – 100

To recap, the study suggests that the transparency on the financial services market has increased dramatically with the new and evolving means of communication. However, there is still a long way to go until the full transparency of the market[168] is reached.

One of the implicit assumptions of the model presented above is that the search agent providing the means to perform a simultaneous search has a complete market overview, i.e. he will include all suppliers in the market in his comparison and as a result will find the least expensive supplier in the market. However, as discussed above, empirical evidence with respect to the German financial services market suggests that there is no search engine in the market that provides a complete market overview. Therefore, the basic search cost model will be extended to account for this condition.

3.4.2.8   Extensions of the Basic Search Cost Model

In the light of these empirical findings, obviously, the former simultaneous search problem and method exhibits sequential characteristics. If a consumer cannot be sure to get the least expensive product as a result of the simultaneous search, he will have to calculate just like in the sequential case whether another search economically makes sense or not. Thus Fig. 16 has to be modified to illustrate the new decision problem.

---

[166] Interestingly, different search agents in some cases yielded the same least expensive product supplier, however, with a different price for the same financial service.

[167] This table is an excerpt of the extensive results in (Kundisch et al. 2001d).

[168] One hint that it might still be a long way is the closedown of moneyshelf.de in November 2001 only after roughly 14 months of being online. Moneyshelf was an online marketplace established by Deutsche Bank AG to provide „the full transparency of the financial market" (Frey 2000). After the closedown of moneyshelf.de most functionality has been integrated in the Deutsche Bank 24 website under the brand of "Deutsche Bank 24 Moneyshop".

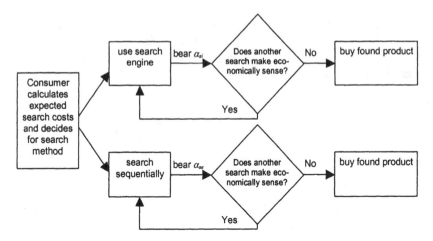

Fig. 17. Consumer Search for Homogeneous Products Revisited

In a very simple setting it can be shown that the *simultaneous/sequential search* method will still be preferred over the pure sequential search by the consumer.

(AS) Search Agent
Let m denote the number of search agents in the market. Each of the $m \leq n/2$ search agents is able to close exclusive contracts[169] with at least 2 of the n product suppliers.[170] Furthermore, search agent $j = c, c+1, \ldots$ yields $p_j = j$ as the least expensive offer.

Fig. 18 illustrates this new setting (analogously to Fig. 15, p. 39). Obviously, the division of the prices in the range between $p_c+m \ldots p_e$ between the m search agents is irrelevant for the decision problem in this scenario.

---

[169] Waiving the assumption of exclusive contracts makes the decision process much more complicated. Sampling from the assumed distribution in assumption (AM) generates a mathematically unhandy distribution. In this scenario, a general preference for one of the search methods cannot be shown either.

[170] To offer a comparison function at least two product suppliers have to be under contract.

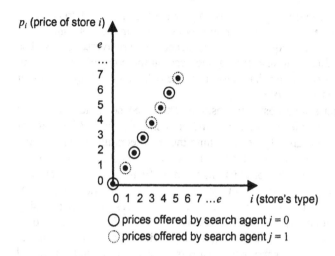

prices offered by search agent $j = 0$
prices offered by search agent $j = 1$

Fig. 18. Supplier Prices, Store Distribution, and Search Agents

Expected total costs of the simultaneous/sequential search $TC_{si/se}$ are then given by[171]

$$
TC_{si/se} = \begin{cases} p_c + \dfrac{-1 + \sqrt{1 + 8 \cdot m \cdot \alpha_{si}}}{2} & \text{if } \alpha_{si} < \dfrac{m-1}{2} \\[3ex] \alpha_{si} + \dfrac{p_c + p_{c+m}}{2} & \text{if } \alpha_{si} \geq \dfrac{m-1}{2} \end{cases} \tag{3.10}
$$

Apparently, the preference for the simultaneous/sequential search method will hold in case search costs for both methods are the same. The special case where $m = 1$ represents the scenario already discussed above (compare Eq. (3.9)).

$$
TC_{si/se} > TC_{se} \qquad \text{for } \forall m,n \tag{3.11}
$$
$$
\text{s.t.} \qquad \alpha_{si} = \alpha_{se}
$$

After having extended the basic model, some fundamental limitations of the analysis will be discussed in the following section.

3.4.2.9   Limitations of the Analysis

In general a search agent will have an information advantage compared to a consumer. (Rothschild 1975) has shown that in many cases the qualitative characteristics of optimal search strategies with known distribution of prices are equal to those where the customer at first knows little or nothing about the distribution of prices but learns about the prices during his search.

---

[171] The derivation of Eq. (3.10) is analogous to Eq. (3.1) - (3.7).

The assumed risk-neutrality of the consumer will often not hold true. Many people prefer a certain result (here: the simultaneous search in the basic model) to an uncertain event (here: the sequential search), hence they are averse to risk. The model can easily be adjusted to also taking into account the consumer attitude towards risk. Given the assumption that consumers are risk adverse, they will favor the simultaneous search even more.

It was assumed that search costs are positive. This need not hold true for all Internet surfers. Many people enjoy surfing and browsing the WWW looking for good deals or just for pleasure. Hence, searching the Internet could provide a customer with utility, which may outweigh opportunity cost of time and online fees.

Even when buying commodity products like simple financial services, price is often not the only important factor that influences the buyer's decision. For example reliability, security and reputation of the financial services provider probably are relevant factors that customers take into account.[172] Also price was taken to be a concrete attribute, however, research suggests that price perceptions are malleable. These behavioral and psychological aspects of price were not addressed above.[173]

3.4.2.10 Conclusion

The customer decision process for using either a sequential or a simultaneous search method in a commodity market has been examined. In the context of a sequential search, the outcomes reveal that the reservation price is not only the price where a consumer is indifferent to searching another time and buying the product in hand. It also represents the expected total costs comprising the costs of the search process itself and the expected product price. If suppliers knew the distribution of the prices in the market and the reservation price of a consumer, they could provide – if appropriate – the consumer with a guarantee that another search does not make sense economically.

It has been shown that both approaches to examining buyer search behavior in (electronic) commodity markets can be comfortably combined. In the absence of special search charges by search agents, a strong preference for the simultaneous search method could be shown. In this case, a strong pressure on the prices in the commodity market should be observable since the simultaneous search always

---

[172] Along with this hypothesis see e.g. (Brynjolfsson and Smith 2000), (Kulkarni 2000).

[173] See e.g. (Monroe 1990), (Moorthy et al. 1997) and references therein for research on this topic. See (Beatty and Smith 1987) and references therein for a review of empirical studies concerning buyer search effort from an involvement perspective. See (Wilde 1980) for a paper emphasizing the much needed interdisciplinary approach – integrating consumer research and economic models – concerning consumer search behavior. Moreover, an empirical study due to Kogut provides evidence that simple marginal search theory, i.e. reservation price strategy, does not adequately predict individual behavior (Kogut 1990). In contrast Urbany (1986) provides empirical evidence that is consistent with the theory due to (Stigler 1961). More references on experiments in information acquisition can be found in (Lawrence 1999).

yields the least expensive supplier. Hence, a decision for a market entry will only be economically sound when the entrant is able to offer the homogeneous product less expensive.

Taking up again the basic theme of this section – the new quality in communication – it can be said that it is highly questionable whether competing on price will be a sustainable business model in electronic commodity markets in the future. This is supported by (Kulkarni 2000), who also comes to the conclusion that "...a firm's informational advantage is generally likely to diminish in the long run in view of the recent advances in IT: This is because IT has greatly reduced the costs of disseminating and acquiring information." New strategies – like building customer trust relationships or differentiate by individualized services and products – may have to be found to successfully compete in such a marketplace.

3.5 Summary

In summary, on the one hand the rapid development in modern information and communication technology, especially the Internet, leads to new organizational models and increasing competition in the financial services industry that is also supported by (de)regulation. On the other hand there is a growing number of people who have no demand for traditional financial solutions, because their income situation does not fit into the assumption of periodically constant income streams. In consequence a lot of innovative products that cover the needs of the described group of customers are likely to appear in the future. In the next chapter recent developments in the financial services industry and strategic options for financial services firms will be discussed based on these findings.

4 Strategic Options[174]

> "Would you tell me, please, which way I ought to go from here?"
> "That depends a good deal on where you want to go," said the Cat.
> LEWIS CARROLL, Alice's Adventures in Wonderland

Having discussed mega-trends of the financial services industry, the strategic options for companies that operate in this dynamically changing business environment will be the issue of this chapter. In the end, it seems to come back to Porter.[175] From a strategic point of view[176], the decision is whether to pursue gaining cost leadership, to differentiate the offered services from other competitors or to serve just a niche market. The niche market strategy in terms of products, a specific customer group or a regional market as a generic strategy does not apply in the context of this book, since the focus is on larger entities such as German universal banks with a broad customer base[177], which would have difficulties revoking their decision at short notice to serve the mass market.[178,179]

---

[174] The basic idea of this chapter is based on (Buhl et al. 2000a). However, the scope of the differentiation strategy described there is much narrower compared to the life-cycle solution provider approach that is suggested here.

[175] (Porter 1985, 1996 1998). See (Coyne and Subramaniam 1996) for some criticizing comments on this traditional approach. However, due to the relative stability of both the suppliers and the needs of the customers in the financial services industry, the traditional approach is still applicable here.

[176] On „strategic fit", i.e. the coherence of the decisions associated with a strategy, see e.g. (Macharzina 1999), (Porter 1996, 1998). See (Wolfersberger 2002) for a discussion of „strategic fit" and a general strategic analysis of the financial services market.

[177] It depends on the point of view, whether the German private customers financial services market is defined as a mass market or a niche. From a global perspective this would not be the case, but certainly from a national one. Here, the scope is the German private customers financial services market.

[178] See (Straub 1990).

[179] Of course, there is still the opportunity to sell parts or the whole business with private customers to a different financial services provider. Since it is the objective to develop a strategy that facilitates a financial services provider to earn adequate returns for its shareholders in the *private customer market*, this option will not be further considered here.

4.1 Cost Leadership: Mergers and Acquisitions

The majority of the 1990-95 bank mergers were at best a wash and at worst a keen disappointment, an apparent triumph of managerial adrenaline over management intelligence.

K. SMITH, MITCHELL MADISON GROUP, 1998

Fostered by the changing market environment that was presented in the last chapter, the financial services industry has seen a large number of mergers in the last couple of years.[180,181] Scale effects are the dominant factor in most mergers and acquisitions (M&A) deals. (Weimer and Wißkirchen 1999) estimate that two thirds of all M&A deals in the financial services industry followed this rationale, only each fifth M&A was a cross-border deal and another fifth pursued diversification. The relative unimportance so far of cross-border deals has been analyzed by (Focarelli and Pozzolo 2001), who find that although cross-border M&A in the banking industry have also risen in recent years, the share of cross-border M&A among banks still being only about half that of non-financial firms.[182] Table 5 shows some megadeals in the international and German financial services market in order to provide a rough picture of the size of the big deals in that sector in recent years.

Table 5. Mergers in the International and German Financial Services Market[183]

Buyer	Target	Year	Volume in billion $
Chemical Banking Corp	Chase Manhattan	1995	14.5
First Union Corporation	CoreStates Financial	1997	16.8
Nations Bank	Bank America	1998	61.6
Banc One	First Chicago	1998	34.0
Deutsche Bank	Bankers Trust	1998	10.0
Royal Bank of Scotland	National Westminster	1999	42.7
Chase Manhattan	J.P.Morgan	2000	41.0
HypoVereinsbank	Bank Austria	2000	7.3
Bank of Scotland	Halifax	2001	41.0
Allianz Holding	Dresdner Bank	2001	20.7

---

[180] On triggers and reasons for this development also see (Schierenbeck 1999a). See (Kaufmann 1999) who attributes the M&A activity in the European financial services industry especially to the introduction of the Euro as single currency.

[181] The global value of M&A transactions across all industries has soared from $365 billion in 1987 to $3,490 billion in 2000. The financial services industry has been the third most attractive industry worldwide for M&A transactions with a total value of M&A deals of $364 billion in 2000; see (Jansen 2001).

[182] They suspect that this is because of the importance of asymmetries in banking relationships and regulatory restrictions.

[183] The table is an excerpt of multiple tables in (Jansen 2001), information provided in (Milbourn et al. 1999) and information taken from the BBC news archive at http://news.bbc.co.uk/.

According to the European Central Bank the transaction volume of European M&A in the banking sector has increased from 1990 to 1999 by 23,2% annually on average.[184] Particularly in the late 1990s the pace and volume of M&A in the financial services sector accelerated spectacularly: There were more M&A transactions in Europe between 1998 and 2000 than during the 14 years before.[185] The number of European banking institutions fell from 12,378 in 1990 to 8,395 in 1999, a decrease of roughly 5% per year on average.[186] In terms of the number of credit institutions, Germany is the undisputed leader in the EU. Fig. 19 shows the chronological development of the number of credit institutions in Germany between 1980 and 1999.

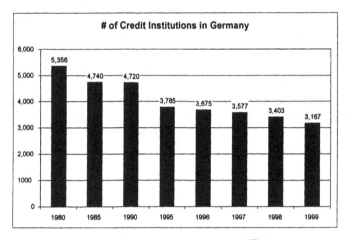

Fig. 19. Number of Credit Institutions in Germany[187]

Analogously to the development in the whole EU, a sharp decline can be recorded in the last 20 years. However, there is still much room for further concentration in Germany.[188] With over 3,000 credit institutions in 1999 it has more than the next three countries in this ranking – France, Italy, and Austria – taken together.[189] At the same time the CR5 – a measure for the concentration in an indus-

---

[184] See (European Central Bank 2000b).
[185] See (Beitel and Schiereck 2001).
[186] See (European Central Bank 2000b).
[187] Figures taken from (European Central Bank 2000b).
[188] Thus the predicted "endgame in financial services" by (James et al. 1997) is by and large not over yet.
[189] See (European Central Bank 2000b), (Kohlhaussen 1999).

try[190] – in the financial services industry was just 15.01 in Germany, compared to 69.20 in France, 48.33 in Italy or 39.58 in Austria.[191]

In literature a number of different motives for M&A deals are distinguished:[192]

- *Monopoly hypotheses*: M&A activity is due to an expected increase in market power and less competition.
- *Tax hypotheses*: M&A activity is due to realizable tax advantages.[193]
- *Information hypotheses*: M&A activity is due to inefficient capital markets.
- *Neoclassical hypotheses*: M&A activity is either due to realizable synergies, i.e. economies of scale or economies of scope or due to inefficient management of the target.
- *Management theories*: M&A activity is due to managers with bounded rationality acting on behalf of their self-interest.
- *Transaction cost theory*: M&A is due to an assumed higher allocation efficiency because of lower transaction costs within a corporation.

None of the above listed approaches to explain M&A activity may convince on its own from a theoretical point of view.[194] Likewise, the extensively available empirical evidence does not exclusively support one of the above approaches. Thus it may often be a number of different factors that contribute to a M&A activity being implemented.[195]

How successful is such a growth strategy historically? Although each deal is different, may have its own logic and is accompanied by specific environmental factors and restrictions, it is noteworthy that the majority of deals has to be classified as failures. While it is apparently impossible to positively decide about success or failure of an integration, the results are consistently discouraging across

---

[190] CR5 is the five-firm concentration ratio, which represents the share of industry sales accounted for by the five largest firms in the market. Another commonly used variable is the Herfindahl-Hirschman Index (HHI) which equals the sum of squared market shares of each firm in the industry; see (Carlton and Perloff 1994). The HHI for the German financial services market based on the total deposits to non-banks was a mere 0.0090 compared to 0.1333 for France for instance; see (European Central Bank 2000b).

[191] See (European Central Bank 2000b). Sweden and the Netherlands with a CR5 of 83.49 and 83.37, respectively, mark the most concentrated financial services markets in Europe.

[192] For more details on the different hypotheses see (Huemer 1991) and references therein. For different categorizations see e.g. (Jansen 2001), (Bernet 1999), (Carlton and Perloff 1994), (Schmitz 1993), and (Jervis 1971). (Macharzina 1999) provides a very nice and comprehensive overview on rationales for M&A transactions.

[193] See e.g. (Auerbach and Reihus 1988).

[194] For a detailed discussion and references for studies presenting empirical evidence see (Jansen 2001), (Huemer 1991).

[195] See (Jansen 2001).

the empirical studies and regardless of the applied research method.[196] This makes a merger in such a dynamic environment a high-risk-venture instead of giving the newly formed company some relief. Instead of presenting and reviewing numerous studies, some quotes of secondary research – summarizing empirical material – with special emphasis on the financial services industry shall make the point here:[197]

- "Up to 40% of mergers fail to capture their identified cost synergies."[198]
- "In Europe one year after the merger or acquisition of financial institutions, there can be as much as a 90% valuation gap between the most successful and the least successful mergers. In the US, the stock price performance of three-quarters of acquirers lagged that of their peer group by more than 20% within two years of making an acquisition. After five years, the stock price performance gap increased to more than 30%."[199]
- "Study after study has shown that up to 80 percent of M&A deals completed during the 1990s failed to justify the equity that funded them. [...] And while growth may be a stated objective in three out of four mergers, a study of 193 transactions between 1990 and 1997 worth at least $100 million found that only 36 percent even maintained revenue growth through the first quarter after announcement. By the third quarter, 89 percent has succumbed to a slowdown, with a median revenue decline of 12 percent.[200]
- "The analysis of the most recent deals (1998 - 2000) reveals that shareholder returns of acquiring banks become significantly negative thus being more consistent to research being conducted in the US-banking sector. Moreover, we find that especially the larger as well as the European cross-border deals are value destroying, which should be an alarming signal against the background of the creation of a more efficient European market."[201]
- "Thus, based on scientific evidence, it is hard to make a compelling case for banks to merge to get bigger, either to reduce costs or improve profitability [...]. Similarly, there is also lack of empirical evidence that expansion of scope in banking has been beneficial [...]."[202]
- "The empirical success rate of bank mergers is a mere quarter."[203]

---

[196] See particularly (Schenk 2000), (Beitel and Schiereck 2001), and (Jansen 2001) for extensive reviews of empirical studies. (Calomiris 1999) discusses methodological problems in such studies and comes to the conclusion in contrast to most other publications that efficiency gains are large in bank consolidation.

[197] (Schenk 2000) provides some ideas why economically unproductive mergers are so omnipresent given the bad track record over the last decades. On efficiency of M&A in the financial services market also see (Neuberger 1998).

[198] (Bekier et al. 2001a).

[199] (Viner et al. 2000).

[200] (Bekier et al. 2001a).

[201] (Beitel and Schiereck 2001).

[202] (Milbourn et al. 1999).

[203] See (Weimer and Wißkirchen 1999), translation of German text.

- "These results paint a pessimistic picture. It appears that failure is widespread, mediocrity considerable, and success only occasional. [...] Evidently, too many mergers, inside as well as outside the banking industry, are to be qualified as economic failures."[204]

A very interesting finding is that success or failure of mergers seem to be independent of the growth dynamic of the industry, the size of the deal and even the experience of the acquirers.[205] A number of reasons contribute to these failures:[206]

- *Retention of key talent* is one of the prime challenges in an integration process.[207] However, "key employees usually receive inquiries within five days of a merger announcement – precisely when uncertainty is at its highest."[208]
- *Labor productivity* may decline severely during an integration process. Tyco CEO Dennis Kozlowski states the following: "People are normally productive for about 5.7 hours in an 8-hour business day... any time a change of control [such as a merger] takes place, their productivity falls to less than an hour."[209]
- *Customers may also defect* if they get the impression that the merger will constrain their bargaining power, reduce service levels, or cause a loss of key relationships.[210]
- *Time pressure* and the *necessity of confidentiality* before a deal is announced prevent a profound "due diligence", thus unpleasant and costly surprises may pop up in the post deal phase.[211]
- The whole new organization may be stalled due to *inside orientation* in the post deal phase. The best employees are busy merging the two or more entities, i.e. integrating the IT systems, training the employees to use the new systems, creating a new corporate identity, crafting a shared vision, and developing a new

---

[204] (Schenk 2000).

[205] See (Bekier et al. 2001a, 2001b). However, (Beitel and Schiereck 2001) find that cumulated abnormal returns depend on time and on the size of the deal.

[206] For another list of risks associated with M&A see (European Central Bank 2000b). (Jansen 2001) distinguishes three areas for acquisition problems: (1) *overoptimistic assessment of the situation*, (2) *bad planning process*, and (3) *personal, cultural, and organizational integration problems*.

[207] See (Kay an Shelton 2000), (Kohlhaussen 1999), and (Börner 1998).

[208] (Kay and Shelton 2000).

[209] (Bekier et al. 2001a).

[210] See (Bekier et al. 2001a), (Kohlhaussen 1999). For the merger of "Schweizerischer Bankverein" and "Schweizerische Bankgesellschaft" a customer defection rate of 20% is expected (Börner 1998). (Klein and Nathanson-Loidl 2000) report about defection rates between 5 and 30% and they also discuss how the defection rate can be lowered based on their experience in the merger between the "Bayerische Hypotheken- und Wechsel-Bank AG" (Hypo-Bank) and the "Bayerische Vereinsbank AG" (Vereinsbank) to form the "Bayerische Hypo- und Vereinsbank AG" (HypoVereinsbank).

[211] A prominent example of such an unpleasant surprise was the necessary provisions of DM 3.5 billion for loan losses turning up in the former Hypo-Bank books after the merger between Hypo-Bank and Vereinsbank; see (Anonymous 1998b). This merger had an estimated value of DM 9 billion; see (Anonymous 1997b).

corporate culture, while competitors can focus on the market and establish or strengthen trust relationships with customers.[212]
- There is no evidence that increased growth results in steadily *declining average costs*.[213] Significant fixed cost effects are only verifiable at small banks with total assets of around $3 billion.[214] At least, exceeding $25 billion the average cost curve is already very flat or even upward sloping.[215] Particularly transactions between a transaction volume of $450 million and $2.2 billion with an average of $1.06 billion are significantly value creating for bidding banks whereas particularly larger transactions significantly destroy value.[216][217]
- Post-merger integration costs are often underestimated.[218]

Based on these findings, it seems that a merger is a high-risk venture in the dynamic market environment sketched in Chap. 3.[219] Therefore it is argued that merging is an inferior and defensive strategy, particularly if it is a cost-driven merger between two large entities[220] aiming at the realization of scale effects.[221] Interestingly, a McKinsey study even provides empirical evidence that customers in the financial services market are not as price sensitive as one might assume.[222] Moreover, in the long run, cost leaders offering commodity products may not be able to generate shareholder value, because competition is driving prices and thus

---

[212] See e.g. (Kohlhaussen 1999).

[213] See e.g. (Rolfes 2001), who questions that there are cost degression effects with respect to the number of employees, the number of customers, and the service volume. However, there is strong degression effect between cost per customer and customers per employee.

[214] See (Kohlhaussen 1999).

[215] See (Schenk 2000).

[216] See (Beitel and Schiereck 2001).

[217] (Kohlhaussen 1999) attributes this assumed shape of the average cost curve to the increasing complexity with increased size of the deal and to *X-inefficiencies* in big organizations. On *X-efficiencies* see (Leibenstein 1966).

[218] See e.g. (Weimer and Wißkirchen 1999).

[219] A discussion of success factors and processes for a successful M&A in the financial services industry can be found in (Seidel 1995) or in the excellent merger guide by (Penzel and Pietig 2000). (Looser 1999) also provides some ideas about how a merger can be turned into a successful transaction. See (Wagner 1991) particularly on the integration of a bank and an insurance company.

[220] Entities with an asset size that exceeds $25 billion. Above this size, the average cost curve is supposed to be flat or even upward sloping. See (Schenk 2000).

[221] In fact the nature of the recent wave of mergers is classified as being more defensive, with retrenchment and cost-cutting receiving higher priority; see (Bank for International Settlements 1999). (Börner 1998) is also skeptical about M&A as the appropriate response to strategic problems.

[222] See (Flur et al. 1997). They come to the conclusion that the "size of the genuinely price-sensitive customer segment is small." They add that "consumers often don't understand the full price of a financial product, focusing instead on a single component of it." This leaves a lot of space for financial services providers to utilize this behavior by focusing on the perceived price for a product.

profit margins down.[223] This holds especially true with regard to web-based commodity markets as laid out in Sec. 3.4.2. In addition, an enormous number of M&A activities is needed in the German financial services market to really form an entity that has a significantly high market share to experience large cost reduction effects. Thus one big deal will not suffice but several deals are necessary, each bringing along cultural and other problems in great quantities. Finally, such a defensive reaction to market trends seems inferior compared to a possible aggressive action that influences and sets market trends. In the next section an aggressive action will be suggested, i.e. a differentiation strategy[224] in this context.[225]

4.2 Differentiation: Life-Cycle Solution Provision

The market for financial services is still dominated by a product and supply side view instead of a customer driven and solution oriented view. Because most financial services companies are organized around products, they have failed so far to fully leverage their relationships with customers and their superior knowledge about their customers' lifecycle behavior.[226] To differentiate from competitors, a life-cycle solution provision strategy is suggested, that focuses on the customer relationship as the most valuable strategic asset. The relationship manager becomes the trusted solution provider instead of a traditional product seller for a customer and delivers superior consultation quality for all customer segments. This does not mean that each customer should have access to all channels and all financial services at will. Instead, an economically sound consideration with respect to the expected life time value of each customer has to decide about the financial services and channels a specific customer is offered.

It is important to note the difference between a cost leader producing commodity banking products and a solution provider producing highly individualized and

---

[223] See e.g. (Gölz and Göppl 1999). Also see Fig. 2 on p. 3.

[224] In the context of financial services providers (Süchting and Paul 1998) call it a "preference strategy" that aims at continuously increasing the utility of the offered services for the customer.

[225] Many practitioners as well as researches agree with the need to differentiate in the financial services market. See e.g. (Buhl et al. 2000a), (Bühler 1995, 1997), (Woodhouse and Weatherill 2001). (Brunner 1993) and (Wiemann 1993) identify the need to differentiate by intangible factors such as quality of consultation services. Superior quality and strict quality management is independently from the pursued strategy a key success factor; see e.g. (Schierenbeck 1997). (Buzzell and Gale 1987) find that a high quality of service has significantly positive effects on turnover, return on sales, and market share. (Geiger 1993) talks about the need to differentiate via soft factors such as service and advice.

[226] The life-cycle solution provider approach relates to the concept portrayed in (Wiemann 1993) but has a broader scope. This will be described in more detail in Chap. 5.

tailored solutions for the customer.[227] On the one hand, in the future the first one might not even have customer contact anymore and will just serve as a "production bank"[228] for the solution provider delivering commodity banking products. In a competitive environment prices will be driven down to marginal costs. Hence, in the long run most financial services companies pursuing a cost leader strategy will not be able to generate an adequate shareholder value. In the extreme, just a handful of globally operating production banks may remain, which have sufficient scale. On the other hand, the solution provider or relationship manager takes care of a highly valuable asset: The contact with the customer, which includes a lot of information about his preferences and objectives as well as his trust. Information can be gathered, formalized and processed in order to achieve a win-win-situation for the customer as well as for the solution provider, since particularly tailored solutions can be offered by data warehouse and data mining techniques.[229] Fig. 20 illustrates the position of the relationship manager within the value network.

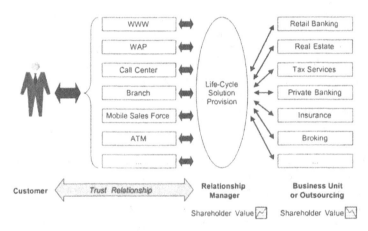

Fig. 20. Life-Cycle Solution Provider and Suggested Shareholder Value Implications[230]

Focusing on superior service delivered to the customer seems to be reasonable since it is reported that 65% of customer defections are due to service quality issues whereas just 15% due to the fact that a customer found a cheaper product.[231] And according to (Bowen and Hedges 1993) customers did not perceive very big differences among banks, which may emphasize the need for real differentiation.

---

[227] See (Buhl and Wolfersberger 2000a). On *individualization* and *personalization* see (Schackmann 2002).

[228] See (Buhl and Wolfersberger 2000b) and (Kohlhaussen 1999).

[229] On data-based marketing in the financial services industry see e.g. (Hassels 1997). On data warehousing and CRM in general see (Kuhl and Stöber 2001).

[230] See (Buhl et al. 2001), modified. The graph also relates to (Süchting 1994).

[231] See (Bowen and Hedges 1993). Surprisingly, "banks and customers tend to disagree about where they stand on the quality spectrum. Most banks believe that they are 'above average,' whereas most customers say their banks are 'average'.".

It is vital for a solution provider to have some independence from the "production banks", since regulative, legal, institutional and other settings may change (quickly). In result, the ingredients, i.e. financial products and related information, of solutions may change at the same pace. These changes should not force the customer to switch to a new supplier, as a sophisticated solution provider should instead be able to adjust his processes of finding a solution and eventually identify new cost leading "production banks" that deliver the needed products at the best price.

Regardless of whether a company decides to focus on costs or to differentiate, it has to make trade-offs in competing. Thus a company not only has to choose what to do but at the same time what *not* to do.[232] Leveraging IT and the new means of communication on net markets, some researchers concluded that serving the mass market as a cost leader and pursuing a differentiation strategy are not mutually exclusive strategies anymore.[233] It has been assumed that applying state-of-the-art IT in all business processes enables a company to pursue a *hybrid strategy* of mass customization, thus being a cost leader and at the same time being able to differentiate from competitors. However, in the long run these new means of communication will not provide for a competitive advantage but they will just be a necessity to stay in business.[234] Nevertheless, IT is an important enabler for strategies and will play an important role in the life-cycle solution provision approach.[235]

Since the business of individual financial consultation exhibits no empirically evident economies of scale and scope[236], the size of the solution provider is not at the center of the interest and there seems no need to merge in order to be successful in the market.

Differentiating by superior (life-cycle solution) services has to be explained in more detail. So far, just the very basic idea of life-cycle solution provision and the enabling role of IT has been sketched. The next chapter will deal with these issues in much more detail and will discuss how a relationship manager should leverage his customer relation by making best usage of a life-cycle solution provision approach.

---

[232] (Porter 1996).

[233] See e.g. (Piller and Schoder 1999). (Porter 1998) calls this position "stuck in the middle".

[234] Already in the beginning of the nineties when electronic banking was still in its infancy (Straub 1990) concluded that it would not suffice for making a mark against competitors. This opinion is shared e.g. by (Eilenberger and Burr 1997). However, (Furash 1994), (Devlin 1995) see an opportunity to differentiate by offering electronic sales channels.

[235] See (Lian 1995) and (Eilenberger and Burr).

[236] See e.g. (Berger et al. 1993), (Lang and Welzel 1996), (Spremann and Buermeyer 1997). In tendency, the costs are proportional to the number of serviced customers.

5 Life-Cycle Solution Provision

Banking is essential, banks are not.
BILL GATES

As outlined above, the traditional financial services market is characterized by a poor quality of consultation and service – not only for retail customers, but also for high end customers in private banking[237] – and an increasing customer willingness to switch banking affiliations resulting in a strong pressure on margins. At the same time financial services firms are facing increasing risk from continuously increasing volatile global markets.[238]

How can a modern financial services provider gain a sustainable competitive advantage by differentiation under such circumstances? To answer this question, first the status quo with respect to marketing strategies[239] has to be presented. Traditionally, segmentation strategies[240] have been widely applied: Customers are clustered into groups that share a few characteristics, such as monthly income or liquid assets. After the clustering these groups are targeted with specifically tailored marketing activities according to the assumed group characteristics. Fig. 21 exemplarily shows a typical segmentation pyramid of customers – here in terms of wealth management categories, such as "assets under management held by clients".

---

[237] On (the poor quality of) performance reporting in the private banking customer segment see (Buhl et al. 2000b).

[238] See e.g. (Gebhardt et al. 1993), (Anonymous 2002e). See also the development of the VDAX, the volatility index for the German blue chip stock market index DAX. Data may be accessed at http://www.deutsche-boerse.de.

[239] Following (Buzzell and Gale 1987) strategy is defined as "The policies and key decisions adopted by management that have major impacts on financial performance. These policies and decisions usually involve significant resource commitments and are not easily reversible.".

[240] (Woodhouse and Weatherhill, 2001), (Kollenda 1992), (Scheer 1989) describe segmentation approaches in the financial services industry. (Bühler 2000a) presents and criticizes common segmentation strategies in the banking sector. On different concepts to customer segmentation see e.g. (Krafft and Albers 2000).

Fig. 21. Wealth Management Pyramid[241]

Segmentation always takes place based on information about the customer and his situation. Generally speaking, data about customers are extensively available but cannot be utilized appropriately when targeting specific customers with fitting financial services. The lack of an appropriate vision and strategy that tackles this issue results in a lack of appropriate information processing systems. Thus financial services providers usually define a small number of different customer segments and assign their customers to these segments. Therefore, customers get really fitting financial services just by chance since they most often will have (completely) different needs and preferences with respect to the variety of different financial services. These needs and preferences cannot be captured using broad segmentation approaches, even though the necessary data would be available somewhere in the organization. Fig. 22 illustrates this situation on a more abstract level. Here, the segmentation approach is based on customer objectives that may be either oriented more quantitatively or more qualitatively.

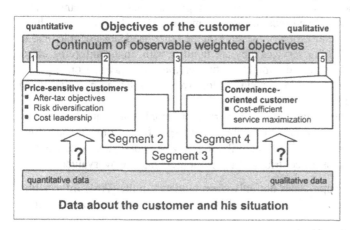

Fig. 22. Traditional Segmentation Approach[242]

---

[241] See (Woodhouse and Weatherhill 2001). The mass market segment was added by the author.

[242] Graph taken from (Buhl and Wolfersberger 2000a).

Of course, customers could circumvent this situation by investing in a search and information process[243] to identify the fitting financial services on their own. This is a time-consuming and complicated process, since the available product spectrum and related information is sheer inestimable[244] as well as the problem space is often rather complex. However, even if customers knew what they wanted and asked for these services, financial services providers sometimes would not offer these services to them. One example might be a customer who wants to get private banking services. Even if he asked for these services, he would not become a private banking customer if he did not satisfy certain criteria such as a minimum level of assets.

Most segmentation approaches result in qualitatively similar offerings in different areas of financial services. (Bühler 1997, 2000a, 2000b) also criticizes these commonly applied segmentation approaches with respect to foregone profit contribution opportunities for a financial services provider. He particularly emphasizes the following points:[245]

- A customer may decide against more comfortable and thus generally more expensive variants of financial services only due to the fact that he does not satisfy one of the segmentation criteria. These potential profit contributions are lost for the financial services provider.
- A customer often exhibits hybrid buying behavior. This means with respect to one product category e.g. current account that he might be very price-sensitive whereas with respect to other product categories such as mortgage loans he might be well willing to pay premium prices if he gets a superior consultation service. Segmentation approaches generally do not provide for such hybrid behavior.
- Segmentation approaches that are based on criteria such as liquid assets or constant monthly income may result in an overemphasis of asset management. This may result in a biased and thus mediocre consultation quality on the one hand and in a wrong specialization of the staff on the other hand since people tend to recommend products or services they are familiar with. In a reinforcing effect the financial services provider might get further and further away from a potential vision of being a solution provider. Moreover, cross-selling potential is not utilized in such a setting.
- Segmentation criteria that focus on historical or actual profit contribution may be misleading for future profit contributions of specific customers. Customers that currently show a poor profit contribution may be undervalued whereas customers with a high profit contribution at the moment may be overvalued.

So, segmentation approaches not only seem outdated in the (Post) Information Age and – if at all – only fit a very small share of the customers, they also may

---

[243] For a search cost model in the financial services industry see Sec. 3.4.2 and references there.

[244] See e.g. (Bühler 1997).

[245] The main ideas of these points are taken from (Bühler 1997, 2000a, 2000b). However, the more detailed explanations and examples come from the author.

have a negative impact on the firms bottom line. Of course it should not be concealed that segmentation approaches also have a number of merits:

- Most financial services companies have not been able so far to utilize the valuable data of their customers: This is true for reasons of the (terabyte) data volume in their operational legacy systems. Segmentation dramatically reduces complexity for the information systems.
- Segmentation reduces complexity for employees.
- Segmentation may be experienced by some customers as an honor. For instance, private banking customers might feel superior with regard to retail customers that cannot get the same quality of service.
- Segmentation may offer the opportunity for a multi-branding strategy[246] more easily.

The first two points are becoming less and less important due to the advances in IT. One the one hand powerful IT is nowadays able to process terabytes of data and on the other hand and user-friendly information systems that are rich in information can substantially support the work of a financial advisor.

The third point is quite a weak argument, since customers mainly decide based on the service quality they perceive and not based on the status they receive compared to other customers.

Though segmentation approaches nicely fit with a multi branding strategy, there are other strategies that can also be applied in a multi-branding setting. For instance by offering different qualities of service levels with a different brand assigned to each service level. Thus segmentation is not a necessity for a multi-branding strategy.

Therefore, in the following a vision and consequently a strategy addressing the discovered inefficiencies in the approach discussed above – also taking into account the findings of Chap. 3 – will be presented.

---

[246] A multi-branding strategy was pursued by Deutsche Bank AG until recently. Three brands were marketed under the Deutsche Bank Group: *maxblue* as the online discount broker, *Deutsche Bank 24* for retail clients, and *Deutsche Bank Private Banking* for high net worth individuals. With Josef Ackermann as the successor to Rolf E. Breuer as CEO, this multi-branding strategy has been abandoned.

5.1 Vision

Before presenting the vision[247] for a life-cycle solution provider, Table 6 provides a quick overview of the paradigm shift that has to take – and at some institutions is already taking – place in the financial services industry in order to generate an adequate return for shareholders with the private customer business.

Table 6. Paradigm Shift in the Financial Services Industry[248]

Traditional banking ⟶		One-to-one banking
Assign standardized products to customer segments	Goal	Satisfy customer needs
Products	Center of interest	Customers
Quantitative, not integrated	Data about customers	Quantitative and qualitative, integrated across channels
Customer is the end of the value chain	Processes	Customer is an integral part of the value chain
Cluster analysis	Marketing Methods	Deduction of preferences

Based on this paradigm shift, the question still remains what vision and corresponding strategy is superior in a market with established competitors and new entrants that increasingly adapt to this new situation and pursue some kind of one-to-one approach. The following is the guiding vision for a financial services provider with a substantial and broad customer base in the Post Information Age:

> A successful financial services provider in the Post Information Age acts as a *one-stop shop solution provider* treating each customer as an *individual* with his needs and preferences. Customers are offered the *choice* of qualitatively different financial services via *multiple channels*. They are serviced according to their needs and preferences applying a *life-cycle service and consultation approach*, but taking into account their expected *customer lifetime value*. Financial consultation services are *priced directly* according to their consumption of resources.

This rather long vision sketches how a successful financial services provider in the Post Information Age might gain a sustainable competitive advantage. How this vision translates in strategic building blocks will be the issue of the next section. The structure of that section follows the terms in italics in the vision statement.

---

[247] On crafting a vision in general see e.g. (Henzler 1992). An excerpt can be found in (Bühler 1997).

[248] The table is taken from (Fridgen et al. 1999). A similar table can be found in (Hawkes 1995).

5.2 Strategy

> But if any area of business deserves the extra effort, surely it is strategy.
>
> KEVIN P. COYNE, SOMU SUBRAMANIAM, 1996[249]

5.2.1 One-Stop Shop Solution Provider

Since many financial services for private customers have become commodities over the last decade(s)[250] and margins have become razor thin over time[251] – and there is no trend reversal foreseeable – selling these commodities only generates an adequate return for the shareholders if enormous scale effects can be realized. There is hardly any German financial services firm that has this (global) scale to realize these effects.[252] Thus it seems much more promising to focus on providing for solutions instead of products. This will strengthen the trust relationship between the customer on the one hand and make the product providers less important on the other hand.[253] The most valuable asset in this setting is the trust relationship to the customer. Then cross-selling potential can be utilized and changing legal and tax circumstances do not change this relationship. This issue has already been brought up in Sec. 4.2. Due to the new means of communication is has become increasingly easily for a *solution provider* to collaborate with *several product suppliers*. Generally speaking, if changes e.g. in taxation laws occur, most often also the bundle of financial products that constitute an optimal solution for a specific customer problem will be altered. Accordingly, the solution provider may have to cancel the relationship to one of the product suppliers on the one hand and establish a new relationship to a different product provider that is now needed for the optimal solution on the other hand. Since the solution provider is located between the customer and the product suppliers (see Fig. 20, p. 62), he is in the relatively comfortable and independent position to adapt to such changing situations.

---

[249] (Coyne and Subramaniam 1996).

[250] See e.g. (Drucker 1999). (Süchting 1998) even talks about that Investment Banking services are nowadays sometimes assigned to transaction instead of relationship banking.

[251] See e.g. (Deutsche Bundesbank 2001), (European Central Bank 2000), (Fischer and Rolfes 2001).

[252] See Sec. 4.1 on concentration figures for the German financial services market.

[253] For instance (Ausfelder et al. 1999) note that independence from product suppliers increases the credibility of the consultation service.

If sound solutions are to be provided, it is inevitable to provide for *one-stop shopping*.[254] Otherwise the full cross-selling potential cannot be utilized and fitting solutions for the customer according to his preferences and needs cannot be generated. In state-of-the-art value networks or so-called virtual organizations, it is not necessary that the solution provider produces all financial services in-house. However, if substantial parts of the business are outsourced, it might be more difficult for the solution provider himself to maintain access to valuable data about the customer.

Indeed many customers have an affinity to one-stop shopping opportunities. (Watson et al. 2000) find in an Internet user survey that 75% of respondents who are online consumers and 43% of respondents who are offline consumers express their interest in purchasing all of their financial services from a single source.

The nature of the products that are sold at the one-stop shop solution provider is quite diverse, particularly if banking *and* insurance products are considered. In tendency, banking products are purchased whereas insurance products have to be sold.[255] This makes a consultation approach with no relation to specific products even more important (see Sec. 5.2.5).

A solution as a bundle of financial services only generates real value add if it is tailored to the specific needs and preferences of the customer, i.e. it constitutes an individualized solution.

5.2.2 Individualization

A solution is generally connected with a corresponding problem of a specific customer. Therefore, a solution consists of a customer-specific bundle of individually tailored financial services.[256] The customer thus has to be an integral part of the value chain and is referred to as *prosumer* (producer + consumer) instead of consumer.[257]

Throughout the book, the needs and preferences of a customer have often been talked about. Fig. 23 broadly summarizes these needs and preferences and impressively illustrates that it is a challenge to take them all into account when trying to find individualized fitting solutions for a specific customer. However, it also

---

[254] Also see Fig. 20, p. 62. On one-stop shopping in the financial services industry see e.g (Jansen 1992), (Geiger 1993), (Spremann and Buermeyer 1997). (Reitinger et al. 1997b) call it *one-stop financial shopping*. Apparently, it is also possible for a financial services provider to focus on some instead of all needs and offer related services such as retirement planning. However, if customers appreciate the comfort of just dealing with one financial services provider – and they surely will have more diverse needs along their life cycle – this strategy seems inferior.

[255] See e.g. (Seebauer 1993).

[256] See (Betsch 1999), who states that a needs-oriented approach will be the only successful one in the future.

[257] The term *prosumer* was first introduced by the futurologist Alwin Toffler in 1980; see (Toffler 1980). Also see (Lehmann 1998).

shows that a segmentation approach most often will not even partially be able to satisfy these needs and preferences

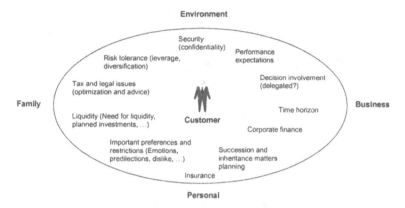

Fig. 23. Needs and Preferences of Customers with Respect to Financial Services[258]

Individualization can only be as good as the knowledge about the customer that is present at the time of the production process of the financial service. There are a lot of interaction points with the customer and most often it is not that there are too few data but that the data are not integrated for instance in a data warehouse. Valuable qualitative data and deduced knowledge is particularly available from customers' web usage and from personal communication with staff in call centers, branch offices or the mobile sales force. Utilizing these data using appropriate IT such as current data warehouse[259] and data mining technologies may help to significantly improve that situation with corresponding effects on the bottom line (see Fig. 24).[260]

---

[258] Figure taken from (Gagnebin 2001), translated and slightly modified.

[259] See e.g. (Hassels 1997), (Kuhl and Stöber 2001), (Steiner 1999), also see Sec. 5.2.4.

[260] (Kopper 1998) also emphasizes the need to apply state-of-the-art IT to utilize available information about the customer. In addition, he stresses the importance of taking advantage of each single customer-bank-relationship and thus deduces the necessity for a needs-oriented marketing approach. At the same time he deduces a product-oriented marketing approach, which seems contradictory.

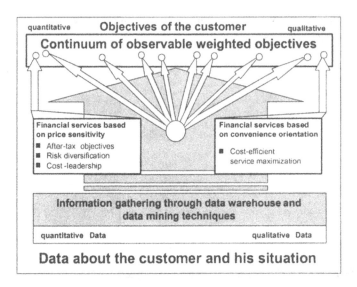

Fig. 24. Customer Objectives and Available Data[261]

However, there is no such thing as a free lunch. Individually targeting and servicing customers is a time and resource consuming process, particularly if it involves personal contact on the phone or face-to-face. Therefore, the decision about the effort that is invested in each single customer relationship has to be a sound business decision. The basis for such a decision should be the expected customer lifetime value, which will be discussed in Sec. 5.2.6.

There are circumstances where a complementing strategy besides individualization is beneficial. If a customer relationship is still in its infancy, there will often just be very few data about this customer. Thus targeted marketing activities are difficult and will often not really fit the needs of this customer, potentially even resulting in customer distress. Moreover, if a customer does maintain an account with a financial services provider that is not his primary relation, the financial services provider most likely will have a biased picture of this customer and his needs and preferences. For instance in the area of banking, more than one third of all banking customers maintain at least a second account.[262] Therefore, operating with a complementing *strategy of choice* seems promising.

---

[261] Graph taken from (Buhl and Wolfersberger 2000b). The graph is modified in so far that Buhl and Wolfersberger talk about *price sensitive customers* or *convenience oriented customers*. Here, the emphasis is that different financial services are offered on different qualitative levels to the same customer.

[262] See (Institut für Demoskopie Allensbach 2002), (Krämer 2002), or Fig. 46, p. 163.

5.2.3 Strategy of Choice

To circumvent the situation that customers are not offered services they would like to consume (Bühler 1997, 2000a, 2000b, 2000c) proposes a strategy based on choice and self-selection. Though in the eyes of the author it might not be a successful move in itself, it seems to be a promising approach if complemented by individualization efforts like those sketched above. The idea is to offer different service levels that provide for different levels of customer value for the same category of financial services, e.g. borrowing. Then the customer can choose from different service levels to satisfy his needs. He might choose a discount product with respect to a current account, but for his retirement planning he may be willing to pay more to get a face-to-face and detailed consultation service. Fig. 25 exemplarily illustrates the idea of the strategy with three different service levels and three lines of business.

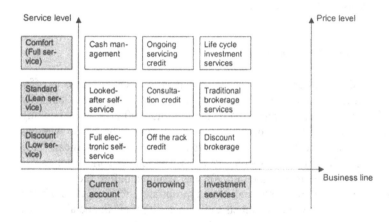

Fig. 25. Stepped Offers Based on Price and Quality of Service[263]

There are a number of advantages connected with this approach:

- Customers have a choice, which in itself is already a nice feature of this strategy from the customer's point of view.
- Customers can exhibit hybrid buying behavior.
- No customers are explicitly excluded based on predefined criteria, but the self-selection just functions over price and the perceived expected value of the service.
- Due to self-selection, customers reveal valuable information about their preferences, particularly if the customer relationship is still in its infancy and just few data are available about the customer for a good individualization approach.

---

[263] Figure is based on (Bühler 2000a) and (Bühler et al. 1999).

- There is enough room for new pricing policies. Advice and consultation services may now be priced according to their inherent value they provide for the customer (also see 5.2.7).

When offering different variants of a service it is important though that the customer can up- and downgrade hassle-free. A customer that has experienced the discount variant of a service may suddenly realize the value of advice from a personal financial advisor. Thus it should be easy to switch between variants upscale. It does not pose a problem either if a customer desires to downgrade on a variant with less service. Since the pricing model (see Sec. 5.2.7) ensures that services are directly paid for, it is not possible to exploit the system.

In short, on the one hand targeting interesting customers with individualized offers and on the other hand offering different levels of service for a potential self-selection are two important strategic building blocks to exceed customers expectations. Apparently, the services have to be marketed via communication channels, which will be the issue of the next section.

5.2.4 Multi-Channel Approach

Today, more and more customers expect their financial services provider to offer various communication channels.[264,265] (Schüller and Riedl 2000) cite a study by Booz Allen Hamilton where it is predicted that in the future 60-80% of all banking customers want to use different channels to interact with their bank, whereas 10-20% are either pure direct banking customers or pure branch customers. They also come to the conclusion that in such a setting the branch network is not an expensive liability – as sometimes in the mid 90s was assumed before the first Internet wave came down – if structured and used appropriately.[266] And although the number of customers using online channels to interact with their financial services providers is still increasing sharply, face-to-face contact stays very important – particularly if a customer plans to purchase financial services that are in need of explanation.[267] Interestingly enough, it seems that customers preferring to use mul-

---

[264] A collection of current articles about multi-channel banking can be found in (Basler Bankenvereinigung 1999), (Schmoll and Ronzal 2001). (Betsch 1999) also believes that sales approaches in the financial services market in the future have to be multi-channel approaches.

[265] A systematic categorization of different channels in banking can be found in (Schierenbeck 1999b). He distinguishes *stationary sales* (Branch, bank shops), *mobile sales* (mobile sales force, mobile branch) and *direct sales* (phone, Internet, direct mail).

[266] (Bekier et al 2000) also find that "US banks identified physical channels as the most defensible source of competitive advantage over attackers."

[267] For instance (Flur et al. 1997) find that "81 percent of middle-income consumers claim they would prefer to purchase life insurance face to face in a representative's office."

tiple channels to interact with their financial services firm are more attractive in terms of spending.[268]

Financial services providers that offer multiple channels to their customers have to acknowledge this as part of a comprehensive and integral marketing concept.[269] A real multi-channel strategy is only possible in a multi-dialog IT-environment. Therefore the integration of new sales channels into a decentralized branch-centered network is a highly demanding structural challenge.[270] It is very important, though, to preserve data consistency between all these different channels. Just imagine that a customer buys stocks using the Internet channel and afterwards asks his personal advisor where to put his stop-loss limit. If the personal advisor has no clue about this stock purchase, customer satisfaction might suffer severely.[271] Thus there must be an integrated database and a respective controlling system that serve each channel and are served by each channel themselves. An appropriately applied controlling system ideally should provide information based on which a decision about channels and services that should be offered to specific customers can be made. Successful financial services providers of the future thus will have to learn to optimally utilize the information flood resulting from interactions of the customer with the financial services provider via multiple channels.[272]

Using Internet/Intranet-technologies as an integration platform for all the channels suits these needs very well. Customer data – both quantitative (hard) operational data and qualitative (soft) – that come in via different channels can be filtered, and relevant customer information can be gathered in a data warehouse. These relevant and consistent customer information are then made accessible at all customer interfaces, i.e. at all different channels.[273] Moreover, the data gathered in the data warehouse can be analyzed by applying data-mining technologies, e.g. to identify interesting customers.

Fig. 26 schematically illustrates the multi-channel approach.

---

[268] (Anonymous 2002d) cites a study by Greenfield Online that reveals that customers who used the channels *Internet*, *mail-order* and *physical store* spent roughly 70% more than customers, who just used one of these channels. Whether these findings also apply to the financial services market cannot be assessed based on that study.

[269] On integration issues of the virtual and physical operation see (Gulati and Garino 2000). In the context of a multi-channel approach in the financial services market, a complete integration seems favorable. (Wölfing and Mehlmann 1999) describe the architecture of a transaction management system for banks in a multi-channel setting.

[270] See (Albert 2000).

[271] On customer satisfaction in services markets see e.g. (Quartapelle and Larsen 1996), on customer satisfaction in general see e.g. (Homburg 2001). On the need to integrate different channels also see (Essayan et al. 2002). They also find that the online channel is making customers more profitable.

[272] See e.g. (Bernhardt and Hofferbert-Junge 2002).

[273] See (Fridgen 2003), who elaborates on customer centric information system in the financial services sector in great detail.

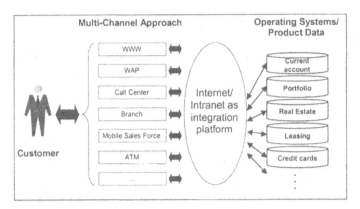

Fig. 26. Multi-Channel Approach with an Internet/Intranet Integration Platform[274]

It should be noted at this point that the Internet/Intranet integration platform by no means puts the Internet at the center of customer interaction activities. It should rather be the financial advisor in the branch who ideally is the central access point among the variety of channels. He should participate in the profit contributions coming from all other (often electronic) channels. So, he has the right incentives to make customers migrate to (lower-cost) online channels for simple transactions and use his sparse time for relationship-building services. Apparently, the old view of "Banking is People" remains or even becomes more important.[275]

Current empirical material also supports that a multi-channel approach is becoming increasingly vital. For instance, the Boston Consulting Group finds that 88% of all Internet users[276] are browsers – which means they look online for the products they might want to purchase offline. 24% of all Internet browsers claimed that they bought the product and brand they had found online. With respect to financial services, 16% of the Internet users always or frequently browse online before purchasing a product offline.[277] This makes a compelling case for a multi-channel approach. However, offering all services via all channels and add channels as they become technically available will not be successful in the long run. A negative example certainly is the provision of mobile financial services, which have so far just cost millions of Euros without any return on investment.[278] Although financial services providers have developed and introduced lower-cost

---

[274] Figure taken from (Buhl et al. 2001), modified.

[275] See e.g. (Süchting 1998). On job specification and qualification development of financial advisors for private customers see (Schütte and Höfle 1998). See (Holmsen et al. 1998), who propose three distinct models for channel management.

[276] As of January 2002, there are an estimated 446 million Internet users; see (eMarketer 2002).

[277] See (Rasch and Lintner 2001).

[278] One of the numerous examples is the Mobilbank founded at the beginning of 2001 as a joint venture between the telecommunication firm Mobilcom AG with one of the six UMTS licenses in Germany and LBBW to offer mobile financial services. The project was stopped at the beginning of February 2002.

channels such as ATM or the Internet in recent years, they have found out that generally total distribution costs have increased.[279]

Therefore, the question of which service should be offered via which channel is an important issue. Back in 1984 (Chandler et al. 1984) with respect to multi-channel approaches predicted the following: "As a greater number of tailored and more dedicated channels emerge, it is likely that most products will be delivered through a broad range of channels in order to meet the service needs of various customer segments [...]." In addition, they determined key factors that help to find the most effective distribution approach. Almost 20 years later this approach still seems to apply. As Fig. 27 shows, on the one hand *product characteristics* and on the other hand *customer characteristics* have to be taken into account to determine the appropriate channel.

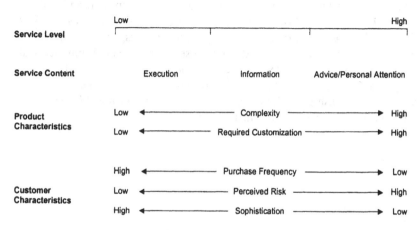

Fig. 27. Key Factors Determining Most Effective Distribution Approach[280]

Fig. 27 nicely illustrates that different customers may want to use different channels for the same services and the same customers may want to use different channels for different services. Obviously, the cost of providing these different levels of service varies greatly: Personal attention through a branch officer or a mobile sales force may provide for the most interactive and adaptive but also the most costly service on a high level, whereas electronic channels such as ATM or WWW are characterized by very low marginal costs of another transaction but can only provide for a comparatively low service level.

The new channels should not only be seen as passive reactions to changes in life conditions (see Sec. 3.3) or tools in order to reduce costs. In fact, they can contribute to high-level financial solutions by collecting information about the customer. Especially the WWW should be used as a source of information because information about the customer's interests can be collected that is not influenced by an advisor and with the WWW the time between contacts with the cus-

---

[279] See e.g. (Bekier et al. 2000), (Eilenberger and Burr 1997).
[280] Figure taken from (Chandler et al. 1984).

tomer can be reduced dramatically. If changes in the customers interests are identified, the financial services provider can react very fast and suggest financial solutions. All in all, the WWW can be used as a high quality information source about the customer if the financial services providers are able to collect high value information. For this it is necessary to design and implement web-tracking systems that go far beyond standard abilities like counting the number of page views or visits.[281] Hence not only the technical information mentioned before but also meta information about the content he is interested in has to be tracked to find out about the customer's interests.[282]

Financial services can broadly be divided in *transaction services* (such as a money transfer) and *relationship services* (such as a consultation concerning a mortgage loan). Whereas transactional services have to be fast, cheap, secure, and proximate[283], relationship services[284] have to be personal, competent, and individual.[285] Thus all channels that offer fast self-service capabilities, such as ATM or WWW, are well suited for transactional services, whereas especially a branch or the mobile sales force can focus on relationship services.[286] Though transactional services are a necessity to stay in business for a one-stop shop financial services provider (see Sec. 5.2.1), the real potential to differentiate can only be realized by individualized relationship services (see Sec. 5.2.2). A promising differentiation approach are life-cycle oriented consultation services.

---

[281] A comprehensive customer tracking model is presented in (Fridgen and Steck 2002).

[282] Intelligent concepts for marking content with semantics based on XML or other meta languages have to be developed for this. In Sec. 6.2 a content model will be presented that may be used to match a customer's interests with finance-related content.

[283] On the cost of a transaction via different channels see (Schierenbeck 1999b) who refers to a study by Booz Allen Hamilton. The Internet channel is by far the cheapest (US$ 0.13) compared to the branch being the most expensive (US$ 1.08).

[284] Relationship services include all consultation services.

[285] See (Instenberg-Schieck 1999), who argues that a coexistence of transaction and relationship banking is possible and even advantageous.

[286] See e.g. (Chandler et al. 1984) for a proposed linkage between channels and products with respect to financial services.

5.2.5 Life-Cycle Consultation Approach

Life-cycle oriented savings and consumer behavior of individuals has a strong effect on demand for financial services. There are a number of theories that try to explain the life-cycle savings and consumer behavior, i.e. the allocation of resources over time.[287] Although the theoretical treatments of this topic provide valuable explanations of savings and consumer behavior over time, they are of limited value with respect to consultation services and real life cycles of individuals and their financial problems. Still, all models acknowledge the fact that consumers exhibit different savings and consumption behaviors according to their life cycle. Fig. 28 exemplarily illustrates a customer's life cycle and related financial needs.[288]

---

[287] The *life-cycle hypothesis* due to (Fischer 1930), (Modigliani and Brumberg 1954) provides for linkage between the consumption plans of an individual and his income and income expectations as he passes from childhood, through the work participating years, into retirement and eventual decease. The *permanent income hypothesis* proposed by (Friedman 1957a, 1957b) suggests that, however variable their income, consumers will attempt to smooth out the pattern of their consumption. Both models neglect uncertainty, which is introduced in the contributions by (Merton 1992) about *optimum consumption and portfolio selection in continuous-time models*. ((Merton 1992) is an omnibus of several articles by Robert Merton. In this context the contributions in Part II of that book are relevant.) A different direction is taken with a further development of the models mentioned above: (Shefrin and Thaler 1988) propose a *behavioral life-cycle hypothesis*, trying to incorporate behavioral sciences, notably psychology to better explain actual observable behavior of investors (also see (Goldberg and von Nitzsch 1999)). Another related concept is that of the *human capital based life-cycle concept* by (Spremann and Winhart 1998), (Spremann 1999). It emphasizes the need to include human capital in the asset allocation decision along the life cycle. There are numerous further developments concerning all models, which will be neither listed nor discussed here.

[288] Another very nice illustration of a hypothetical consumer financial life cycle can be found in (Parja et al. 2000).

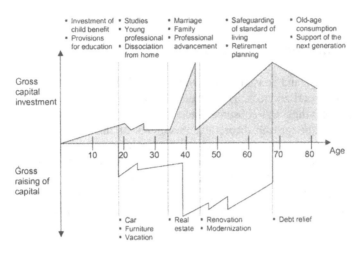

Fig. 28. Schematic Illustration of an Exemplary Customer's Life Cycle[289]

Although there may be life stages where the probability of specific needs is comparatively high and with it the affinity to specific financial solutions, each customer's life cycle is very individual. The needs are highly dependent on life circumstances: It makes a great difference with regard to a customer's needs whether he has a family and children or whether he lives as a single.[290] However, it is not only family issues that influence the need for financial services but also life events such as a sudden inheritance. Moreover, the sophistication level or the attitude towards risk[291] may change over time, resulting in different needs for financial solutions.[292] (Stracke and Geitner 1992) allude to the fact that though the static life-cycle concept[293] may provide valuable insights and be a basis for consultation services, due to changing demographic and social changes, the need for individual consultation approaches is rising.

---

[289]   Figure taken from (Tilmes 2000). A very similar figure can be found in (Stracke and Geitner 1992).

[290]   See e.g. (Tilmes 2000) for a special family-life-cycle concept. (Epple and Ramin 1993) discuss consequences for financial advice based on life-cycle considerations. They base their recommendations on an empirical study about the customers in the German financial services market in 1991. (Laternser 2000) reports that life-cycle approaches have already replaced traditional bankbook investments. On the life-cycle concept with respect to financial services in general see (Stracke and Geitner 1992). A typical life cycle for a physician and its consequences on the need for financial services can also be found therein. A detailed life cycle for a physician can also be found in (Hassels 1997).

[291]   See (Kraus 2002) for a typical development of the attitude towards risk along a life cycle.

[292]   See e.g. (Spremann 2000).

[293]   Static in terms of the typical unchanged order of life stages of a citizen of a western industrialized country: school, training/education, young professional, marriage, children, children leave home, retirement, death of spouse.

(Nowak 1999) even suggests that considering a life cycle in order to target the right customers with the right products via the right channel at the appropriate time is not enough. The customer should be seen in his whole personality. She proposes a *habitat-oriented marketing approach*.[294] This approach surely has its merits when it comes to targeting the right customer segments with the right products. However, here the *type* of the service itself is the center of interest.

Operationalizing the life-cycle approach for the customer as well as for the financial services provider, the concept of *financial planning*[295] seems to suit very well.[296] Following (Tilmes 2000) financial planning is defined as a comprehensive consultation service, which is organized as a structured planning process (see Fig. 29). Financial planning shall enable private persons in their roles as economically acting individuals, households or entrepreneurs to substantiate and optimally achieve their financial objectives caused by occurred or expected life events.[297]

Fig. 27 schematically illustrates the financial planning process.

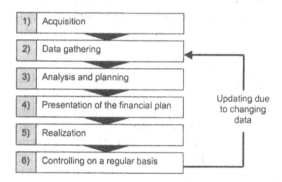

Fig. 29. Process of Financial Planning[298]

---

[294] On milieu structures in Germany between 1981 and 1994 as well as 1998 see (Nowak 1999).

[295] In the following the terms *financial planning* and *wealth management* are used interchangeably.

[296] The connection between life-cycle considerations and financial planning is also made in Anglo-American literature. See e.g. (Garner et al. 1996), who state "Rather than viewing financial planning as a one-time activity, we think of it as a series of steps you take at certain times in your life to make life's events more financially manageable.".

[297] On *financial planning* see e.g. (Tilmes 2000), (Böckhoff and Stracke 1999), (Perridon and Steiner 2002), (Kruschev 1999), (Reitinger et al. 1997a, 1997b), (Kraus 2002). Especially (Kruschev 1999) provides a nice discussion about the advantages and disadvantages of financial planning.

[298] Figure is based on (Böckhoff and Stracke 1999), (Tilmes 2000), and (Richter 2001). On *rules of orderly financial planning* see (Richter 2001). They include *completeness, individuality, integration, correctness, understandability, documentation, compliance with principles of the profession* (integrity, confidentiality, objectivity, neutrality, competence, and professionalism). In his illustration (Tilmes 2000) distinguishes a *customer* and a *supplier* perspective. The latter one is the center of interest in this book.

After the customer acquisition (potentially supported by CRM methods), all relevant data about assets, liabilities, and insurance contracts as well as consumption objectives, expected life events and other relevant information have to be gathered in order to get a holistic picture of a specific customer. Generally speaking, instruments such as the *private balance sheet,* the *private income statement* and the *private liquidity plan* are used to illustrate the current and expected situation of the customer.[299] Simulations are used to check on the insurance against events such as occupational disability. One of the most demanding tasks is the *analysis and planning phase,* since an individually tailored financial solution has to be developed for a specific customer. The resulting financial plan has to be discussed with the customer and eventually an agreed-on solution plan may be realized. It is important though that financial planning is not a one-time event but that the plan is updated on a regular basis. If actual values considerably differ from the reference values, exceeding a threshold value, an adaptation has to be performed. Particularly this controlling loop ensures customer retention and regularly repeated business. Even though this concepts sounds appealing it is surprising that just very few financial plans have been accomplished so far in the German financial services market.

(Böckhoff and Stracke 1999) assume that roughly 2,000-3,000 comprehensive financial plans have been accomplished so far. (Reitinger et al. 1997a) state that according to recent studies 6,000-8,000 were performed between 1987 and 1997. This stands in contrast to the estimated 2.7 Mio wealthy private households that potentially have a demand for comprehensive financial planning services.[300] And more and more practitioners seem to recognize that the mass affluent customer segment should be targeted with financial planning services,[301] since many of these customers eventually may become private banking customers.[302] Apparently, there is an immense business opportunity that may be utilized. However, introducing financial planning on such a broad basis makes the appropriate support with IT crucial. Today, there are already a number of (very) sophisticated products in the market,[303] but they mostly lack a sound support of the *analysis and planning* phase

---

[299] See e.g. (Tilmes 2000), (Böckhoff and Stracke 1999).

[300] See (Tilmes 2000).

[301] See e.g. (Fuchs and Girke 2002), (Maguire et al. 2001), (Ausfelder et al. 1999). (Tilmes 2000) cites a number of empirical studies performed in the US market that deal with demand factors of financial planning services. Taxation issues as well as retirement planning are the two reasons mentioned most often. Retirement planning is an issue that has gained increasing attention in Germany in recent years (see Sec. 3.2), which is a hint that the demand for financial planning services is also on the rise.

[302] See (Ausfelder et al. 1999). Certainly, not every customer needs a very comprehensive financial plan also taking into account business and private assets. On different financial plans see e.g (Tilmes 2000).

[303] Examples include the detailed and comprehensive financial planning applications by MWS Braun GmbH (http://www.mwsbraun.de) or Microplan GmbH (http://www. micro-plan.de). A comprehensive and up-to-date market overview on financial planning software is available to subscribers of "bankmagazin" (also see http://www. bankmagazin.de).

and – if at all – a well-designed *controlling loop*. To facilitate closing this gap, a product model is presented in Sec. 6.3 to support the analysis and planning phase.[304]

Having talked imprecisely about private banking customers and the mass affluent segment but also having argued why these segmentation approaches are outdated, the question remains which customers should be actively targeted with financial planning services.

5.2.6 Customer Lifetime Value[305]

So far, in addition to cost-oriented merger strategies discussed above (see Sec. 4.1), financial services firms on the marketing side have been trying to concentrate on *high net-worth individuals*.[306] These are usually defined as having high income, high property or both. In many cases, for instance in the early years of Germany's Advance Bank this strategy has failed due to low willingness of these high-end customers to switch banking affiliations. Thus for the entrant per capita acquisition costs were quite high. Other income-/property-based segmentation strategies have also failed due to the fact that (because of lack of consultation service) interesting customers could not be retained.[307] In contrast, successful exceptions on the financial services markets such as MLP AG concentrate on potentially interesting customers such as students of business administration, computer science and engineering, invest heavily in winning them early and accompanying them along their (often freelance[308]) career with increasingly sophisticated (and profit generating) financial products and services. Using IT as an enabler and pursuing the life-cycle oriented strategy sketched above seems very promising for the following reasons:

- Particularly (potentially) interesting customers are often convenience-oriented and prefer – given a trust-relationship – financial services bundled by one supplier instead of spending their scarce time on shopping around and coordinating multiple suppliers (also see Sec. 5.2.1).
- Financial services firms pursuing a strategy of investing in long-run trust relationships with (potentially) interesting customers are facing lower costs, because it is much cheaper to sell additional products to existing customers along their life cycle instead of winning new interesting customers.

---

[304] The idea to support the financial planning process with IT is not new though. An IT-enabled financial planning approach based on a customer's life cycle was already proposed e.g. by (Wiemann 1993).

[305] Parts of this section are taken from (Buhl et al. 2001).

[306] Also see Fig. 21, p. 65.

[307] Also see p. 64.

[308] Also see Sec. 3.3.

- Appropriately individualized bundles of financial services are usually advantageous for both the supplier and the customers for reasons of taxation and diversification as it has been have shown in a number of studies.[309]

Thus such a long-run strategy applied to customers becoming interesting in the future seems promising to European and particularly German financial services firms as a differentiation strategy on global markets. How can a financial services firm decide whether a customer is interesting or not?

The concept of *customer lifetime value*[310] is a relatively young discipline compared to other marketing strategies. It emphasizes the need to view the customer base of a firm as its assets (*customer equity*), thus turning from a product-centric towards a customer-centric view. Customer lifetime value (CLV)[311] is strongly interrelated with the individualization and the life-cycle consultation approach both discussed above. Companies have to acknowledge that a customer relationship evolves over time. Each customer has his own preferences and needs and is located at a different status in his own life cycle as well as in the life cycle with respect to the relationship with his financial services firm.

CLV denotes the expected value that a customer contributes to the value of the firm along his (potential) relationship with the firm.[312] Mathematically, the CLV is the expected discounted net cash flows that are assigned to a specific customer relationship.[313] The total of all CLVs of a firm is its customer equity.[314] The concept of CLV makes an important point in emphasizing that it is not about customer orientation at all costs, maximal customer satisfaction and customer loyalty of all customers.[315,316] It rather provides an invaluable basis for the decision about how much should be invested in a customer relation from the supplier's point of view.[317]

---

[309] See e.g (Buhl et al. 1999a), (Buhl et al. 1999b), (Buhl and Wolfersberger 2000b), (Satzger and Kundisch 2001), (Schneider and Buhl 1999), (Schneider 1999a), (Will 1995).

[310] On *customer lifetime value* see e.g. (Stahl et al. 2000), (Blattberg et al. 2001), (Günter and Helm 2001), (Dzienziol et al. 2001), (Dwyer 1989), (Rust et al. 2000), (Tomczak and Rudolf-Sipötz 2001), (Rudolf-Sipötz 2001).

[311] See (Dwyer 1989).

[312] The definition of CLV used here is clearly from the perspective of the supplier. The value a customer assigns to a relationship with a firm is not considered explicitly in this book.

[313] See e.g. (Dwyer 1989), (Helm und Günter 2001).

[314] See (Rust et al. 2000).

[315] (Helm and Günter 2001).

[316] Linking the multi-channel and CLV approach, (Albert 2000) emphasizes the need for an integrated multi-channel approach to perform a times series analysis under life-cycle considerations is an important concept.

[317] On methods to determine the customer value see e.g. (Helm and Günter 2001), (Stahl et al. 2000). A very thorough treatment of this topic can be found in (Rudolf-Sipötz 2001).

Having the theoretical methods to manage a customer base, the question is not only about which customer relations should be worked on with respect to existing customers but also *what kind of new customers* should be attracted *at what time*. Generally speaking, the first part of the question can be answered quite easily: Obviously, customers with a high expected CLV should be attracted.[318]

The question has to be raised, when in the life cycle it is a good time to target a potential customer. Companies should not wait until postgraduates apply for their first jobs after their studies to approach them with appropriate services.

- Firstly, it is quite difficult to approach postgraduates since the university as a communication and networking platform cannot be utilized anymore.
- Secondly, a majority of postgraduates will already have at least one relationship to a financial services firm due to their jobs during their studies. If they have made good experiences with their current firm, they might be at least reluctant to switch. Thus acquisition cost will be much higher for these relationships.

Therefore, firms should approach (high) potential customers as early as needed to build a relationship. Here, the university and chairs in particular, lend themselves preeminently as a communication and networking platform. This holds true not only for recruiting purposes, where the struggle for the best brains gets also harder every day, but also for building long-term customer relationships.[319] One example is the (so far) very successful approach of MLP, a German financial intermediary that focuses its marketing efforts mainly on graduates.[320]

Another promising approach may be to offer highly standardized products for company pension plans.[321] If this bulk business can be handled by appropriate IT, it should be possible to turn this offering in a successful business model in itself. However, the real benefit stems from the opportunity to leverage the vast amounts of data a financial services provider gets the hands on when managing these retirement plans. Again, using a powerful data warehouse and accompanying data mining technologies, potentially interesting customers can be identified and targeted with comprehensive financial planning services.

According to a study by (Hawkes 1995) less than 30% of financial services firms hold information on customer needs and preferences and only 20% hold information on CLV. Even worse (Tomczak and Rudolf-Sipötz 2001) find that only 3% of respondent firms in a recent survey calculate CLVs for their customers based on a 10-year horizon. This indicates the need to invest in appropriate information systems on the one hand and shows the unutilized potential for a differentiation strategy on the other hand. With successful relationship management it is not only possible to identify and select the most valuable customers, but also to

---

[318] (Blattberg et al. 2001) formulate the rule that customers should be acquired „as long as the discounted future value of the customer exceeds the acquisition costs for that customer.", which from a finance and investment perspective makes perfectly sense.

[319] On long-term relationships in the financial services market with respect to banking structure and policy see (Haubrich 1989).

[320] However, recently at the stock market, MLP has suffered severely.

[321] See e.g. (Flieger and Frischmuth 2002).

increase margins, because of reduced costs for customer care and increasing selling numbers or prices (for individual products). Pricing will also be the issue of the next section.

5.2.7 Pricing: Business Model[322]

Historically, the simple selling of financial products was too often denoted as *advice*, whereas the *structuring know-how* as the real value add of a financial services provider was often seen as a friendly auxiliary service without separated pricing. Due to cross-subsidies, the customer paid in fact too much for the transaction and too little for the real advice services in this scenario.[323]

Therefore, a pricing scheme is proposed that is not based on cross-subsidies but on direct charges for the value of the service that has been produced. But it is not only about the circumvention of these subsidies. If financial planning services are to be offered on a broad scale, it is important that objectivity and neutrality[324] are guaranteed in order to maintain a trust relationship with the customer. Moreover, due to the probably higher expenses compared to traditional financial consulting in terms of information systems, human resources and organization[325], a direct pricing scheme seems favorable.[326,327]

Certainly, market conditions cannot be neglected: In the German financial services market it has generally not been common to charge for consultation sessions so far. Therefore, fee- instead of commission-based pricing should be introduced stepwise and very cautiously without, however, losing sight of the objective. The different levels of service that are offered according to the above-described strategy of choice also makes it easier to charge for the higher level services (see Sec. 5.2.7).[328] This should result in a higher cost transparency for the customer and less volatile – since independent from any transactions – revenues for the supplier. If introduced appropriately, it may even lead to additional revenues.[329,330]

---

[322] On the commission scheme see e.g. (Meier 2000).

[323] (Instenberg-Schieck 1999).

[324] See (Richter 2001).

[325] On organizational issues see (Kruschev 1999).

[326] See (Eder 2002).

[327] In the US market, fee-based pricing has been common already for a couple of years now; see (Sestina 1991).

[328] (Meier 2000) presents three different consultation-based fees: Consultation fees per unit of time, flat consultation fee based on consultation intensity and all-in rates.

[329] See e.g. (Eder 2002).

[330] On pricing models in financial planning see also (Kruschev 1999).

5.3 Summary

In the preceding sections a vision and an accompanying strategy were developed for a German financial services provider with a broad customer base. If the financial services firm succeeds in replacing usual segmentation strategies by a potential-oriented CLV strategy ensuring that competence of its consultants fits to the customer, individualized life-cycle solution provision is feasible. For increasingly competent customers and complex financial problems along their life cycle appropriate solutions with substantial advantages for both the customer and the financial intermediary can be provided.

In the next chapter two concepts will be presented that have already been mentioned above and that may facilitate a financial services provider turning the strategy into reality.

6 Concepts for Life-Cycle Solution Provision

Having laid out a vision and a sustainable strategy for a financial services provider in the (Post) Information Age in the preceding chapter, two important concepts will now be presented and discussed that may facilitate and contribute to the implementation of the strategy described above. The first one, a *content model* for the financial services market, aims at keeping a customer better informed about financial services by facilitating the individualization of finance-related content distribution, thus contributing to solving a *financial problem in the broader sense* with respect to information needs. The second one, a *product model*, facilitates the process of generating an individualized solution to a customer's *financial problem in the narrower sense*, i.e. the need for an intertemporal liquidity distribution.

IT plays a very important role in the implementation of the strategy and particularly of these two concepts due to various reasons:

- Financial services are immaterial, i.e. they are just information and therefore are preeminently suited for IT-enabled processing.
- The solution space for financial problems is very complex. Profound product know-how as well as knowledge about superior combinations of financial products has to be present to generate superior solutions.[331] Enormous CPU power is needed to generate good solutions for a customer.
- Financial services often have repetitive character since investment strategies have to be controlled over time. If the ex post performance is significantly different from ex ante performance expectations, the investment strategy has to be adapted. Therefore, the relevant information has to be stored and made accessible for a controlling process.
- A complex and fast-changing environment with respect to national taxation and other laws makes it nearly impossible to provide good consultation services without the support of an appropriate information system.
- The time of a personal financial advisor is expensive and his ability to take care of customers is limited. Therefore he should be able to focus on value added instead of standardized undemanding activities.

---

[331] See e.g. (Buhl et al. 1996).

- There are significant scale effects that may be realized utilizing appropriate information systems. One prominent example with respect to the customer interface – not related to the two concepts – is an online money transfer application.[332]

Though this list of items is definitely not exhaustive, it should become clear that applying appropriate IT is not just a nice-to-have but a necessity to survive in the market. However, in contrast to Internet boom times at the beginning of the third millennium, economic considerations must be the guidance for any investment decision into IT. Even though the indirect effects on the profitability – such as contributing to building trust and loyalty towards a financial services provider – of an IT venture and its contribution to the overall objectives of the organization can often not be determined with exactness, a thorough cost/benefit analysis should be accomplished for each project. In the following, two models – a content and a product model – will be presented in which it seems reasonable to invest scarce resources due to promising scale effects as well as substantial improvements for CRM with respective positive effects on trust and loyalty. Both aim at providing a customer with an individualized solution to his financial problems, the first one with respect to informational needs, the latter one with respect to desired cash flow streams.

The chapter is organized as follows: After these introductory remarks, the general research framework is presented in Sec. 6.1. Special parts of this general research framework, namely the content model (Sec. 6.2) and the product model (Sec. 6.3) are covered in the subsequent sections. A brief summary concludes this chapter (Sec. 6.4).

6.1   Research Framework

The problem of providing customers with individualized solutions to their problems is very complex.

Firstly, the customer himself has to be modeled and a machine-readable representation of his (changing) preferences and (latent) needs has to be provided.

Secondly, the quite different financial products in terms of cash flow effects, risk, and complexity, to name just a few, have to be modeled in order to generate a sound bundle of financial products based on the customer's needs.[333] A financial problem is often only the second step with respect to an overall problem or need.

---

[332] In fact, the scale effects on the one hand and the cost reduction effects on the other hand seem to be massive, since German HypoVereinsbank offers a special checking account where the customer gets a credit of 0.26 Euros for each transfer performed by using technical communication channels such as online banking or ATM. See (Dzienziol et al. 2002) for a contribution that deals with multi-channel pricing in the financial services sector.

[333] On the issue of bundling financial products see Sec. 6.3. Also see a seminal contribution by (Will 1995) with respect to IT-related issues.

As already stated in Sec. 2.3, customers do not really have a financial problem in the first place, but it is generally the result of an explicit or latent need. Once this need – for instance to have a car at one's disposal – is identified, it is the challenge to provide the customer with a good financial solution in order to satisfy this need. Generally speaking, a customer has a great variety of needs that translate into consumption objectives. Thus the problem of financial dispositions with respect to these objectives are also quite diverse.

Thirdly, a customer not only wants financial products, he also wants to be informed about finance-related issues and financial products. There are various reasons why a customer might want to be informed.[334]

- He wants to be informed about companies and markets he has already invested in.
- He wants to be informed about companies and markets he is interested in and considers investing in.
- He expects that solutions to his financial problems are properly explained to him.
- He is looking for advice on how to invest his money.
- He is looking for general information on specific topics such as taxation, monetary policy, and legal aspects.
- He wants to be informed about changes in the value of his assets and liabilities as well as in his expected cash flows.

Certainly, this list is not exhaustively enumerative but it shows that the *informational needs* of a customer can have various reasons and that it is not an easy task to individually offer a customer the *right content* at the *right time* using the *right communication channel*.

Fourthly, there are various channels that can be utilized to distribute pieces of content as well as to sell financial products to specific customers. Each channel has its own characteristics and restrictions.

Finally, intelligent matching algorithms are needed to combine the customer with the products and contents, i.e. matching[335] has to take place based on the information provided in the customer, content, channel, and product models.

Fig. 30 depicts the general framework of the research approach.[336]

---

[334] A McKinsey study provides evidence that consumers want to be informed: "While consumers show little interest in shopping for financial services, they do have a growing appetite for education regarding PFS [personal financial services] products, particularly if it is marketed around a significant life event such as retirement or sending your children to college." (Flur et al. 1997).

[335] See e.g. (Pau and Gianotti 1990), (Bibel 1993), (Kirn and Weinhardt 1994), (Rehkugler and Zimmermann 1994) for basic information about matching algorithms and knowledge representation in the financial services domain.

[336] A similar approach can be found in (Probst and Wenger 1998).

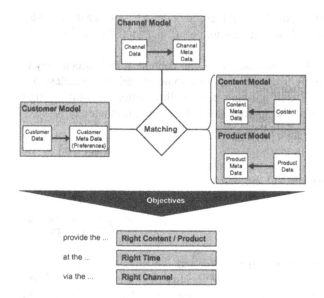

Fig. 30. General Research Framework

The framework consists of four models. They all have in common that they already provide for an inference pre-process (step one). These inference pre-processes generate meta data about the modeled objects. In a second step meta data of the different models are matched to individually provide pieces of content or products to a specific customer. The main advantages of this approach are the following:[337]

- Reduction of complexity.
- More precise specification of the matching algorithms.
- Different inference processes can follow different paradigms.
- 2-step approach (pre-process and matching) provides for more flexibility.
- Processes of knowledge generation can be traced more easily.

It should be mentioned though that there is a major deficiency affiliated with this approach. Since inference pre-processes have to be performed in all models, the matching itself cannot take place in real-time. At first glance, this might not pose a severe problem. However, most consultation processes, particularly the face-to-face ones, are (ideally) an extremely interactive process where a lot of highly relevant and valuable information is generated during the consultation process. Upfront the approach described above does not account for information generated during a consultation session.[338]

The focus in this contribution will be the right hand side of Fig. 30, i.e. the content and the product model. The concept of a state-of-the-art customer model that

---

[337] For a detailed discussion of the advantages see (Fridgen et al. 2000a).
[338] This fact has already been criticized in (Buhl et al. 2002).

is compatible with the other models is not focused on here.[339] A consistent and applicable channel model is still an open research issue that should be tackled in the future.

In the next section the focus will be put on the content model, which may be used relatively independently from the applied customer model. Nevertheless, any content model is no end in itself but aims at providing customers with the right content at the right time using the appropriate channel, i.e. it is inherently based on assumptions and knowledge about the customer.

6.2   Content Model[340]

> I only ask for information.
> CHARLES DICKENS

In the following, a content model will be suggested, which ensures that the information about the available content needed to identify the right one for a specific customer is accessible for an automatic matching process. An intelligent solution to a customer's problem in finance typically consists of multiple components one of which surely is domain-specific background information, which will be referred to as content in the following. Though content will always be part of a solution[341], frequently there will be other components, such as a financial product or a combination of products.

In the Information Age, access to information 24 hours a day and seven days a week is ubiquitous. With the rapidly spreading technology of mobile data transfer, for example cellular telephony, the location of the customer becomes irrelevant for his access to information. Content providers and intermediaries have the means to serve their customers better than in the industrial age: content can be delivered to the customer via multiple communication channels 24/7, if the customer wants to

---

[339] The interested reader is referred to (Fridgen et al. 2000a), (Fridgen et al. 2000b). For more basic contributions about user modeling see (Mertens and Höhl 1999) and (Woywod 1997) and references therein. On customer modeling with special emphasis on the financial services industry also see the forthcoming dissertations (Fridgen 2003) and (Volkert 2002). Michael Fridgen and Stefan Volkert have worked in the same publicly-funded research group FAN (Forschergruppe Augsburg-Nürnberg) as the author himself.

[340] The presented content model is based on joint research efforts with Peter Wolfersberger, Elisabeth Klöpfer, and David Calaminus. The model was presented and discussed with the German and international IS community at the FAN 2000 conference and the 34th Annual Hawai'i International Conference on System Sciences 2001; see (Kundisch et al. 2000), (Kundisch et al. 2001a), and (Kundisch et al. 2001b).

[341] Financial services are in need of explanation. Therefore, information of the customer is a very important issue form the perspective of the financial services provider (Nader 1995). On the *Theory of Financial Intermediation* with respect to informational problems see (Süchting and Paul 1998).

be informed. However, the time and effort a customer can spend gathering and absorbing information becomes the limiting factor. For instance Kerscher states that the customer is interested in problem solving information because of an increasingly difficult search process[342]. Therefore, new methods of filtering and providing information have to be developed, enabling information providers to deliver the right content at the right time via the right channel, thus optimizing customer benefit by using his scarce time and effort efficiently for his information, or even exceeding customer expectations by actively delivering important and urgent content. In fact, there seems to be a high demand especially for finance-related content in the WWW. GVU's 10th Web User Survey Graphic found out that 25% of the people who use the WWW want to access financial materials on a daily basis.[343] More than 45% of the respondents of the same survey felt that they were not able to find the information they were looking for. Hence customers either have the alternative to search for content[344] or they can leave it up to the financial services firm to provide them with relevant information.[345]

Generally, a financial services firm can provide its customers with a great variety and quantity of self-produced and externally purchased content[346] such as research, market reports, and CFO interviews just to name a few. For the decision, if a special content is the right one for the customer with respect to the above formulated objectives, meta information about the customer as well as information such as the subject of the content and other content meta information have to be considered. To automatically match pieces of content on the one hand and the customer's interest and effort limits on the other hand by an inference mechanism, fixed attributes are needed, which have to be known at the design-time of the matching rules. Hence, a customer model, a channel model and a content model as well as intelligent matching-rules have to be developed to satisfy the informational needs of customers.

Though literature shows an ongoing discussion about ontologies and technologies to build such ontologies in order to achieve semantic categorization and se-

---

[342] See (Kerscher 1998). On customer satisfaction with respect to financial services also see (Nader 1995). On customer satisfaction in services markets see e.g. (Quartapelle and Larsen 1996). On customer satisfaction in general see e.g. (Homburg 2001). (Bühler 1993) presents a framework to measure customer satisfaction in the financial services industry.

[343] See (GVU 1998). In Germany at the end of 2000 even 33% of the people who use the WWW want to access financial materials on a daily basis. See (Anonymous 2001d).

[344] With respect to standardized financial products this might become increasingly convenient over time (see Sec. 3.4.2). However, with respect to finance-related content the opposite seems to be true. For instance due to advances in IT, content is produced and made available thousandfold on the Internet making it ever more hard to find the information one is looking for.

[345] On syndication as a viable business model see (Werbach 2000).

[346] (Randle 1995) states the following about the financial services industry: It "is now the business of providing convenient access to information about money and swift [...].".

mantic linkage of web documents[347], there is a lack of a finance specific content model, i.e. comprehensive ontologies for finance-related content. In the following it is the objective to contribute to close the gap with a model for content on finance-related issues, which is suited for the matching of information to specific customer problems.[348] This is realized by identifying relevant attributes which describe finance-related content. The values of the attributes are mainly derived by an IT-enabled inference process directly from the content by methods of automatic content analysis and partly by human content managers.[349]

Before getting into the details Example 6.1 shall illustrate how content may be individually targeted at specific customers. Though Example 6.1 is quite simple it should become clear that a thorough knowledge about the customer, his situation, and his preferences as well as about the content is necessary to perform that task.

Example 6.1: Table 7 shows two different customers with (assumed) respective (latent) informational needs.[350]

Table 7. Customers and Informational Needs (Example 6.1)

Customer with (latent) informational need	Provided Content
A family father wants to put money aside for his retirement and to secure the education of his children. He is conservative but considers stocks as having the best long-term growth perspectives.	Market research about blue chips in the national currency and pension funds is provided.
A young single loves to speculate in high tech stocks. He is willing to take high risks in order to have the chance of receiving high returns.	Latest material on an IPO of a dot.com-company is provided.

Two relevant questions seem obvious when reading Example 6.1:

- What meta information is needed to be able to match customer's needs with available content?
- How can this need for specific meta information be derived?

The latter question will be addressed in the following section, the first one in subsequent sections.

---

[347] For a description of the state-of-the-art see e.g. (Weikum 2001), (Mädche et al. 2001) and the literature referenced there.

[348] The issue of *content management* in general will not be covered here; see e.g. (Schumann and Hess 1999).

[349] This approach relates to the concept of mediating electronic product catalogues described in (Körner and Zimmermann 2000).

[350] Note that it is not claimed that the inherently applied matching rule in the example is correct. It shall just show that different customers have different informational needs. The content model provides the relevant data that may be used in a variety of different matching algorithms in order to match content with customer's preferences.

6.2.1 Methods

Necessary content attributes are deduced by arguing from the customer's point of view, since it is the customer's needs which have to be satisfied with the matching process using these attributes. This is done by finding valid arguments why a certain attribute contributes to the objectives discussed in the following paragraphs.

Although it could well be the case that an attribute contributes to more than one of the three objectives the attribute is added to the catalogue of relevant attributes after identifying at least one contribution. Generally, it is not discussed why rejected attributes do not contribute to an objective. Both of those two issues mentioned above are part of identifying matching rules. There might be attribute candidates which seem close at hand but on closer inspection are either redundant or their value is not derivable from the mere content itself. In these cases it will be argued why they are not needed as attributes. For identifying the right point of time and the right channel combination to deliver this piece of content, not only relevant content attributes will be identified, but also a concept for a multi-channel distribution architecture will be presented.

The presented approach belongs to both the discipline of information filtering (IF) and of information retrieval[351] (IR). Whereas IR generally deals with a stable information space and users having varying information needs, IF deals with a dynamic information space and users having a relatively stable information need.[352] In the context of this framework, it has to be dealt with both a highly dynamic information space and changing user needs, since on the one hand finance-related content is produced thousandfold in a minute and on the other hand customers marry, change jobs, grow older, etc. The challenge here is to match the characterizations (meta information) of content[353] with (changing) user profiles. Among other things these profiles include representations of the user's informational needs.

It has to be stated that the identification of the content attributes is done by theoretical discussion and lacks empirical evidence in the first place. Nevertheless, this procedure may serve as a good starting point for building hypotheses for further empirical research, which seems to be underrepresented in scientific literature in this specific area.

---

[351] For up-to-date concepts in IR see e.g. (Baeza-Yates and Ribeiro-Neto 1999) and references therein.

[352] See e.g. (Wondergem et al. 1997). A nice collection of articles about IF can be found in (ACM 1992).

[353] To be more precise, for the purpose of matching, the information objects are weakly characterized, i.e. different information objects may have the same characterization. See e.g. (van Bommel and van der Weide 1998).

6.2.2 Right Content

The right piece of content for a customer is the one which satisfies the customer's explicit and latent informational needs and matches his mental abilities as well as his current situation and environment.

While explicit informational needs are easily assessable by online profiling techniques or by using a questionnaire, the assessment of latent informational needs is not quite as easy. However, a financial services firm normally has access to a vast amount of customer information, which can be used with the help of data mining techniques to identify future customer's informational needs. To match the identified customer's interest with the subject of the content, content providers on the market already use subject catalogues and match the content to the *subject terms*. When a relevant subject for the customer is identified, matching can be triggered for content with the categories in question. Those catalogues normally are flat lists of keywords (or subject terms), subsets of which are attributed to pieces of content. These are already very well suited for matching content and customer with respect to subject dimension (see Fig. 31).

Concentration on the nearby contract in financial futures markets: A stochastic model to explain the phenomenon
Journal of Economics and Finance; Murfreesboro; Fall 2000; Gunter Bamberg; Gregor Dorfleitner;

Volume:	24
Issue:	3
Start Page:	246-259
Page Count:	14
Document Type:	Feature
Source Type:	PERIODICAL
ISSN:	10550925
Subject Terms:	Studies
	Stochastic models
	Financial futures
Classification Codes:	9130: *Experimental/theoretical*
	3400: *Investment analysis & personal finance*
UMI Article Re. No.:	JOEF-6-5
UMI Journal Code:	JOEF

Abstract:
A stochastic model is developed to explain how the early unwinding propensity of market participants in financial futures markets can lead to a strong concentration of the trading volume on the nearby contract. In this model the position closing behavior of the market participants is captured by three distribution functions. The concentration process works under many realistic specifications of these distribution functions.

Fig. 31. Query Result of ProQuest ABI/INFORM Database[354]

Some information providers already deliver *language* and length information along with information about the *author, type information* of the text (research report, rumor, etc.) and the *source* of a piece of content (see Fig. 31). There might be customers with strong preferences for or aversions to specific authors or sources. For example a scientifically oriented person might reject reading any yel-

---

[354] The database is accessible at http://proquest.umi.com.

low press article. Therefore source and author information should be incorporated into the set of relevant attributes for the matching process.

Obviously, *language information* is also mandatory to provide readable information for the customer: Who would like to read this book in German?

As already argued above, time is a scarce resource and hence bothering the customer with articles too long or with poor information density contributes to customer dissatisfaction. Thus *length* is a key attribute.[355]

Type information about the content might also be vital to help the customer assess its reliability and objectivity. As Fig. 32 shows, some providers already provide type categories like for example "commentary" or "review", which state that the content does not represent objective information. So, content type should be included in the catalogue of attributes.

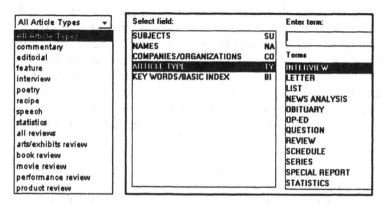

Fig. 32. Content Types at ProQuest (left) and New York Times (right)

It is quite clear that temporal information as the *release date* of the content has to be available additionally to provide topical news and information and to signal the expiration of the content. Finding the right time of expiration of a piece of content is very important for customer satisfaction. However, it is much too complex to be modeled solely by one content attribute, since there are several different situations and possible triggers for the expiry of a piece of content. Expiry usually originates from the environment rather than from the content itself: finance specific content is regularly outdated by the market, additionally it can be outdated by changes of tax laws or other events. Therefore an attribute *expiry date* cannot be added to the content model. In Sec. 6.2.5 some ideas are presented which might contribute to ensure timely expiry of the content.

So far attribute candidates have been considered which are already derived and provided by content providers. However, exclusively taking into account the attributes mentioned above endangers customer satisfaction. When reading a piece

---

[355] This will be an issue later when discussing the order in which pieces of content should be presented to a customer.

of content, there are numerous other factors which influence the attitude of the customer towards the content.

If the customer needs a recommendation, a mere informing content would waste his time and effort if a recommending piece of content could be presented instead. In contrast, if the customer only wants to be informed, he might even feel distressed when reading recommendations. To avoid this, each piece of content needs to be categorized in terms of its *recommendation level*, which is low if only information about a subject or product is given, or high if the customer is urged to buy a product.

In some countries, recommendations must be handled with care. Especially if the content is about risky assets, there might be legal restrictions.[356] Content providers might be hold liable for (wrong) recommendations within the content. Moreover, it is generally a valid question whether for instance content about high-risk stock options should be delivered to a person, who is rather averse to risk and not versed in the subject anyway. To avoid this, it seems at first glance to be a good idea to introduce a content attribute like *risk*. On closer inspection, this turns out to be unnecessary. The already introduced subject catalogue usually provides information about the products and markets mentioned in a piece of content. With the newly introduced attribute *recommendation level*, liability problems can be avoided by appropriate rules within the rule base. Content concerning inappropriate products due to risk assessed by volatility measures or ratings, can also be sorted out.

Example 6.2: Consider a conservative customer and a content with the subject "NASDAQ stocks options" and a high recommendation level. The provided information about the content comprises sufficient information about the risk involved for the customer and the liability risk for the provider.

Assigning the value "high" to an attribute *risk* would also produce redundancy and thus would not be efficient.

Just like at the *recommendation level*, the customer with respect to the *level of specificity* might want to receive general information about a subject rather than special information about a certain product or topic. If for example, the customer wants to inform himself about retirement planning, he will not be satisfied with a recommendation to buy a life insurance from the ACME insurance company. On

---

[356] For instance in Germany the German Securities Trading Act (Wertpapierhandelsgesetz) requires financial services in Section 31, Paragraph (2) "1. to demand from their customers particulars of their experience or knowledge of transactions intended to be the subject of investment services or non-core investment services, of the aims they pursue with those transactions and of their financial situation; 2. to furnish their customers with all pertinent information, in so far as this is necessary to protect their customers' interests and with regard to the type and scope of the intended transactions. [...]" Furthermore, Section 32 states: "Investment services enterprises or related enterprises may not 1. advise customers of the investment services enterprise to purchase or sell securities, money-market instruments or derivatives if and to the extent that such advice is not in conformity with the customers' interests [...]".

the other hand, if he only wants to be informed about a certain product or service, he might not want to be bothered with content of a more general nature. The generality of information is of great importance, but normally not treated within the already established methods of cataloguing subjects of content mentioned above. A flat subject catalogue does not necessarily contain information about generality or specificity of the content. In order to achieve this, the catalogue has to be at least hierarchical, i.e. with categories and subcategories. However, hierarchies have the problem that subcategories become redundant when they are subcategories to different supercategories. Therefore an attribute categorizing the specificity of the content is proposed. If a piece of content belongs to more than one subject category, a measure of multiple category specificity could be a fuzzy approach to categorization with the subject catalogue, where the association degree would be a specificity measure for the respective category.

The customer's expertise level can be matched and deliberately raised by introducing an attribute *sophistication level* of the content and treating it properly within the matching algorithm: On the one hand a slight raise within the sophistication level of the content above the customer's present expertise level will tend to raise his expertise level. On the other hand, customers get frustrated or even aggressive if they do not understand a text because of too many scientific or technical terms, or for instance too complicated a syntax within the content.

In the preceding section, content attributes that help to identify *the right content* for a customer were derived. In the following, attributes are identified which help to distribute this content via multiple channels. Moreover approaches to put the identified relevant pieces of content for delivery in an order are presented. First the involved matching and distribution processes are sketched, and consequently a multi-channel distribution architecture is presented.

6.2.3 Right Time and Right Channel

Having categorized content with ten attributes to determine *the right content* (inference process I_{1B}, see Fig. 33), the matching process I_2 with customer meta data takes place.

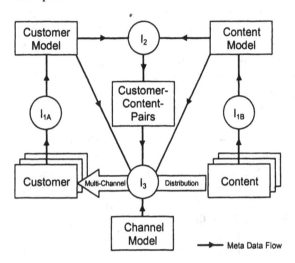

Fig. 33. Information Flow and Inference Processes

Meta information is derived by the already mentioned pre-processing inferences I_{1A} and I_{1B}, respectively. It is important to note that the matching I_2 can be triggered both customer model- and content model-driven. That is, on the one hand new content and on the other hand a changing or new customer profile may trigger the matching process. It is necessary to facilitate both types, since it may be necessary based on new information to act immediately. Example 6.3 shall elucidate that both scenarios are relevant and important.

Example 6.3:
Content-driven: In a pre-market report it is expected that the Microsoft stock will most likely plunge heavily at the stock market. A specific customer holding a big position in his portfolio of this stock should be informed as soon as possible to allow for actions.
Customer-driven: In November, a customer marries, which he reports to his financial services firm. Since different taxation laws apply for married couples, the customer should be informed about the new opportunities before year end.

Depending on the trigger for the matching process, matching output is either a prioritized list of contents per customer if customer driven, or a list of customers to be delivered per content if content driven. The amount of content pieces to be received by a distinct customer has to be restricted, so that it can be handled by the distribution process and suits the information processing capability of the customer, i.e. the time and effort he wants to spend consuming finance-related content. A static assessment of relevance for a specific customer might also be misleading as Example 6.4 illustrates.

Example 6.4: Three different pieces of content *a*, *b*, and *c* haven been identified to be relevant for a specific customer, i.e. they are *the right content*. Fig. 34 illustrates different expected utility functions[357] for these pieces of content with respect to time. Content *a* might be the case of ad hoc news with stock price relevant information about a stock the customer owns. Such information diffuses very fast in the market and already a couple of minutes later it might be worth much less than it was initially. Content *b* might contain a long-term market outlook for the European steel market, in which the customer plans to invest. Content *c* contains information about tax-saving opportunities before year end. It can even turn out that a content *not* presented may harm the customer's wealth due to foregone opportunities as shown in case *c*.[358]

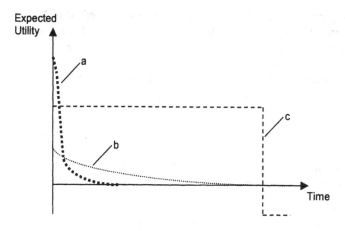

Fig. 34. Different Content Utility Functions for a Specific Customer Dependent on Time

To derive a prioritized list of contents for a specific customer, some theoretical approaches shall be presented in the following. Given a result set of various pieces of content, the question of ranking, i.e. the order of importance, is quite a challenging task. This problem has lately been discussed in a number of contributions.[359] In the following, two approaches, namely Maximal Marginal Relevance (MMR) and Incremental Searcher Satisfaction Model (ISSM) will be presented.

---

[357] Here, *expected utility* denotes the utility the customer is expected to realize within his financial sphere due to the consumption of the piece of content.

[358] Also see (Whinston et al. 1997). In their taxonomy of digital products they introduce the criterion *timeliness*. "Time-dependent products lose value rapidly [...]. Timeliness is critical to daily news, stock quotes, and other information needed for quick decision-making."

[359] See e.g. (van der Weide et al. 1998), (van der Weide and van Bommel 1998), (Carbonell and Goldstein 1998), (Varian 1999). Furthermore, see (Berger et al. 1999).

Consequently, they will be discussed with respect to search cost theory, which will provide some interesting insights in this context.

Both approaches deal with the problem that a result set based on a query generally contains more than one piece of content. Conventional IR systems basically just rank the pieces of content in a result set by maximizing relevance to the (user) query. Note that there need not have been an explicit user query to trigger a matching process as already stated above. Clearly, a ranking just based on the relevance dimension will not take into account a customer's preferences with respect to his informational needs. Perhaps he might prefer to drill down on a narrow topic whereas a different user may prefer to get a panoramic overview bearing relevance to the query. Especially, customers with high opportunity costs may not be satisfied with (partly) redundant pieces of content presented to them.[360] Hence, a customizable method, taking into account these aspects might be advantageous.[361]

One important step into the right direction is provided by the method of Maximal Marginal Relevance (MMR) due to Carbonell and Goldstein.[362] They propose (re-)ranking a result set based on a function that is constructed as a linear combination of two similarity functions.

Let C denote a document collection[363], Q a query or a user profile[364], R a set of documents, and Θ a relevance threshold[365], below which no documents will be retrieved. It follows that

$$R = IR(C, Q, \Theta).\qquad(6.1)$$

Based on result set R, S denotes either a subset of documents in R or initial knowledge of a specific user, i.e. it may represent a user profile.[366] D_i is the i'th

---

[360] (Varian 1999) emphasizes the basic property of the economic value of information. He states "the interesting thing about the economist's notion of value of information is that it is only new information that matters. [...] another document with the same information has no incremental value. This is quite different from relevance as it is usually defined since duplicate documents may well be relevant to a choice problem, even though the second instance of the relevant document is certainly not valuable." (van der Weide et al. 1998) call it *law of repetition*. $x \in S \Rightarrow I(S,x) = 0$, where $I(S,x)$ is interpreted as the increment in searcher satisfaction when document x is presented after set S has already been presented.

[361] See e.g. (Carbonell and Goldstein 1998).

[362] The following paragraphs are based on (Carbonell and Goldstein 1998).

[363] Note that in the contribution of (Carbonell and Goldstein 1998) they just refer to documents. However, the approach can be relatively easily extended to cover all kinds of content such as video clips, audio files, pictures.

[364] This a nice feature of this method since it fits the presented framework: user profiles are matched with content meta information.

[365] Θ may be either a degree of match or a number of documents.

[366] In their contribution, Carbonell and Goldstein just talk about S as a subset of R. In contrast (van der Weide et al. 1998) point out that "S can also be interpreted as previous personal knowledge [...] (sometimes also-called a user profile)".

document in R and λ the measure for the weight for novelty. Sim_1 is a similarity metric used in document retrieval and relevance ranking between documents.[367] Sim_2 may be the same metric as Sim_1. For the specific purpose of determining novelty, Sim_2 may however be a different metric. Based on this notation, the linear combination can be constructed.

$$MMR \overset{def}{=} Arg \max_{D_i \in R \setminus S} \left[\lambda Sim_1(D_i, Q) + (1 - \lambda) \max_{D_j \in S} Sim_2(D_i, D_j) \right] \qquad (6.2)$$

Like S, λ may also be derived from the user profile. If a user prefers maximal diversity, λ is set to 0. For the initial retrieval process, λ is set to 1. For intermediate values of λ a user gets a sampling of the information space around the query (smaller value of λ) or potentially overlapping or reinforcing relevant documents (higher value of λ). Hence, MMR greatly helps to rank documents according to customer preferences thus resulting in an increase in customer satisfaction.

The Incremental Searcher Satisfaction Model for IR[368] points in the same direction, but focuses on a more fundamental approach to differential relevance. Hence, elementary properties are formulated and proven, which overall leads "to a better understanding of the nature of ordering documents in IR"[369]. (van der Weide et al. 1998) point out that their approach is especially well-suited for an application in dynamic and distributed archives, such as the WWW. It is based on a relative need function, which expresses an informational need in relation to previously presented documents or initial knowledge. Due to the similar objectives of ISMM and MMR, the formal ISSM shall not be laid out here.[370]

Another very important issue in the ranking process is the limited time and effort a customer can spend consuming content. These limiting factors should also be taken into account for the delivery of the right content. Unfortunately, the above-described approaches do not provide for such features. Moreover, the similarity measures generally yield some fixed value, whereas in practice it is often known with just some kind of probability distribution whether a piece of content might be relevant for a customer or not. Here, search cost theory may give some important insights into the IR domain.

Obviously, there are costs caused by the consumption of each piece of content, such as online fees, opportunity cost of time, and telephone charges. In addition, relevancy values will be a distribution instead of a fixed value. The application of search cost theory in this context is due to (Varian 1999), who suggests applying Weitzman's *Pandora's Problem*[371]. To briefly recap *Pandora's Problem*: There

---

[367] See e.g. (van Rijsbergen 1990) or (van der Weide and van Bommel 1998) for similarity measures.

[368] This paragraph is based on (van der Weide et la. 1998) and (van der Weide and van Bommel 1998).

[369] (van der Weide et al. 1998).

[370] Moreover (van der Weide et al. 1998) emphasize that the MMR approach can be incorporated in the ISSM.

[371] See (Weitzman 1979).

are initially a number of closed boxes. Each box contains a potential reward that is independent of other rewards. Costs arise when opening a box and its content only becomes known after a specified time lag. At each stage Pandora must decide whether or not to open a box. By applying dynamic programming[372], a straightforward optimal policy can be derived:[373]

- *Selection Rule*: If a box is to be opened, it should be the closed box with the highest reservation price.
- *Stopping Rule*: Terminate search whenever the maximum sampled reward exceeds the reservation price of each closed box.

Interestingly, the reservation price is not the expected value/reward of the box. In fact, the optimal search strategy can easily involve opening a box with a low expected value/reward before opening a box with higher expected value. The reason is that each box has an option value, which increases with the riskiness of choices. Thus the superior strategy might be to look at risky choices early in the search process.[374] A simple example shall elucidate the applicability of the approach described above to IR and IF problems.

Example 6.5: A customer with high opportunity cost of time logs into the Internet. While logging in, a query based on his specific profile – revealing a preference for retirement planning subjects – is generated. The query yields a result set with a number of documents about retirement planning that may be presented one after another in, for instance, a pop-up-window to this customer. Which document should be presented first?

The result set of n documents in Example 6.5 corresponds to the boxes in Pandora's Problem. There is also a time lag t_i in consuming the document since reading takes some time. It is by far not sure how satisfied the customer will be after reading a piece of content (uncertain but estimated reward R_i). In contrast, no upfront cost c_i arises for the customer when consuming a document.[375] To make it really simple, assume for a moment that customer satisfaction is just based on the level of sophistication of a document under the condition that the subject is interesting for this customer. Moreover, the appropriate level of sophistication is determined in a binary way: it is either appropriate with probability p_i with respect to the initial knowledge of a specific customer or it is not appropriate with probability $(1 - p_i)$ leading to a reward of 0.[376] Let r denote the discount factor per unit of time and z_i the reservation price.

---

[372] See e.g. (Bellman 1957).
[373] See (Weitzman 1979).
[374] See (Varian 1999).
[375] However, the financial services provider may have to pay by piece of content viewed. This will have no relevance in the customer decision process.
[376] To include customer distress about a delivered content that was inappropriate with respect to his sophistication level, one could also assume a negative reward here.

Based on the basic condition for Pandora's Problem[377]

$$c_i = e^{-r_i} \int_{z_i}^{\infty} (x_i - z_i) dF_i(x_i) - \left(1 - e^{-r_i}\right) z_i \tag{6.3}$$

it follows that the reservation price z_i in the situation described above is given by

$$z_i = \frac{e^{-r_i} R_i p_i}{1 + e^{-r_i} p_i - e^{-r_i}} = \frac{R_i p_i}{e^{r_i} - 1 + p_i}. \tag{6.4}$$

And the expected reward er_i (or net payoff) of the i'th document is given by

$$er_i = e^{-r_i} R_i p_i. \tag{6.5}$$

Two interesting conclusions can be drawn in this context:

- Firstly, with other things being equal, the reservation price decreases with increasing length of the document. It seems to be reasonable to assume a direct positive correlation between length of a document i and the time t_i needed by a customer to consume the document. Other things being equal $(R_i = R_j$ and $p_i = p_j)$ it follows that $z_i > z_j$ for $t_i < t_j$, $t_{i,j} > 0$, and $r > 0$.
- Secondly and perhaps a bit less intuitive at first glance, for the same expected net reward and length of the document, the document which offers a *smaller* probability of success should be presented first.[378] Here, option value comes into play. Probability is smaller but potential reward is higher, hence there is a higher option value affiliated with that document. Thus $z_i > z_j$ for $er_i = er_j$, $t_i = t_j > 0$, and $p_i < p_j$.

Example 6.6: Suppose the query in Example 6.5 yields just two "right documents". Both have roughly the same length ($t_i = t_j = 0.25$). Based on the user profile, the estimated reward for the customer with document 1 is 5 ($R_1 = 5$) and with document 2 is 10 ($R_2 = 10$). The respective probabilities are $p_1 = 0.5$ and $p_2 = 0.25$. The discount rate is 0.1. Thus the expected reward is 2.44 in both cases. However, the reservation price z_2 is 9.1 in contrast to z_1 being 4.8. Hence, document 2 should be presented first.

In short, it has been shown that ranking pieces of content just based on the relevance level will not suffice to achieve a high level of customer satisfaction. In fact, a ranking just based on relevancy may even cause customer dissatisfaction through the redundancy of (at least partly) overlapping contents. The proposed approaches offer a way to deal with this problem. Of course, it is still a challenge to determine the values for the rewards and the probability of a successful presentation, and the application of such a model does not provide any insights in the channel selection process upfront.

---

[377] See (Weitzman 1979). Here, x_i denotes the potential reward with probability distribution function $F_i(x_i)$.

[378] Also see (Weitzman 1979).

For further processing, the prioritized result list is decomposed into customer-content-pairs. The following part will focus on the distribution of these pieces of content to the corresponding customer using the appropriate channel combination at the right time, which is enabled by the inference process I_3 (see Fig. 33).

When using the expression *channel*, one should be very precise about what is meant when referring to it. Often Internet, branch or call-center, just to name a few, are referred to as *channels*[379]. For the purpose of this section, this is by far not sufficient. The Internet offers a number of different *services* (and respective *protocols*), such as WWW (HTTP), Wireless WWW (WAP), email (SMTP) just to name a few. For content distribution, it makes a significant difference which of these services are used. The technical characteristics of the devices used by the customer also clearly restrict the presentation of the content or even make it impossible. For example, most cell phones currently do not support the display of colored content. However, if the cell phone is just used to connect a laptop with the Internet, completely different presentation circumstances have to be taken into account and should be utilized. Therefore, a *channel* in the terminology used here is always a *combination of the presentation device and the used service to transmit the data.*

Clearly, understanding a channel as a combination of a service and a presentation device requires a very good knowledge of the devices the customer owns or has access to. For instance, the cell phone Nokia 6510 offers different presentation options compared to an Ericsson T68.[380] If the distributed content cannot be displayed correctly on the site of the customer, it will cause customer distress. Since it is not the objective to exhaustively list all channels, i.e. all service-device-combinations here, the argument will just be illustrated on an exemplary basis.[381]

Apart from the mentioned differences within the technical characteristics of the channels, customer access time and direction (push or pull) are also relevant channel characteristics. For example a call via cell phone might be the fastest way to contact a customer, and content can be pulled and pushed through this channel. While the popular GSM (Global System for Mobile Communications) paging service SMS (Short Message Service) has similar access time, it does not offer personal contact. WWW access is pull, but not always available to the customer, thus customer access time on average will be longer. These channel characteristics have to be taken into account for the decision about the appropriate distribution channel for a given content, according to its urgency and importance. Sometimes a single channel might be less suitable than a combination of channels. For instance if an urgent and important content is too long for transmission via cell-phone

---

[379] See e.g. (Buhl and Wolfersberger 2000a).

[380] For instance in contrast to the Nokia 6510, the Ericsson T68 offers a color screen allowing for the display of colored charts.

[381] For a framework for adaptive content delivery, see (Ma et al. 2000) and (Yang et al. 2000). The decision engine proposed in (Yang et al. 2000) roughly takes the same approach as presented here. See (Edwards et al. 2001) on system performance issues with respect to dynamic content generation on the WWW.

(more precise: SMS), transmission of the content via email (SMTP) and a short note by SMS to check email might be the right solution.

Thus the first task the inference process I_3 (see Fig. 33, p. 100) has to accomplish is to classify each incoming customer-content-pair with respect to the importance and urgency of the content for the customer. The second is to select the appropriate combination of channels according to this classification, select the values of the other relevant content model attributes as well as information about the customer, and thirdly it has to adapt content in case it is not yet in a suitable form for the appropriate channel combination. Therefore, a three-layer architecture is proposed for the distribution layer which performs I_3. Fig. 35 illustrates this three-layer architecture. Technically, those layers are referred to as sub-layers of the distribution layer.

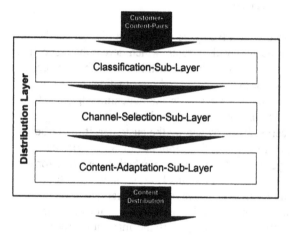

Fig. 35. Distribution Layer Overview

6.2.3.1 Classification Sub-Layer

As stated above, the first step in distribution is classifying the content with respect to its *urgency* and *importance* within the context of the customer's current situation. The concepts of urgency and importance are well-known from time-/self-management literature[382] and are needed to decide about the appropriate combination of channels for the distribution of content. Concerning urgency, the system has to decide about the time frame for the customer to get knowledge of the content. Considering importance, a decision must be made as to what degree it must be ensured that the customer receives and understands the content.

---

[382] See e.g. (Covey 1990).

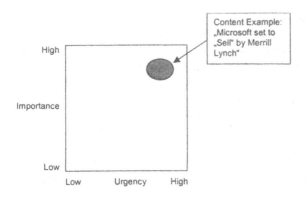

Fig. 36. Urgency-Importance-Classification of Content

With this classification, a place within the space depicted in Fig. 36 can be assigned to each content. This can be achieved by rules, which derive the respective value of urgency and importance from constellations within the attribute values of the content and the knowledge about the customer and his situation. For example, if a content has been matched to the customer, with the matching triggered from the market side, the subject of the content can give a valuable hint about urgency. For instance if the content concerns shares owned by the customer, it might be vital to deliver the content within a time going from minutes to hours from the trigger event. If it is about a change within the tax system which is relevant for the customer, and the deadline for reaction is six months later, it might as well be sufficient to deliver the content within the next 7 days (also see Example 6.3).

The level of importance can also be derived by using content attributes and information from the customer model. For example, if the matching process has identified a content about the latest development within the stock market as relevant but the customer does not have stocks in his portfolio (but his interest in stock issues has been recorded within the customer model), it could be nice for the customer to receive the content, although not receiving it at all would not damage his wealth either. The formal specification for the establishment of the rules cannot be enumerated completely here and is subject to further research.

The last paragraph exemplarily illustrated how attributes of the content model and the customer model can be used to derive the levels of importance and urgency. Ideally, this urgency classification provides a time frame for the content to be accessed by the customer. The next part will illustrate how these two dimensions affect the right choice of the combination of distribution channels trying to get as close as possible to the optimal delivery time. Thus the question of right time and right channel are strongly interrelated.

6.2.3.2   Channel-Selection-Sub-Layer

The selection of the appropriate distribution channel combination for a given customer-content-pair has to be based on the technical channel characteristics and restrictions as well as on information about the content, the customer, and the attributes *importance* and *urgency* as dealt with in the last paragraph. It also requires a
lot of detailed knowledge about the customer, the channels he uses and how they
are used by him. Fig. 37 gives an overview of information that is needed to take
the channel combination decision.

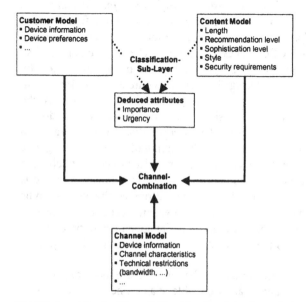

Fig. 37. Input for the Channel Combination Selection – Process View

Within the identification of the right channel combination, four groups of channel characteristics have to be taken into account.[383]

First of all, the *technical restrictions* of the channels have to be considered. As
one important issue, the security requirements imposed by the customer have to be
met by the channel characteristics. This especially applies to the Internet, where
not encrypted IP-packages travel along unpredictable and uncontrollable routes
and thus could be spied out by anyone eager to do so. If sensitive data has to be
transmitted, secure protocols such as HTTPS or SSL may be used as far as the
WWW is concerned, or emails can be encrypted using for instance PGP. So, the
attribute *security requirements* should be added to the attribute list. With respect
to the level of confidentiality, the security requirements may be high, moderate or
low. Generally speaking, the more personal information (such as the status of the

---

[383] For technical issues concerning multimedia content delivery, see e.g. (Wagner et al.
1999) and (Kießling et al. 2001).

portfolio) the content contains, the higher the security requirements have to be. Another important technical channel restriction to be taken into account are display features of the respective channel. The file format of the content will also play an important role here. Depending on whether it is a video, an audio file or just plain text, it makes a big difference for the requirements of the device used by the customer. Hence, the attribute *style* should be added to the attribute list. Length information will also help to determine which channel is appropriate for a specific piece of content. For instance, the SMS service is restricted to 160 characters, and some POP-servers (the receiving servers for emails) restrict single emails to 5 MB in order to be able to process the mail spool for a high number of users.

The second group to be considered are *customer preferences for channel usage*. Does he like using email as a means of communication between the financial services firm and himself or does he prefer printed material that comes to his home by traditional mail? Perhaps a CEO makes his secretary check his emails and so does not want to have information about his personal financial dispositions sent by email. Time windows set for channel usage by a customer are also very important, e.g. for a young father who does not want to be phoned after 7 pm because the phone might wake up his children or a stylish person who does not want to do any business at lunchtime. But the content attributes *sophistication level* or *length* of a content already mentioned above also influence the timing of delivery. It might be disturbing for the customer to receive a complex or long piece of content delivered by a phone call from his financial consultant during his lunch break, when he is trying to relax from the stress of his job. Hence, those attributes always have to be set into the context of channel usage restrictions to ensure customer satisfaction and avoid customer disturbance. Lots of cases can be imagined where time restrictions apply, and it is quite important for customer satisfaction that those restrictions are not violated.

The third group of channel characteristics to be regarded are those of *potential customer access time*. Not all channels are accessible at any time by the customer, so there is always a time lag between the initiation of a transmission process and the reception of the content by the customer. This lag varies from channel to channel. Cellular phones e.g. might well be the fastest, most direct and with respect to the access time most predictable way to communicate with a customer, whereas the average time between two visits on a personalized website may be quite long and rather unpredictable, as is the interval for some people between two checks of their email account.

The fourth important group of channel characteristics to be thought about is the degree to which a *personal or even face-to-face-contact* with the customer should and can be established. For important and sophisticated content it might be vital that the customer not only receives it, but also fully understands its consequences to his situation. To ensure this, establishing a connection with the possibility of immediate feedback might be necessary. It might even be essential to establish face-to-face contact for content involving a special degree of trust or personal recommendations.

Sometimes it is necessary to use characteristics of different channels at the same time. In this case, channels have to be combined, and content may have to be adapted to channels it was not originally suited for. Consider a customer who likes communicating by email as well as by using services such as WAP or SMS on his mobile. Now take a content that has been classified as very important as well as very urgent for the customer. However, the content may be in the PDF-file format and may contain twenty pages. Thus it cannot be delivered on the customer's mobile phone. Using the email-channel, i.e. the SMTP service and a desktop or laptop as a device might be the appropriate channel, but then the high urgency has to be indicated to him by means of another channel. For example sending an SMS on the mobile phone to notify the customer that an important email can be found in his inbox will signal its urgency. A short hint of the email-subject within the SMS might also be a valuable content adaptation for the customer. This illustrates very well that there are circumstances under which one channel will not suffice to account for the classification of the content but channel combinations have to be used.

6.2.3.3   Content-Adaptation-Sub-Layer

In the content-adaptation-sub-layer, the content to be delivered to the customer has to be adjusted to the channel combination selected for this task. In general a content will not be suitable for all the channels of the selected channel combination. Vital information has to be brought into a suitable form for the channels the original content is not suited for. This could for example be the SMS notification with a hint of the subject of the content and the advice to check the email inbox for further information. Or it could be the covering note in an email the content, which e.g. might be a PDF-file, is attached to. Thus the original content itself is not changed but just the information necessary for the distribution has to be generated in this layer and transmitted by the respective channel of the selected combination. To change the format of the content itself or just selecting some paragraphs of the text which are highly relevant for the customer[384] is subject to further research and will not be discussed here. As the content-customer-pairs have passed all three sub-layers, the actual content distribution can take place.

---

[384] In fact, the above presented MMR approach due to (Carbonell and Goldstein 1998) may also be used for text summarization.

6.2.3.4   Relevant Attributes

In the paragraphs above multiple content attributes were derived by arguing from the customer's point of view. The complete list is summarized in Table 8. Although exhaustiveness and consistence of the model, as mentioned above, cannot be guaranteed the argumentative approach is at least a good starting point for empirically identifying the attributes necessary for achieving customer satisfaction.

Table 8. Complete Attribute List for Content Model

Objective	Attributes
Right Content	Author, Source, Subject Categories, Language, Release Date, Content Type, Recommendation Level, Specificity, Sophistication Level, Length
Right Time	Subject Categories, Length, Sophistication Level
Right Channel	Subject Categories, Length, Content Style, Security Requirements, Recommendation Level, Sophistication Level
Complete Attribute List	Author, Source, Subject Categories, Language, Release Date, Content Type, Recommendation Level, Specificity, Sophistication Level, Length, Content Style, Security Requirements

After having presented the relevant attributes in the next section the application of the presented model will be discussed.

6.2.4 Application

In this section a visionary implementation design as well as the first steps towards the realization of this vision in the context of a project with Deutsche Bank AG will be presented. The discussion is restricted to a single channel application, namely the WWW service which also was the objective within that project. A discussion of the lessons learned from the project concludes this section.

6.2.4.1   Implementation Vision

Based on this model, the right hand side of Fig. 33 can be refined, discussing the processes that have to be performed to facilitate the whole matching process I_{1x} and I_2.[385] Fig. 33 shows that an inference process has to be performed in order to derive content meta information that can be used for a matching process. This pre-

---

[385] The objects *Output* and *Customer* are not depicted in Fig. 38 and Fig. 39 for reasons of simplification and clearness. Abstracting from institutional settings, Fig. 33 gives an overview of the relationships between the content and customer model and their related objects.

processing is already partly performed by content providers (step 1, for this and the following steps see Fig. 38[386]).

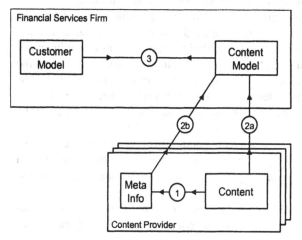

Fig. 38. Process Design – Vision

For instance content categorization is done and content length is determined by most content providers (see Fig. 31, p. 96). Relevant attributes to describe finance-related content have been enumerated and discussed in Sec. 6.2.2 and Sec. 6.2.3. Certainly, not all these attributes (see Table 8, p. 112) have been captured by content providers up to now.[387] Furthermore, the semantics of the derived meta information is not standardized among content providers. For instance content provider A may save the number of words for the length of an article whereas content provider B may store the number of pages.

Thus a second pre-processing has to be performed. Except for the subject terms and type of the content, all other attributes may be derived by a standardized and IT-enabled inference process (step 2a). In contrast, subject terms and type are (partly) determined by human content managers and for cost reasons these values should not be derived for each content again but the already determined ones should be used. Consequently, for the subject terms and type, an additional standardization process has to be performed in order to receive consistent meta information (step 2b). This process adapts the different terms and types to a major catalogue maintained by the financial services firm. The standardized pre-processing for the remaining attributes can be performed in at least two different settings. First, the content providers can send their content to the financial services firm and

---

[386] Note that from the content provider's perspective the object *Meta Info* can also be seen as a content model.

[387] There are various methods for automated text categorization. (Yang and Liu 1999) present, discuss, and compare the following five methods: *Support Vector Machines*, *k-Nearest Neighbor classifier*, *neural network approach*, *Linear Least Squares Fit mapping*, and *Naive Bayes classifier*. In (Yang 1999) twelve methods are compared. Also see references in (Yang and Liu 1999) and (Yang 1999).

the remaining meta information may be derived there. Second, meta information can be derived at the content providers' sites using an inference process provided by the financial services firm. Finally, the matching can take place (step 3).

In summary the matching process is based on consistent meta information which has been mostly derived by an automated inference pre-process. The approach convinces by its flexibility and modularity. New attributes may be easily introduced or already established attributes may be altered by simply adjusting the standardized inference pre-process provided by the financial services firm. New content providers can also be added to the framework without difficulty. The new content provider has either to be equipped with the standardized pre-process or he just sends the content to the financial services firm. Nevertheless, its subject terms and type information have to be included into the semantics of the financial services firm's subject index and type information. The meta information deduction is widely independent of the content providers as well as of the employed customer model.

It is also important to note that *content provider* does not stand for a certain industry, but a role, which can be played by several companies belonging to very different industries.

6.2.4.2 *Practical Experience and Implementation at Deutsche Bank*

The focus of the following section will lie on the practical project experience gained at Deutsche Bank AG, where such a system has been implemented. The individualization efforts comprise the steps I_{1X} and I_2 depicted in Fig. 33.

The current market situation implies an adaptation of the visionary solution described above. Content providers currently are neither willing to send their content for a pre-processing to the financial services firm nor allowing the financial services firm to equip the content providers with a standardized pre-process. Therefore, the concept of the *master index* had to be introduced. The master index – as a new element in Fig. 39 – is a union set of the (subject) categories and attributes that are provided by Deutsche Bank's content providers. That is, the master index serves as a central reference catalogue of meta information categories and attributes that comprises all individual catalogues of the different content providers and is used in the matching process. Note that the master index is just a representation of different subject categories and attributes and their possible values.

Step 1, namely the inference pre-process at the content providers, has already been described above. To prepare a matching, a customer profile of the customer model is populated with fitting items out of the master index (step 2).

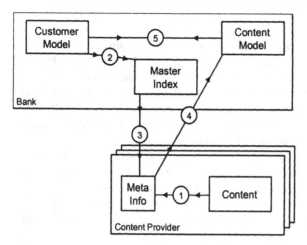

Fig. 39. Implementation Scenario at Deutsche Bank

In result, a query is generated that is sent to the content providers (step 3). In case the specific customer is already quite well-known by the system, the query will be more specific as if only some general preferences have been derived so far. For example, if it is known that a customer is interested in U.S. high tech stocks, a query will deliver much better results compared to the situation where just a general preference for U.S. stocks is assumed. Due to missing standardization the result set of a query may vary extremely concerning fit between the result of the query and the customer. For instance, if a content provider just offers a few categories, a query will not deliver high quality results. To cope with the problem of non-standardized categories, attributes, and inference processes at Deutsche Bank, an implementation of an intelligent layer is planned, which adapts each query to the specific content provider's attributes and categories before it is sent.

The result set of each content provider is sent back to Deutsche Bank (step 4), where another matching (step 5, analogously to I_2 in Fig. 33, p. 100) with the customer model takes place.[388] This is necessary since in the Deutsche Bank setting, a priori, it is not sure how the result set will look like due to not standardized inference processes at the content providers' sites and due to differing categories and attributes.

In the course of the project at Deutsche Bank AG, one of the lessons learned was that players on the financial services market are keen on the application of individualization and personalization concepts in order to intensify their customer relationships and thus achieve sustainable and unique selling positions. Moreover, it could be shown that state-of-the-art technology already enables such concepts. With vital parts of the vision sketched above being implemented, the project at Deutsche Bank is a big step in the right direction towards efficient CRM.

---

[388] Note that the content model in the Deutsche Bank scenario differs in so far from the visionary content model described above that it does only contain the result sets with the values of meta information based on the master index.

Nonetheless, there remain three major deficiencies:

- The concept of the master index portrays just an interim solution, since it has to cope with inconsistency and standardization problems. It is necessary to have just one consistent inference process (I_{1B}, see Fig. 33) based on standardized subject categories and attributes. However, most likely, it will still take some years until this may be achieved. Therefore, the master index is a helpful concept right now, even if Deutsche Bank cannot influence the categorization and inference processes used at the content providers' sites.

- In terms of the subject categories, already quite good meta information about the content is available, whereas on the remaining attributes, this is not the case. In addition to the already provided attributes, such as *length* or *language*, it is inevitable to provide the above enumerated attributes (see Table 8, p. 112), like *sophistication level*, *recommendation level* or *specificity*, in order to be able to fully match the customer's preferences with the right content at the right time in a multi-channel environment.

- At Deutsche Bank, the implemented system just allows for personalized one-to-one marketing and relationship management via the WWW channel. However, comprehensive CRM has to serve all available channels in order to satisfy customers' needs (also see Sec. 5.2.4). Nevertheless, since the Internet may serve as an integration platform and once the basic functionality and implementation is understood and tested, the system may be relatively easily adapted to comprise the remaining channels.

With these concluding remarks for the application scenario at Deutsche Bank, some limitations of the analysis and prospects for further research activities are presented.

6.2.5 Limitations and Prospects for Further Research

First, the content model is domain-specific, hence the suggested attributes might not necessarily be valid in other contexts. However, based on the presented analysis, a transfer to other knowledge domains can be comparably easily performed. The underlying technique and methodology will stay the same: *fixed attributes*, an *inference pre-process*, and *arguing from the customer's perspective*.

Second, though both practical experience and theoretical models tend to support the perspective that it is well worthwhile investing in such one-to-one marketing concepts and performing CRM, it is quite difficult to provide an accurate cost/benefit-analysis which would support the vision. Conducting a thorough and correct analysis is not possible since the efforts will only pay off in the long run due to more satisfied and loyal customers.

Third, the presented approach so far just includes the possibility to extract meta information for each piece of content and then match these meta data with information about specific customers. In the future, summarizing and matching several related documents with customers' preferences might become necessary.[389]

Fourth and most important, it is not possible to prove theoretically that the chosen attributes are indeed the relevant ones. This should not be a prohibitive obstacle to performing such kind of research. In case it turns out that one or more attributes are either missing or dispensable, the model may be easily adapted to the new set of relevant attributes.

With these limitations of the model the attention will be drawn to prospects for further research. One of the most important tasks in the future will be to conceptually combine the models of the framework. Special attention has to be put to the matching algorithms that will serve as the glue that holds the different models together. One possible design for the customer and content model is to represent each piece of content and each customer as a software agent.[390] This would facilitate the opportunity to have both customer and content driven triggers that cause a new matching process. In the financial services industry, the suggested design has already been successfully applied in a distributed multi agent environment in the German National Science Foundation (DFG) funded research project ALLFIWIB and a similar approach at Advance Bank.[391]

The expiry of content is also challenging. On the one hand it should be possible that content agents themselves interact with each other to determine whether one of them is outdated by the other. For instance a content agent containing meta information about an old quarterly report of a specific company should be terminated by a content agent that contains the meta information about the new quarterly report of the same company. On the other hand, market or legislative-driven events should generate expiry agents that screen content agents and determine whether they are outdated or not. For instance, the above mentioned example of the latest judgment in the MICROSOFT trial might trigger the creation of an expiry agent that terminates all content agents that contain meta information about earlier hearings. Modularity, maintainability as well as scalability are just some advantages of an agent-based approach. However, the scale of Deutsche Bank may require new methods and tools in order to reach an acceptable performance and security.

---

[389] (Ando et al. 2000) e.g. propose and implement a multi-document summarization technique by visualizing topical content. (Radev et al. 2000) propose two new techniques for summarization of multiple documents – cluster-based sentence utility and cross-sentence informational subsumption. These concepts relate to the above-described MMR technique due to (Carbonell and Goldstein 1998).

[390] (Wondergem et al. 1998) propose a multi-agent environment where each user and user profile, respectively, is described by a number of user agents. Resource agents also derive document characterizations from a set of documents which belongs to an information source. Also see (Wondergem et al. 1997) for an earlier article on this topic. On the state-of-the-art with respect to *cooperating intelligent software agents* see (Kirn 2002).

[391] See e.g. (Buhl and Wolfersberger 2000a), (Einsfeld and Will 1996), (Buhl and Will 1998), (Buhl et al. 1993).

Moreover, in the field of ranking and importance and urgency classification there is still a lot of space for further research. An integrated approach, taking into account the timeliness of the piece of content in the context of importance and urgency considerations has not even been established on a sound theoretical basis, let alone a practical implementation.

Finally, for validation and gradual improvement of the content model, empirical evidence on the relevance of the identified attributes is necessary.

6.2.6 Conclusion

A model with respect to finance-related content has been presented. The model has been put in the context of a general one-to-one marketing framework comprising a customer model, a content model, and a channel model as well as a product model. It has been argued that a number of attributes besides the subject and length of the content have to be derived in order to properly match a customer's preferences. Meta information is mainly derived by an IT-enabled inference process and partly by human content managers. In addition to the model, implementation issues – especially with regard to the project experience at Deutsche Bank – have been addressed and it has been shown that vital parts of the vision can already be implemented with current technology.

6.3   Product Model[392]

> And what a bank has to provide [...] is not only a product A or B,
> but an integral solution that possibly comprises many products and
> consists of intelligent product combinations that are tailored to a specific case.
> ALFRED HERRHAUSEN, 1988[393]

Having shown that information is usually at least part of a solution for a customer problem with respect to financial dispositions, in the following financial products or to be more precise, the process of bundling superior financial products is covered. Due to the quantity of available different products and the accompanying vast number of legal and tax restrictions, it is a challenging task for the financial services provider to recommend the right product or – more often – the appropriate bundle of fittingly configured products to meet a customer's needs.

To facilitate this bundling process an IT-enabled solution will often be a promising alternative in order to generate a superior solution for both the customer and the financial services provider at the same time.

---

[392] The presented product model is based on joint research efforts with Jochen Dzienziol. See (Kundisch and Dzienziol 2002) and (Dzienziol and Kundisch 2002).

[393] Translation from German, see (Herrhausen 1988).

6.3.1 Introduction

Due to the trend towards one-stop shopping in the private and retail banking segments[394], the number of products that may be offered by a personal financial advisor as solutions to a customer problem has increased dramatically.[395,396] One prominent example of this trend in the German financial services market is the takeover of Dresdner Bank AG by Allianz AG in early 2001[397], forming at least on the national level an important one-stop shopping financial services provider with global reach and ambitions. Along with the enlarged variety of products that may be offered, the complexity of finding a superior solution has also risen extremely. In addition, competition has intensified and customers have become more demanding. Thus financial services providers struggle with a more difficult solution process and at the same time with shrinking margins. In recent years, many financial services providers have already found financial planning as a strategy to gain a sustainable competitive edge at least in the customer segment of high net worth individuals. There, financial planning is understood as a financial service that cannot be offered simply as another product like investment funds by the sales force but as a service that has to be offered *before* any recommendation to purchase a financial product can be given.

From the finance perspective, the analysis and planning phase in the financial planning process, i.e. the phase where the recommendations are developed, is the most complex and demanding.[398] There are numerous different products for the optimization available, such as stocks, bonds, funds, leasing, real estate, loans, options, and futures just to name a few. Generally, they differ not only in their cash flow structure and their risk, but also in terms of their legal and tax treatment. Within these broad groups of products there are again many differences in the design of the products. For instance funds may accumulate or distribute profits once a year. Or loans may come with constant repayment or repayment at maturity. These are just two very simple examples. In fact, the opportunities to configure a financial product are often enormous. Particularly leasing contracts offer vast opportunities to exploit advantages for the customer as well as for the supplier under the condition that the contract is intelligently designed.[399]

---

[394] See e.g. (Spremann and Buermeyer 1997), (Geiger 1993). (Breuer 2002) talks about a "renaissance" of the one-stop-shopping idea in the financial services sector. He attributes part of the actuality of the topic to the passage of the Pension Assets Bill in late 2000.

[395] On problems in general, i.e. definition, types, etc. see e.g. (Elbracht-Hülseweh 1985).

[396] (Bühler 1997) concludes that as a result of the product competition a sheer uncountable and confusing variety of financial product variants and innovations has evolved.

[397] Interestingly, back in 1998 Henning Schulte-Noelle, CEO of Allianz group, was not convinced of the one-stop shopping strategy; see (Schulte-Noelle 1998).

[398] See Fig. 29, p. 81.

[399] A number of contributions deals with intelligently-designed leasing contracts. See e.g. (Schneider and Buhl 1999), (Buhl et al. 1999a), (Buhl et al. 1999b).

For an optimization it has been shown that intelligent bundling of standard products or product components may generate significant net present value advantages for both the supplier and the consumer of such an intelligent bundle.[400] However, to be able to intelligently bundle financial products, profound knowledge about single products (*product knowledge*), i.e. their cash flow characteristics, their legal and tax treatment, and obviously, current prices, has to be present at the time of the optimization process. But equally important as product knowledge is profound knowledge of intelligent combinations of these single products (*combination knowledge*). Though there are top-down optimization approaches available concerning some products or for special problems[401], because of its complexity, no *global* top-down optimization approach has been established so far. In fact, financial services providers offering financial planning services usually put a team of analysts and other experts – such as lawyers, CPAs, CFPs, and tax consultants – to the task of optimizing the global financial situation including stocks and bonds as well as real estate and other assets, given the objectives, needs, and restrictions provided by the customer.

This way of dealing with the problem is very human resources intensive, however, particularly in the domain of high net worth individuals the problems are generally of such a high complexity that IT[402] may just support some tasks of these experts in that phase.[403] The results of the analysis and planning phase are then entered back into the financial planning system that supports the other phases of the financial planning process. Even though a complete financial planning service is priced at around 4,000 Euros, financial services providers in Germany cannot cover their costs with this price and are dependent on customers applying the recommendations in their dealings with their private banking branch thus generating commissions in addition to the fees for the financial planning service.

When it comes to customer segments such as private banking customers or even customers from the mass affluent segment, the case is a different one. Here, the problem domain is simpler on average and often in a more structured form. For instance, the inclusion of corporate assets and the utilization of different tax laws concerning corporate assets as opposed to private assets can often be neglected. This makes financial planning for these customer groups a compelling case for an appropriate system support. An underlying requirement to support this process with IT is a common language, i.e. a *meta language*, which can translate

---

[400] See e.g. (Buhl and Wolfersberger 2000b) for an impressive example in the context of products with secure payments. Also see (Schneider and Buhl 1999), (Buhl et al. 1999a), (Buhl et al. 1999b). Another example is the gains that may be realized using Markowitz's portfolio optimization approach; see (Markowitz 1959).

[401] Markowitz's portfolio theory or Capital Asset Pricing Model (CAPM) due to (Sharpe 1964), (Lintner 1965) and Jack Treynor (his article has not been published) are examples that take into account common stocks and risk-free investments such as US Treasury bills.

[402] On the development of financial analysis systems see (Schneider 1999a).

[403] This statement is based on discussions of the author with many financial planning representatives of major German financial services providers.

and represent the needs of the customer on the one hand and financial products that are available to satisfy these needs on the other hand.

In literature a convincing representation language can hardly be found that may serve as a common language in conjunction with a methodology of how to intelligently combine financial products and find superior solutions to the customer's problems.[404] (Will 1995) is one exception that deals especially with such a problem domain. However, Will just considers the case of certain payments, which will not suffice in a financial planning context. In the following a formal representation of financial problems and financial products allowing for the inclusion of risk will be presented that may serve as a basis for a respective application.

Therefore, in the next section the general perspective on financial problems and solutions as well as the proposed solution process is illustrated. Consequently, necessary assumptions for the basic model are formulated (Sec. 6.3.3). In Sec. 6.3.4 the basic model without risky cash flows is presented whereas Sec. 6.3.5 and Sec. 6.3.6 cover starting points to include uncertainty and risk in the process. The identification of the final recommendation for the customer is addressed in Sec. 6.3.7. The model and its applicability is discussed in Sec. 6.3.8, whereas limitations of the approach and prospects for further research are talked about in Sec. 6.3.9 and the main findings are briefly summarized in Sec. 6.3.10.

6.3.2 Problem Solution Process in Financial Planning

Once the data of a customer are gathered for a financial planning service, the real challenge is to come to sound recommendations with respect to the customer's situation. In the recording phase all assets and expected cash flows from salaries for instance as well as objectives and needs that will result in an alteration of the financial situation of the customer are gathered (also see Fig. 29, p. 81). Based on these data and interpreting the desired cash flows as restrictions, such as a constant minimal income to cover life expenditures, an optimization process is triggered. Ideally, the result is a transformed cash flow stream based on the cash flow restrictions of the customer that optimizes a specified objective function.[405] From a mathematical point of view it is a linear or non-linear optimization problem subject to constraints.[406] The objective function in combination with these constraints – both provided by the customer – are called the customer's *financial problem*.

There might be a difficulty defining such a financial problem of a customer[407], since issues like retirement planning are still far in the future for many customers and many needs are of a latent nature or evolve as trendy only over time. Thus the

---

[404] A financial decision support system is proposed by (Palma-dos-Reis and Zahedi 1999), which does not relate to the model presented here, since their system does not support the cash flow perspective which is key in the product model.

[405] On the consultation process between customer and financial advisor see e.g. (Brunner 1993).

[406] On linear and non-linear optimization see e.g. (Neumann 1975).

[407] In the following briefly denoted as *problem*.

financial advisor has the challenging task to identify these needs during the conversation with the customer and assign cash flow requirements to these needs in order to define the problem. Historical data from peer groups can help a great deal in this task and there are already a number of valuable tools[408] available that facilitate this process.[409]

Though the identification of the problem is demanding, the generation of the solution is characterized by at least the same level of complexity. On the one hand it is the task to transform vague and often qualitative needs in quantitative requirements considering cash flows, on the other hand it is the sheer uncountable number of products with often various parameters that can be included in the solution process to determine an optimal solution to the customer's problem. Talking about this solution process, apparently a global top-down optimization approach in form of an algorithm leading to a guaranteed optimal solution will hardly exist. In literature top-down approaches just exist in specific product domains. Examples are Markowitz's portfolio theory[410] (*optimization through selection*) or the design of the discount in a mortgage loan[411] (*optimization through configuration*). Nevertheless, these optimization approaches usually are still subject to a number of restrictive assumptions.[412] In contrast to the availability of top-down domain-specific optimization knowledge, top-down *combination* knowledge is rare and generally remains on a simple and abstract level.[413]

Therefore, the process of determining a globally optimal solution has to be tackled from a different side. To recap, local instead of global optimization knowledge is often available with respect to specific product domains. Hence, it might be advantageous to combine two or more locally optimized products to form a globally superior solution. Particularly if the principle of value additivity[414] holds, locally optimized solutions can be simply summed to form a solution for the customer, which is a very nice feature from a mathematical point of view. A

---

[408]   Examples include the detailed and comprehensive financial planning applications by MWS Braun GmbH (http://www.mwsbraun.de) or Microplan GmbH (http://www.micro-plan.de).

[409]   Therefore, this process step will not be covered in the following. It is assumed that the customer can define the problem himself or the process of defining the problem is sufficiently supported by appropriate tools.

[410]   See (Markowitz 1959).

[411]   See (Wolfersberger 2002).

[412]   For instance Markowitz's portfolio models generally assume discrete returns as normally distributed. However, there is a lot of empirical evidence that this assumption is not realistic. See (Bamberg and Dorfleitner 2001) for a discussion of the impact if log returns are fat-tailed.

[413]   An example might be the CAPM, which includes a risk-free investment opportunity (Tobin separation). As a surrogate for this risk-free investment opportunity Treasury bills are often taken; see (Brealey and Myers 1996). However, there are Treasury bills with different maturities as well as different interests and thus with different liquidity effects for the customer. These unique characteristics of each Treasury bill are not captured in the CAPM.

[414]   See (Brealey and Myers 1996).

heuristic approach[415] that enables both the search for and the integration of *partial solutions* in a bottom-up approach as well as the utilization of available top-down combination knowledge is presented in the following. But first the term "financial solution" has to be defined in more detail.

A *financial solution*[416] consists of a single financial product or a bundle of financial products. If a solution satisfies all constraints, it is called a *feasible solution*. Note that a feasible solution is by no means a *superior solution* a priori. A feasible solution just satisfies all formulated constraints. In an additional step, the superior solution has to be identified applying the objective function to a set of feasible solutions that were generated during the solution process. Thus a superior solution is defined as the best solution from a set of feasible solutions with respect to the objective function. The term *superior solution* is used intentionally instead of *optimal solution* to make clear that the superior solution hopefully will be near the (theoretically) optimal solution, although there is no guarantee that heuristics ensure that an optimal solution is found. Thus *superior solution* is used as an approximation for a theoretically optimal solution. The way of finding feasible solutions and selecting a superior solution from a set of feasible solutions is called *satisfycing* instead of *optimizing*.[417]

If no global optimum can be easily determined top-down, at least knowledge about a local optimum within a specific product domain can be incorporated bottom-up in a (global) solution. In these cases it can be advantageous to include *partial solutions* intentionally even if they are not feasible. The *residual problem* that generally remains if such locally optimized solutions are integrated in the overall solution can be solved in another solution step. Two or more combined partial solutions may solve the (global) problem. One iteration in the process of the determination of a solution is called a *partial solution process step*.

For the solution process it is of great importance whether partial solutions can be calculated separately or whether they have to be calculated taking into account their impact on the overall solution as well as on other partial solutions. For instance if a partial solution provides a very high tax-deductible amount of money, this may have a great impact on other solutions since the marginal tax rate of this customer will most likely be altered by the partial solution mentioned first. In the following it is assumed that the *principle of value additivity* holds.

But the proposed heuristic does not only provide for a bottom-up approach but also for the opportunity to integrate top-down combination knowledge. If such knowledge exits with respect to a specific problem, it can be split up into *partial*

---

[415] On problem solution algorithms see e.g. (Elbracht-Hülseweh 1985), (Klein 1971), and (Ulrich 1976), on heuristic approaches see e.g. (Kaindl 1989), (Lenat 1983), (Streim 1975), and (Pau and Gianotti 1990). The approach presented here belongs to the group of exact heuristic methods, which are suited for an implementation in an information system due to the fact that the problem may be poorly structured but it is well-defined; see (Elbracht-Hülseweh 1985).

[416] In the following briefly denoted as *solution*.

[417] See e.g. (Pinney et al. 1992). On *bounded rationality* and *satisfycing* also see (Schneider 1997) and references therein.

problems. Due to the principle of value additivity, problems can be conveniently split up into partial problems[418] – just like partial solutions can be integrated to form a global solution – that may be solved with local optimization knowledge. If a problem or partial problem is identified as one where top-down combination knowledge is present and can be applied, the system has to recognize that fact and trigger a separation of the problem into partial problems – if necessary.[419] This part of the solution process is called a *process of recognition* (top-down) as opposed to the *process of search*[420] for another partial solution (bottom-up).[421] In conjunction, the solution process is a *hybrid process of search and recognition*[422]. This way of producing superior solutions has a number of merits:

- Established local combination and optimization knowledge is incorporated into the solution process. Thus knowledge that is already available can be utilized.[423]
- New innovative solutions – solutions that no one would have thought of upfront – can be found due to the iterative process of search.[424]
- Since a set of feasible solutions is generated during the solution process, the financial advisor has a number of solutions that may be presented to the customer. This has at least two advantages: First, the customer has a choice and generally, this is already associated with utility. Instead, if a global top-down solution could be determined, just one solution would be offered.[425] Second, a financial solution just considers quantitative factors, but a decision of a customer will be made based on quantitative as well as qualitative considerations. Thus a customer might choose intentionally a second or third best solution from a quantitative point of view.

The problem solution process and the interrelations of the above-described terms *partial solution, residual problem, objective function, superior solution* and *financial problem* are illustrated in Fig. 40.

---

[418] It should be noted though that value additivity is not a necessity in this case but makes the separation much easier.

[419] For instance in the ALLFIWIB project this has been realized by an autonomous so-called *combination agent*; see (Buhl et al. 1996). Combination knowledge will not be covered here, since the formulation and solution of customer problems that take uncertainty and risk into account are the focus at this stage. The issue of combination knowledge remains an open research question.

[420] This is also denoted as *learning by discovery*, see (Lenat 1983) and (Kaindl 1989).

[421] Note that the process of recognition and the process of search are not separated in a way that *either* only search is done *or* only combination knowledge is applied, but that the solution process can and often will be a combination of both. The problem may first be separated using available combination knowledge and subsequently a search process proceeds to find feasible solutions for the partial problems.

[422] See e.g. (Buhl et al. 1996).

[423] See e.g. (Will 1995).

[424] See e.g. (Will 1995).

[425] On *variety seeking behavior* see e.g. (Helmig 2001).

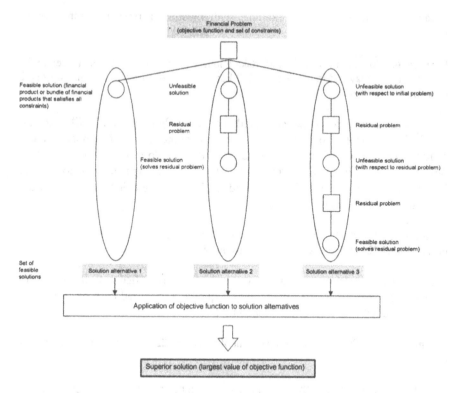

Fig. 40. Schematic Problem Solution Process[426]

A basic requirement for such a solution process being implemented is the formal representation of problems as well as solutions. As (Will 1995) showed, it is advantageous to model problems as well as solutions in the form of cash flows. Using a formal way of representing problems facilitates the use of an appropriate application that may help to find a superior solution. Problems can be broadly distinguished into finance and investment problems.[427]

- *Finance problems* are characterized by the need to transform cash inflows in future periods into a large cash inflow today.
- *Investment problems* are characterized by the need to transform a cash inflow today into cash inflows in future periods.

Most problems of a customer are *mixed problems* since they possess characteristics of both groups of financial problems. Therefore, an objective has to be translated into a form where the problem is characterized by a desired cash flow

---

[426] The general process pattern taken from (Sandbiller et al. 1992) has been modified. In the graph the *process of recognition* is not illustrated, since it will not be the focus of the contribution in this chapter. The interested reader is referred to the discussion in Sec. 6.3.9 and the explanations provided in (Will 1995). See also footnote 419.

[427] See (Sandbiller et al. 1992).

stream. The following simple example shall illustrate a typical customer prob-lem.[428]

Example 6.7: Mr. Smith wants to undertake a longer journey in two years. Therefore, he plans to invest today and in one year 10,000 Euros each. His objective is to maximize the repayment in two years.

However, future cash flows are usually not certain but inherently affiliated with risk. This holds true on the one hand for investment products such as bonds, stocks or funds. On the other hand, a customer is hardly able to formulate an exact cash flow requirement in 25 years from now. However, he might be able to state at least a minimal payment that he will need. Or he might be able to set a maximum cash outflow that he is willing to bear.

Example 6.8: Mr. Smith not only wants to maximize the repayment in two years but de-mands at least 22,000 Euros as a minimal repayment.

Another less restrictive constraint would be that a specified cash inflow has to be exceeded with a specified probability. Equally, a specified cash outflow must not be exceeded with a specified probability.

Example 6.9: Mr. Smith expects a repayment of more than 22,000 Euros with a probability of 90%.

Generally speaking, such problems can be found in various areas of financial consulting, for instance in the domain of financial planning. Refinancing mort-gages constitutes another important area as long as rates are still unknown. All these examples have in common that it is a cash outflow that should not be ex-ceeded (concerning financing problems) or a cash inflow that should not fall short of a specified target value (concerning investment problems).

Example 6.8 and Example 6.9 illustrate two different approaches of formulat-ing uncertain constraints. In decision science, Example 6.8 would be called a *situation under uncertainty*. There are no probabilities associated with different states of the world. The situation in Example 6.9 would be called a *situation under risk*. Objective or subjective probabilities can be assigned to each state of the world. Instead of using the expression *state of the world* in the following, the ex-pression *scenario* will be used. In a meeting with a customer often *best-*, *average-*, and *worst-scenarios* are used to visualize uncertainty or risk in a financial plan-ning situation.

But it is not only the customer who has desires that cannot be expressed by fixed or arbitrary cash flows but also financial products inherently contain risk. The level of future payments is – depending on the type of security or contract – generally not certain but inherently affiliated with risk. Increased return is usually

---

[428] Obviously this is a very simple example in comparison to real world financial planning problems. Still, it shall suffice here in order to illustrate the model. The example will be continued throughout the section on the product model.

combined with increased risk of an investment. Exceptions are contractually agreed-on cash outflows like in mortgage loans. Table 9 shows some data of US stocks and bonds and the affiliated risk in terms of their standard deviation.

Table 9. Investment Risk and Return Data[429]

	Stock Market Returns		Bond Market Returns			
			Short Term Government		Long-term Government	
Time Period	Return	Standard Deviation	Return	Standard Deviation	Return	Standard Deviation
1802-1870	7.0%	16.9%	5.1%	7.7%	4.8%	8.3%
1871-1925	6.6%	16.8%	3.2%	4.8%	3.7%	6.4%
1926-1997	7.2%	20.4%	0.6%	4.2%	2.0%	10.6%

Obviously, stocks showed the better performance but also have a significantly higher associated risk. Risk in this context is not only the potential of losses but just the extend to which the expected return can be exceeded (chance or *upside risk*) as well as undercut (loss or *downside risk*). To configure superior solutions, it is important to also consider risky securities in the solution process, thus the model shall also be capable of taking this fact into account.

Having described the perspective on financial problems and solutions, in the following the basic assumptions of the formal model are presented.

6.3.3 Assumptions

In the following, notation and basic assumptions are introduced to lay the ground and define the restrictions for the proposed (mathematical) formulation of the solution process.

(AF) *Framework*
Future states of the world are denoted as scenarios. In each scenario $j = 1,..., m$ there are certain payments[430] at each point in time $t = 1,..., n$.[431]

(AS) *Solution*
Solutions are represented as ($n \times 1$)-column vectors, where each row marks a cash inflow (positive) or a cash outflow (negative) at a specific point in time t. The solution vector $\vec{s}^{ja}$ is an aggregation of $l = 1,..., b$ partial solutions of a solution alternative $a \in IN^+$ for each point in time t in a scenario j, hence an aggregation of

---

[429] Data taken from http://www.evansonasset.com/index.cfm?Page=14. For more information on historical data on stock and bond returns see (Siegel 1998).

[430] Thus uncertainty or risk is captured by the provision of different scenarios. Within a scenario, however, payments are assumed to be certain.

[431] In the following, pre or after tax payments will not be explicitly distinguished.

the partial solution vectors $\vec{s}^{\,jal}$, thus $\vec{s}^{\,ja} = \sum_l \vec{s}^{\,jal}$. s^{al} denotes the set of all sce-

nario-specific   partial   solution   vectors   of   partial   solution l,   thus
$s^{al} = \left\{ \vec{s}^{\,1al}, \vec{s}^{\,2al}, \ldots, \vec{s}^{\,mal} \right\}$. s^a denotes the set of all scenario-specific solution vectors

of a solution alternative a, thus $s^a = \left\{ \vec{s}^{\,1a}, \vec{s}^{\,2a}, \ldots, \vec{s}^{\,ma} \right\}$.

(APr) *Problem*
The equality and inequality constraints of the optimization problem are modeled
using a $(n \times n)$ problem matrix[432] $\mathbf{P}^j$ and a $(n \times 1)$ problem vector $\vec{p}^{\,j}$.[433] If a problem cannot be solved after a first solution step $(l = 1)$ a residual problem remains
denoted by the residual problem vector $\vec{p}^{\,Ja(l+1)}$ within a solution alternative s^{al}
and solution step l in scenario j.

(AV) *Value additivity*
All cash flows streams are based on the *principle of value additivity*, i.e. "the
value of the whole is equal to the sum of the values of the parts".[434] That has to be
true *within* a partial solution as well as *across* partial solutions, i.e. cash flow
streams can be summed.[435,436]

---

[432] The problem matrix is in case of certainty and uncertainty independent of scenarios, i.e.
       $\mathbf{P}^j$ will be the same for all scenarios. However, in case of risk this changes. Therefore,
       the problem matrix is already introduced as scenario-specific at this point.
[433] See Eq. (6.6) and Eq. (6.10) to see how the coefficients form a set of linear equations
       that can be gathered in a *problem matrix* and in a *problem vector*.
[434] See (Brealey and Myers 1996). The value additivity principle is also denoted as the *law
       of conservation of value*.
[435] Note that if the marginal tax rate is an endogenous variable, a simple aggregation of
       two or more after tax payment streams is not possible; see (Will 1995). Therefore, in
       the following, it is implicitly assumed that the investor's marginal tax rate is exoge-
       nously given.
[436] Note that the principle of value additivity is only assumed for cash flow streams as op-
       posed to an applied decision rule (objective function). Decision rules under uncertainty
       or risk will in most cases not provide for value additivity. However, it is not required to
       have that feature in the model presented here.

Example 6.10[437]: There are three scenarios (*best* ($j = 1$), *average* ($j = 2$), and *worst* ($j = 3$)). An investment today of 10,000 Euros in a fund with European bonds, which is sold two years from now yields 14,000 Euros in the best, 13,000 Euros in the average, and 12,000 Euros in the worst case. This situation may be a partial solution s^{11} ($l = 1$) that can be combined with other partial solutions to form a solution alternative ($a = 1$).

$$s^{al} = s^{11} = \left\{ \vec{s}^{111} = \begin{pmatrix} -10 \\ 0 \\ 14 \end{pmatrix}, \vec{s}^{211} = \begin{pmatrix} -10 \\ 0 \\ 13 \end{pmatrix}, \vec{s}^{311} = \begin{pmatrix} -10 \\ 0 \\ 12 \end{pmatrix} \right\}$$

6.3.4 Model under Certainty[438]

In this setting, there is just one scenario that occurs with probability one. Even if there is just one scenario, the index j will be used throughout this section since the description below will also be used for the cases with uncertainty and risk.

6.3.4.1   The Financial Problem

As mentioned above, the financial problem consists of an objective function subject to a number of constraints. A feasible solution has to satisfy all constraints. These constraints can be represented in a system of linear equations – one equation for each point in time t:

$$P^j_{t1} s^{jal}_1 + \dots + P^j_{tt'} s^{jal}_{t'} + \dots + P^j_{tt} s^{jal}_t + \dots + P^j_{tn} s^{jal}_n + p^j_t = 0 \qquad (6.6)$$

If the coefficients P^j_{ti} and p^j_t are appropriately chosen, the following desired cash flow streams can be formalized:[439]

- *Fixed* payment (Case I): Let k denote the desired value of a payment at time t then only solutions s^{al} are feasible if and only if payment s^{jal}_t has the value k across all scenarios (see Example 6.7). This can be represented in the following way:

$P^j_{tt} = -1, P^j_{ti} = 0$ for $i = 1, \dots, n; i \neq t; j = 1, \dots, m$

$p^j_t = k$ for $j = 1, \dots, m$

Rearranging Eq. (6.6) yields $s^{jal}_t = k$.

---

[437] In this and all following examples concerning the product model, the three zeros for thousand are omitted in vectors and matrices for reasons of clarity and simplicity. Hence, for instance 10 means 10,000 in a vector or matrix.

[438] This section, i.e. the basic model under certainty is based on (Will 1995). It differs from Will's model in terms of a more detailed notation.

[439] Constraints in the form of the following Cases I – III and later on also Cases IV and V have to be satisfied, of course, for the global solution s^a. However, since upfront it is not known whether the first solution process step will yield a feasible solution, s^a is replaced by s^{al} in the following.

- *Arbitrary payment* (Case II)[440]: Feasible are all solutions s^{al} independent of the value of the payment s_t^{jal}. Consequently

$$P_{ti}^j = 0 \qquad\qquad \text{for } i = 1,\dots,n; j = 1,\dots,m$$

$$p_t^j = 0 \qquad\qquad \text{for } j = 1,\dots,m$$

Rearranging Eq. (6.6) yields $0 s_t^{jal} = 0$, which is always true.

- *Desired payment is a multiple of a preceded payment* (Case III)[441]: Let t' denote the preceded point in time ($t' < t$), then all solutions s^{al} are feasible if and only if s_t^{jal} has the value $\alpha \cdot s_{t'}^{jal}$ across all scenarios. Thus,

$$P_{tt}^j = -1, P_{tt'}^j = \alpha, P_{ti}^j = 0 \quad \text{for } i = 1,\dots,n; i \neq t; i \neq t'; j = 1,\dots,m$$

$$p_t^j = 0 \qquad\qquad \text{for } j = 1,\dots,m$$

Rearranging Eq. (6.6) yields $s_t^{jal} = \alpha \cdot s_{t'}^{jal}$.

For each point in time t a constraint in form of the cases (I) – (III) can be formulated and results in n equations in the form of Eq. (6.6). All coefficients P_{ti}^j and p_t^j can be summarized in the problem matrix $\mathbf{P}^j$ and the problem vector $\vec{p}^j$, respectively. Thus for each of the m scenarios there is one problem matrix and one problem vector. A solution is feasible if and only if it satisfies all constraints, i.e. if Eq. (6.7) holds true.

$$
\underbrace{\begin{pmatrix} P_{11}^j & \cdots & P_{1t}^j & \cdots & P_{1n}^j \\ \vdots & \ddots & \vdots & & \vdots \\ P_{t1}^j & \cdots & P_{tt}^j & \cdots & P_{tn}^j \\ \vdots & & \vdots & \ddots & \vdots \\ P_{n1}^j & \cdots & P_{nt}^j & \cdots & P_{nn}^j \end{pmatrix}}_{\text{Problem matrx}} \underbrace{\begin{pmatrix} s_1^{jal} \\ \vdots \\ s_t^{jal} \\ \vdots \\ s_n^{jal} \end{pmatrix}}_{\substack{\text{Solution} \\ \text{vector}}} + \underbrace{\begin{pmatrix} p_1^j \\ \vdots \\ p_t^j \\ \vdots \\ p_n^j \end{pmatrix}}_{\substack{\text{Problem} \\ \text{vector}}} = \mathbf{P}^j \vec{s}^{jal} + \vec{p}^j = \vec{0}
\tag{6.7}
$$

---

[440] This case is particularly useful if investment problems have to be formulated where the future cash inflows are known but not the amount that has to be invested.

[441] This case offers the opportunity to generate a progressive ($\alpha > 1$) or a declining ($\alpha < 1$) payment stream. As (Will 1995) mentions, inconsistent problem formulations are excluded since for each point in time just one reference point in time is allowed.

Example 6.11: Mr. Smith's financial problem based on Example 6.7 can be formalized using the above notation. Taking into account that Example 6.7 assumes just one scenario (situation under certainty), thus $j = 1$, the system of equations according to Eq. (6.6) for the three points in time ($t = 1, t = 2, t = 3$) are

$$P^j_{11} s^{jal}_1 + P^j_{12} s^{jal}_2 + P^j_{13} s^{jal}_3 + p^j_1 = 0 \quad \Rightarrow -1 \cdot s^{lal}_1 + 0 \cdot s^{lal}_2 + 0 \cdot s^{lal}_3 + (-10) = 0$$

$$P^j_{21} s^{jal}_1 + P^j_{22} s^{jal}_2 + P^j_{23} s^{jal}_3 + p^j_2 = 0 \quad \Rightarrow 0 \cdot s^{lal}_1 + -1 \cdot s^{lal}_2 + 0 \cdot s^{lal}_3 + (-10) = 0$$

$$P^j_{31} s^{jal}_1 + P^j_{32} s^{jal}_2 + P^j_{33} s^{jal}_3 + p^j_3 = 0 \quad \Rightarrow 0 \cdot s^{lal}_1 + 0 \cdot s^{lal}_2 + 0 \cdot s^{lal}_3 + 0 = 0.$$

These equations can be summarized in a problem matrix and problem vector (see Eq. (6.7))

$$\underbrace{\begin{pmatrix} -1 & 0 & 0 \\ 0 & -1 & 0 \\ 0 & 0 & 0 \end{pmatrix}}_{\mathbf{P}^1} \bar{\mathbf{s}}^{lal} + \underbrace{\begin{pmatrix} -10 \\ -10 \\ 0 \end{pmatrix}}_{\bar{\mathbf{p}}^1} = \vec{0}.$$

6.3.4.2 Formulation and Solution of Residual Problems

As already mentioned above, it may often be advantageous to utilize local optimization knowledge to configure or select a partial solution that does not solve the initial problem entirely but yields a residual problem. Such a partial solution is called an *unfeasible solution*.

Let $\bar{\mathbf{s}}^{l11}$ denote an unfeasible solution. Apparently, a partial solution $\bar{\mathbf{s}}^{l12}$ that solves the residual problem constitutes a global solution $\bar{\mathbf{s}}^{l1}$ which solves the initial problem. The respective problem vector is determined using Eq. (6.8).

$$\vec{\mathbf{p}}^{ja(l+1)} := \mathbf{P}^j \bar{\mathbf{s}}^{jal} + \vec{\mathbf{p}}^{jal} \tag{6.8}$$

In general, the problem vector $\vec{\mathbf{p}}^{ja(l+1)}$ refers to the residual problem that remains after l partial solution process steps. To be precise, $\vec{\mathbf{p}}^{jal}$ has to be set equal to the initial problem vector for the first partial solution process step ($l = 1$), thus

$$\vec{\mathbf{p}}^{jal} := \vec{\mathbf{p}}^j \quad \text{for } l = 1 . \tag{6.9}$$

Suppose Eq. (6.7) yields the zero vector then the solution process is terminated. If Eq. (6.7) does not yield the zero vector another iteration using problem vector $\vec{\mathbf{p}}^{ja(l+1)}$ (Eq. (6.8)) can be performed integrating another partial solution $l + 1$. This process can be iterated until either there is no residual problem anymore or a specified stopping rule fires, leading to a termination of this solution process without a feasible solution.[442] A stopping rule may be that either a specified CPU time or a specified number of financial products (or product groups) to solve the problem is exceeded. Especially the latter rule strongly depends on the sophistication level of the customer. There the customer model briefly touched on above

---

[442] Alternatively, a process of finding a feasible partial solution *without* taking into account local optimization knowledge but just focusing on solving the residual problem could be triggered, terminating the process with a globally feasible solution.

comes into play again. To provide tailored solutions, knowledge about the customer has to be used in the solution generation process.

Example 6.12: To solve the investment problem of Mr. Smith in the case of certainty $(j = 1)$, a zero bond with the cash flow $\vec{s}^{111} = \begin{pmatrix} -10 \\ 0 \\ 12 \end{pmatrix}$ is considered as the first partial solution $(l = 1)$ within the first solution alternative $(a = 1)$. Inserting this partial solution into the system of equations of Example 6.11 yields $\mathbf{P}^1\vec{s}^{111} + \vec{p}^1 = \begin{pmatrix} 0 \\ -10 \\ 0 \end{pmatrix} \neq \vec{0}$, hence the residual problem

$$\begin{pmatrix} -1 & 0 & 0 \\ 0 & -1 & 0 \\ 0 & 0 & 0 \end{pmatrix} \vec{s}^{112} + \underbrace{\begin{pmatrix} 0 \\ -10 \\ 0 \end{pmatrix}}_{\vec{p}^{112}} = \vec{0}.$$ To solve this residual problem, a short term governmental

bond from $t = 2$ until $t = 3$ with cash flow $\vec{s}^{112} = \begin{pmatrix} 0 \\ -10 \\ 10.7 \end{pmatrix}$ is considered as a second partial solution $(l = 2)$ within the first solution alternative $(a = 1)$. Since $\mathbf{P}^1\vec{s}^{112} + \vec{p}^{112} = \vec{0}$ holds, there is no residual problem. The initial problem is solved by combining the two partial solutions, i.e. $\vec{s}^{11} = \vec{s}^{111} + \vec{s}^{112} = \begin{pmatrix} -10 \\ 0 \\ 12 \end{pmatrix} + \begin{pmatrix} 0 \\ -10 \\ 10.7 \end{pmatrix} = \begin{pmatrix} -10 \\ -10 \\ 22.7 \end{pmatrix}.$[443]

After the basic model has been introduced, the center of interest will now be the inclusion of uncertainty into the model.

---

[443] Again, it should be emphasized that solution s^1 does not need to be a superior solution. It is just a feasible one for the time being.

6.3.5 Model under Uncertainty

To formalize desired cash flows of customers that include a minimal cash inflow
or a maximal cash outflow (see Example 6.8) another case has to be introduced
that leads to inequalities in the system of linear equations.[444] Uncertainty[445] is captured providing for $m > 1$ different scenarios.[446] Even though there is knowledge
about different scenarios, there are no subjective or objective probabilities that
may be assigned to each of the scenarios.

6.3.5.1   The Financial Problem

A constraint in the form of an inequality at point in time t may be formalized using
m inequalities of the following type:

$$P_{t1}^j s_1^{jal} + \ldots + P_{tn}^j s_n^{jal} + p_t^j \leq 0 \qquad (6.10)$$

Accordingly, the so-called *inequality constraint* can be described as follows.

- *Desired payment is a minimum cash inflow or a maximum cash outflow* (Case
  IV): Let v denote the desired minimum or maximum payment, then all solutions
  s^{al} are feasible if s_t^{jal} has at least the value v across all scenarios.[447] Thus,

  $P_{tt}^j = -1, P_{ti}^j = 0$ for $i = 1,\ldots,n; i \neq t; j = 1,\ldots,m$

  $p_t^j = v$ for $j = 1,\ldots,m$

  Rearranging Eq. (6.10) yields $s_t^{jal} \geq v$ for all scenarios j.

Since there may now be equalities in the form of Eq. (6.6) as well as inequalities in the form of Eq. (6.10), a $(1 \times n)$-*inequality row vector* $\vec{u}^T$ has to be introduced to distinguish between fixed payments on the one hand (Cases I and III) and
minimum, maximum or arbitrary payments on the other hand (Cases II and IV).
Therefore, for each payment according to Cases I and III, u_t is set to one ($u_t = 1$).
For the other two cases, u_t is set to zero ($u_t = 0$).

---

[444] It should be mentioned though that (Will 1995) also provides a very short sketch of a
solution approach when dealing with inequalities.

[445] Uncertainty is defined as the absence of knowledge for the decision maker about the
probability distribution on states of the world. This does not necessarily mean that these
probabilities are not available at all. It just states that a decision maker has no knowledge of and no subjective expectation about these probabilities. See e.g. (Krelle 1968)
or (Neuberger 1998). This distinction is originally due to (Knight 1921). Though this
distinction is still widely used, its dubious nature is criticized e.g. in (Arrow 1951).

[446] See e.g. (Wang and Xia 2002), (Rockafellar and Wets 1991).

[447] This case makes also sense in the model under certainty, i.e. if there is just one scenario. The solution process cannot be performed using Eq. (6.7) but the two step solution process using Eq. (6.11) - (6.13) has to be applied.

If there are several different desired payments at one point in time, Case IV is generally more binding than Cases I and III, and these for their part are more binding than Case II. Hence, Case II is overwritten by Cases I and III, and these are overwritten by Case IV. This can occur if a customer mentally distinguishes several financial problems as the following example illustrates.[448]

Example 6.13: A customer might demand a minimum cash inflow for his living expenses of 1,500 Euros per month. At the same time he demands a fixed payment of 1,000 Euros to pay interest on his mortgage loan. Apparently, the resulting problem at that point in time will be a minimum cash inflow of 2,500 Euros per month, thus an inequality constraint.

Even though the coefficients can be gathered again in the problem matrix $\mathbf{P}^j$ and the problem vector $\vec{\mathbf{p}}^j$, there are now two steps necessary to check whether all constraints according to the Cases I - IV are satisfied. In a first step it is checked whether the inequalities hold true. In a second step it is checked whether fixed payment requirements are satisfied. These two steps have to be performed for each scenario.

Step 1:
To check whether the inequalities of the constraints are satisfied (Case IV), the left hand side of Eq. (6.11) has to be smaller or equal to the zero vector.

$$\mathbf{P}^j \vec{\mathbf{s}}^{jal} + \vec{\mathbf{p}}^{jal} \leq \vec{\mathbf{0}} \qquad (6.11)$$

Here, all constraints are considered to be inequalities and it is checked whether at least the desired cash inflow or at most the desired cash outflow holds true for the respective solution.

Step 2:
Further, using the inequality vector, the fixed payment constraints (Cases I and III) are checked. Let $\mathbf{E}_{ij}$ denote the $(n \times n)$ matrix that has all elements equal to zero except for the (i,j)-th's element which is equal to one and let $\vec{\mathbf{i}}$ denote the $(n \times 1)$ vector that has all elements equal to one. $\mathbf{K}$ denotes the $(n \times n)$ matrix which is yielded by a right-hand sided multiplication of the left-hand side of Eq. (6.7) with the inequality vector $\vec{\mathbf{u}}^T$.

$$\left(\mathbf{P}^j \vec{\mathbf{s}}^{jal} + \vec{\mathbf{p}}^{jal} \right) \vec{\mathbf{u}}^T = \mathbf{K} \qquad (6.12)$$

Using Eq. (6.12) it can be checked whether all fixed payment constraints are satisfied.

---

[448]   For the sake of simplicity, it is assumed in the following that there is just one constraint at a specific point in time.

$$\left(\sum_{t=1}^{n} \mathbf{E}_{tt} \mathbf{KE}_{tt}\right)\vec{\mathbf{i}} = \vec{0} \qquad\qquad (6.13)$$

First, a diagonalization operation is performed (term in brackets in Eq. (6.13)). This operation yields a matrix with all elements being zero that are not located on the main diagonal. The elements of the main diagonal of the resulting matrix equal the elements from the main diagonal of matrix $\mathbf{K}$.

Second, multiplying this resulting matrix from the right side with the vector of ones $\vec{\mathbf{i}}$ the main diagonal of the matrix is transformed into a column vector. If and only if this (n x 1)-column vector equals the zero vector and Eq. (6.11) holds true then all constraints are satisfied.[449]

6.3.5.2   Formulation and Solution of Residual Problems

If one of these two steps described above is not satisfied, Eq. (6.8) yields the residual problem. The initial problem matrix $\mathbf{P}^j$ and the inequality vector $\vec{\mathbf{u}}^T$ are not altered and can be used for the next partial solution process step. The following example illustrates the procedure in case of constraints with minimum cash inflow, i.e. with inequalities.

Example 6.14: Suppose that there are three scenarios (best ($j = 1$), average ($j = 2$), and worst ($j = 3$)) like in Example 6.10. Based on the initial financial problem of Mr. Smith (Example 6.7) and the extension in form of a minimum repayment of 22,000 Euros after two years (Example 6.8), a feasible solution has to satisfy the following equations.

Step 1:
$$\underbrace{\begin{pmatrix} -1 & 0 & 0 \\ 0 & -1 & 0 \\ 0 & 0 & -1 \end{pmatrix}}_{\mathbf{P}^j} \vec{\mathbf{s}}^{jal} + \underbrace{\begin{pmatrix} -10 \\ -10 \\ 22 \end{pmatrix}}_{\vec{\mathbf{p}}^j} \leq \vec{0} \quad \text{for } j = 1,\dots,3$$

Step 2:
$$\left(\sum_{t=1}^{n} \mathbf{E}_{tt} \underbrace{\left[\left(\mathbf{P}^j \vec{\mathbf{s}}^{jal} + \vec{\mathbf{p}}^j\right)\vec{\mathbf{u}}^T\right]}_{\mathbf{K}} \mathbf{E}_{tt}\right)\vec{\mathbf{i}} = \vec{0}$$

$$\Rightarrow \left(\sum_{t=1}^{3} \mathbf{E}_{tt} \underbrace{\left[\left(\begin{pmatrix} -1 & 0 & 0 \\ 0 & -1 & 0 \\ 0 & 0 & -1 \end{pmatrix}\vec{\mathbf{s}}^{jal} + \begin{pmatrix} -10 \\ -10 \\ 22 \end{pmatrix}\right)\begin{pmatrix}1 & 1 & 0\end{pmatrix}\right]}_{\mathbf{K}} \mathbf{E}_{tt}\begin{pmatrix}1\\1\\1\end{pmatrix}\right) = \vec{0} \quad \text{for } j = 1,\dots m$$

Can the problem be solved using the fund investing in European bonds ($l = 1$) of Example 6.10, i.e. do both equations hold true? Let the solution alternative be denoted with $a = 2$. It can be shown that Step 1 is not satisfied for all scenarios. (Note that $\mathbf{p}^{j21}$ had to be set equal to $\mathbf{p}^j$ (Eq. (6.9)), since the first (partial) solution ($l = 1$) could not solve the initial problem.)

---

[449] See (Magnus and Neudecker 1988) and (Krapp 2000) on matrix algebra.

$$\underbrace{\begin{pmatrix} -1 & 0 & 0 \\ 0 & -1 & 0 \\ 0 & 0 & -1 \end{pmatrix}}_{\mathbf{P}^3} \underbrace{\begin{pmatrix} -10 \\ 0 \\ 12 \end{pmatrix}}_{\vec{s}^{321}} + \underbrace{\begin{pmatrix} -10 \\ -10 \\ 22 \end{pmatrix}}_{\vec{p}^{321}} = \begin{pmatrix} 0 \\ -10 \\ 10 \end{pmatrix}.$$

Thus the minimum cash inflow constraint is not satisfied. Checking Step 2 using s^{21} also does not yield the zero vector for all scenarios. Thus at least one constraint concerning the fixed payments is not satisfied either. The set of residual problem vectors using Eq. (6.8) is

$$\left\{ \vec{p}^{122} = \begin{pmatrix} 0 \\ -10 \\ 8 \end{pmatrix}; \vec{p}^{222} = \begin{pmatrix} 0 \\ -10 \\ 9 \end{pmatrix}; \vec{p}^{322} = \begin{pmatrix} 0 \\ -10 \\ 10 \end{pmatrix} \right\}$$

If now the short term bond of Example 6.12 is used in a second partial solution process step ($l = 2$), it can easily be shown that the inequalities in Step 1 as well as the constraints concerning the fixed payments (Step 2) are both satisfied. Thus the residual problem is solved and the feasible (global) solution is

$$s^2 = \left\{ \vec{s}^{12} = \vec{s}^{121} + \vec{s}^{122} = \begin{pmatrix} -10 \\ 0 \\ 14 \end{pmatrix} + \begin{pmatrix} 0 \\ -10 \\ 10.7 \end{pmatrix} = \begin{pmatrix} -10 \\ -10 \\ 24.7 \end{pmatrix}; \vec{s}^{22} = \begin{pmatrix} -10 \\ -10 \\ 23.7 \end{pmatrix}; \vec{s}^{32} = \begin{pmatrix} -10 \\ -10 \\ 22.7 \end{pmatrix} \right\}.$$

Though introducing different scenarios into the consulting and solution process marks a significant improvement compared to the status quo, scenarios without scenario probabilities will not suffice for a number of financing and especially investment problems.

From the perspective of the customer, inequality constraints (Case IV) may be too restrictive since a payment must not fall below a specified value. To make sure that this specified value is reached at all costs, the customer may have to sacrifice a lot of potential return. It might be advantageous to be able to show a customer in a consulting conversation how much he has to sacrifice for an increased certainty of minimum cash inflows. So, probabilities would help a great deal to illustrate different constraints and their impact on the sacrificed upside risk. Generally speaking, at least subjective probabilities for scenarios can be obtained from historical data for most traded securities. From the perspective of the solution and decision process, all relevant information that is accessible (without prohibitive costs) should be included in the process in order to improve the quality of the decision. Finally, not only new constraints can be formulated if probabilities are incorporated in the decision process, but it also offers the opportunity to apply more sophisticated decision rules (see Sec. 6.3.7.3).

6.3.6 Model under Risk[450]

So far, desired cash flow structures can be generated that include minimum cash inflows, maximum cash outflows, fixed payments and arbitrary payments by using scenarios to capture the uncertainty about a payment stream. However, the possibly known probability distribution on scenarios has not yet been incorporated in the calculation. A general constraint for a minimum or maximum payment across all scenarios can be very restrictive, particularly in case of very unlikely scenarios, and may restrict the set of feasible solutions far too much. Especially in the context of financial planning services, the used *best* and *worst* scenarios are often very unlikely compared to the *average* scenario, since they are usually based on historical data and mark the worst and best possible outcome over a couple of years or even decades.

6.3.6.1 The Financial Problem

As already mentioned above, less restrictive constraints compared to Case IV can be formulated if probabilities can be assigned to each scenario. Now desired minimum cash inflows with a specific minimum probability and maximum cash outflows with a specific maximum probability can be represented. These constraints are called *probability constraints* in the following. The solution process is by far not so easy compared to the case of certainty and uncertainty and cannot be performed with matrix algebra solely. Therefore, another assumption is necessary.

(AD) *Distribution function and scenario probabilities*
The payment at time t within a (global) solution s^a is a discrete probability variable denoted by S_t^a. The corresponding distribution function is denoted by $F_t^a(x)$[451]. Let w^j denote the probability of occurrence of scenario j, with $\sum_j w^j = 1; w^j \geq 0 \quad \forall j$. This probability is assumed to be constant in time and independent of all partial solutions s^{al} and all other solution alternatives.

---

[450] The model under risk below only distinguishes itself by the introduction of probabilities of occurrence for each scenario. Thus risk is captured in a discrete function. There is no separation between systematic and unsystematic risk (for a description of these terms see e.g. (Steiner and Bruns 2000) or (Brealey and Myers 1996)). The aim is again to ensure minimum cash inflows or maximum cash outflows, i.e. the shortfall risk remains the center of interest. Other risk parameters such as beta, volatility, residual volatility, correlation coefficient, tracking error see (Steiner and Bruns 2000) are at least not covered in the constraints.

[451] l means in this context that the distribution function includes l partial solutions.

To capture cases that are similar to the one described in Example 6.9, another case has to be introduced:

- *Desired payment is a maximum cash outflow with a maximal probability* (Case Va): If v_t denotes the desired maximum cash outflow at time t with the maximal probability w_t^v, then all solutions s^a are feasible if and only if

$$W\left(S_t^a \leq v_t\right) \leq w_t^v \Leftrightarrow F_t^a\left(v_t\right) \leq w_t^v.$$

$W\left(S_t^a \leq v_t\right)$ denotes the probability that S_t^a yields a value that is equal to or below v_t. Even though probability constraints are checked without using matrix algebra, the coefficients of the problem matrix and the problem vector still have to be set to zero for further calculations, thus

$$P_{ti}^j = 0 \qquad\qquad \text{for } i = 1,\ldots,n; j = 1,\ldots,m$$

$$p_t^j = 0 \qquad\qquad \text{for } j = 1,\ldots,m$$

Rearranging Eq. (6.6) yields $0 s_t^{jal} = 0$, which is always true.

- *Desired payment is a minimum cash inflow with a minimal probability* (Case Vb): If v_t denotes the desired minimum cash inflow at time t with the minimal probability w_t^{v*}, then all solutions s^a are feasible if and only if

$$W\left(S_t^a > v_t\right) \geq w_t^{v*} \Leftrightarrow F_t^a\left(v_t\right) \leq \underbrace{1 - w_t^{v*}}_{w_t^v}.$$

Obviously, Case Vb can be transformed into a formulation analogously to Case Va. Analogously to Case Va, the coefficients of the problem matrix and the problem vector are set to zero.

$$P_{ti}^j = 0 \qquad\qquad \text{for } i = 1,\ldots,n; j = 1,\ldots,m$$

$$p_t^j = 0 \qquad\qquad \text{for } j = 1,\ldots,m$$

Rearranging Eq. (6.6) yields $0 s_t^{jal} = 0$, which is always true.

Example 6.15: The probability constraint of Mr. Smith in Example 6.9 – to receive at least 22,000 Euros after two years ($v_3 = 22$) with a probability of at least 90% ($w_3^{v*} = 0.9$) – corresponds to Case Vb and can formally be written as $W\left(S_3^a > 22\right) \geq 0.9 \Leftrightarrow F_3^a\left(22\right) \leq \underbrace{1 - 0.9}_{w_3^v} = 0.1.$

To check a solution s^a on feasibility with respect to a formulated probability constraint at a time t, first the distribution function $F_t^a\left(x\right)$ has to be calculated. Solution s^a comprises all partial solutions s^{al} that have been integrated in s^a so far on the way to find a feasible solution after l partial solution process steps. A separated calculation for partial solutions, like in Sec. 6.3.4 and Sec. 6.3.5 does not suffice here anymore.

Each solution alternative s_t^a at time t is characterized by its payments s_t^{ja} in the various scenarios j and the respective probabilities of occurrence w^j. Summarizing the payments and the respective probabilities into a tupel, a solution for time t (the discrete probability variable) can be written as

$$S_t^a = \left[\left(s_t^{1a}; w^1 \right) \ \left(s_t^{2a}; w^2 \right) \ \dots \ \left(s_t^{ma}; w^m \right) \right]. \tag{6.14}$$

To calculate the distribution function, first the row of tupels has to be sorted ascending dependent on the value of the payment s_t^{ja}. The respective sorting function is denoted by Θ. After the sorting, the resulting tupels have the form $\left(s_{t,c}^a; w_{t,c}; j_{t,c} \right)$, where c denotes the rank among the tupels after the sorting took place and $j_{t,c}$ denotes the rank according to the scenarios before sorting. The coefficient t in $w_{t,c}$ reflects for which point in time the sorting took place.

$$\Theta\left[\left(s_t^{1a}; w^1 \right) \ \left(s_t^{2a}; w^2 \right) \ \dots \ \left(s_t^{ma}; w^m \right) \right] = \left[\left(s_{t,1}^a; w_{t,1}; j_{t,1} \right) \ \dots \ \left(s_{t,m}^a; w_{t,m}; j_{t,m} \right) \right] \tag{6.15}$$

Having sorted the tupels, an accumulation of the probabilities is now necessary to get the distribution function. This operation is denoted by Φ.

$$\Phi\left[\left(s_{t,1}^a; w_{t,1}; j_{t,1} \right) \ \dots \ \left(s_{t,m}^a; w_{t,m}; j_{t,m} \right) \right] \tag{6.16}$$

$$= \left[\left(s_{t,1}^a; \underbrace{w_{t,1}}_{w_{t,1}'}; j_{t,1} \right) \ \left(s_{t,2}^a; \underbrace{w_{t,1} + w_{t,2}}_{w_{t,2}'}; j_{t,2} \right) \ \dots \ \left(s_{t,m}^a; \underbrace{\sum_c w_{t,c}}_{w_{t,m}'=1}; j_{t,m} \right) \right]$$

The corresponding distribution function can be written as

$$F_t^a(x) = \begin{cases} 0 & \text{for } x < s_{t,1}^a \\ w_{t,1}' & \text{for } s_{t,1}^a \leq x < s_{t,2}^a \\ w_{t,2}' & \text{for } s_{t,2}^a \leq x < s_{t,3}^a \\ \dots & \\ 1 & \text{for } s_{t,m}^a \leq x \end{cases} \tag{6.17}$$

Graphically, the distribution function is illustrated in Fig. 41. Point $\left(v_t; w_t^v \right)$ marks a probability constraint according to Case V.

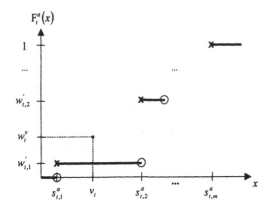

Fig. 41. Distribution Function

Example 6.16: Mr. Smith is offered a funds investing in European stocks as a first (partial) solution ($l = 1$) within a third solution alternative s^{31} ($a = 3$). The funds is expected to yield 35,000 Euros with 25% probability in the *best* ($w_1 = 0.25$), 25,000 Euros with 60% probability in the *average* ($w_2 = 0.6$), and 18,000 Euros with 15% probability in the *worst* scenario ($w_3 = 0.15$) in 2 years. Solution S_3^{31} at time $t = 3$ can be written as $[(s_3^{131} = 35; w^1 = 0.25)(s_3^{231} = 25; w^2 = 0.6)(s_3^{331} = 18; w^3 = 0.15)]$. Sorting this expression yields $\Theta[(35; 0.25)(25; 0.6)(18; 0.15)] = [(18; 0.15; 3)(25; 0.6; 2)(35; 0.25; 1)]$. Cumulating these probabilities yields $\Phi[(18; 0.15; 3)(25; 0.6; 2)(35; 0.25; 1)] = [(18; 0.15; 3)(25; 0.75; 2)(35; 1; 1)]$. The corresponding distribution function can be written as

$$F_3^3(x) = \begin{cases} 0 & \text{for } x < 18 \\ 0.15 & \text{for } 18 \le x < 25 \\ 0.75 & \text{for } 25 \le x < 35 \\ 1 & \text{for } 35 \le x \end{cases}.$$

The distribution function is graphically illustrated in Fig. 42.

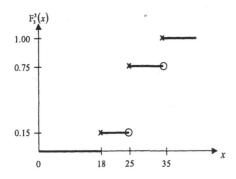

Fig. 42. Distribution Function of Example 6.16

Apparently, the constraint $F_t^a(v_t) \le w_t^v$ is satisfied if point $(v_t; w_t^v)$ is located *on or above* the distribution function. To check whether the probability constraints are satisfied at time t the first tupel $(s_t^*; w_t^*; j_t^*)$ has to be considered where the cumulated probability is above w_t^v.

$$w_t^* = w_{t,c}^{'} : w_{t,c-1}^{'} \le w_t^v < w_{t,c}^{'} \tag{6.18}$$

$$s_t^* = s_{t,c}^a : s_{t,c}^a \in (s_{t,c}^a, w_t^*, j_{t,c}) \tag{6.19}$$

$$j_t^* = j_{t,c} : j_{t,c} \in (s_{t,c}^a, w_t^*, j_{t,c}) \tag{6.20}$$

Thus a condition of the form $F_t^a(x) \le w_t^v$ is satisfied if and only if $x < s_t^*$. That is, for $F_t^a(v_t) \le w_t^v$ to hold, the following statement has to be true.

$$v_t < s_t^* \Leftrightarrow s_t^* - v_t > 0 \tag{6.21}$$

Example 6.17: The offered solution in Example 6.16 has to be checked on the probability constraint of Mr. Smith from Example 6.9. The relevant tupel $(s_3^* = 18; w_3^* = 0.15; j_3^* = 3)$ and the probability constraint $(v_3 = 22; w_3^v = 0.1)$ at time $t = 3$ is shown in Fig. 43.

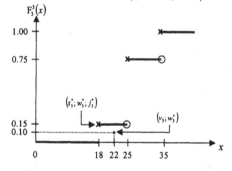

Fig. 43. Probability Constraint in the Distribution Function of Example 6.16

The point $(v_{10} = 15; w_{10}^v = 0.15)$ representing the probability constraint is obviously located below the distribution function $F_3^{31}(x)$. Thus the probability constraint is not satisfied. Formally, Eq. (6.21) yields $s_3^* - v_3 = 18 - 22 = -4 \le 0$. Apparently, in the worst case scenario, another partial solution would have to provide a cash inflow greater than 4,000 Euros in $t = 3$.

Like in the simpler cases mentioned above, there may remain residual problems to be solved as Example 6.17 shows. How can a residual problem formally be described?

6.3.6.2   Formulation and Solution of Residual Problems

If the condition $s_t^* - v_t > 0$ (Eq. 6.21) is not true, this is equivalent to the statement that the solution so far provides for a payment that is too low in scenario j_t^* at time t. Therefore, for another partial solution $s^{ja(l+1)}$ at time t in scenario j_t^* the following condition – ε being some marginal value like 0.01 Euros – has to be true:

$$s_t^{j_t^* a(l+1)} > -\left(s_t^* - v_t\right) \Leftrightarrow s_t^{j_t^* a(l+1)} \geq v_t - s_t^* + \varepsilon \tag{6.22}$$

Apparently, Eq. (6.22) corresponds to Case IV and the constraints formulated there. However, in contrast to Case IV the constraint for a minimum cash inflow and a maximum cash outflow is limited to a specific scenario here. Therefore, scenario-specific problem matrices $\mathbf{P}^{jal}$ have to be introduced that are dependent not only on the scenario but also on the solution alternative a and the partial solution process step l. The integration of a residual problem into the scenario-specific problem matrix and problem vector is accomplished by an *adaptation matrix* $\mathbf{A}^{jal}$ and *adaptation vector* $\vec{a}^{jal}$.

- For each point in time t without a probability constraint and for each point in time t with a *satisfied* probability constraint the elements of the adaptation matrix $\mathbf{A}^{jal}$ and adaptation vector $\vec{a}^{jal}$ are set to zero.
  $$A_{ti}^{jal} = 0 \, ; a_t^{jal} = 0 \quad \forall i, j$$

- For each point in time with a probability constraint that is not satisfied, the elements of the adaptation matrix $\mathbf{A}^{jal}$ and adaptation vector $\vec{a}^{jal}$ have to be altered according to the following rules
  $$A_{ti}^{j_t^* al} = -1; \qquad\qquad A_{ti}^{j_t^* al} = 0 \quad \forall i \neq t; \qquad A_{ti}^{jal} = 0 \quad \forall j \neq j_t^*, i$$
  $$a_t^{j_t^* al} = v_t - s_t^* + \varepsilon; \qquad a_t^{jal} = 0 \quad \forall j \neq j_t^*$$

Thus the residual problem vector can be calculated as

$$\vec{p}^{ja(l+1)} = \mathbf{P}^{jal}\vec{s}^{jal} + \vec{p}^{jal} + \vec{a}^{jal} \tag{6.23}$$

and the corresponding adapted problem matrix as[452]

$$\mathbf{P}^{ja(l+1)} = \mathbf{P}^j + \mathbf{A}^{jal}. \tag{6.24}$$

In contrast to Sec. 6.3.4 and Sec. 6.3.5 it is not sufficient here to check whether another partial solution just satisfies the constraints of the residual problem. Instead, it is inevitable to check the constraints also based on the complete aggregated solution, since the last integrated partial solution may alter the ranking of the tupels in Eq. (6.15) and thus may yield a different result based on Eq. (6.16).

---

[452] Note that in Eq. (6.24) it is always the initial problem matrix $\mathbf{P}^j$ that is used to determine the problem matrix for the solution step $(l+1)$.

Example 6.18: The proposed solution in Example 6.17 was unfeasible. Another partial solution ($l = 2$) s^{32} has to provide in the *worst* scenario a cash inflow after two years ($t = 3$) that is greater than 4,000 Euros ($v_3 = 4$), i.e. $s_3^{332} > 4 \Leftrightarrow s_3^{332} \geq 4 + \varepsilon$.[453] The constraints concerning the two fixed payments today ($t = 1$) and in one year ($t = 2$) were satisfied. To formally determine the residual problem, first the adaptation matrices A^{j31} and vectors $\vec{a}^{j31}$ have to be determined.

$$A^{131} = A^{231} = \begin{pmatrix} 0 & 0 & 0 \\ 0 & 0 & 0 \\ 0 & 0 & 0 \end{pmatrix}; \quad A^{331} = \begin{pmatrix} 0 & 0 & 0 \\ 0 & 0 & 0 \\ 0 & 0 & -1 \end{pmatrix}; \quad \vec{a}^{131} = \vec{a}^{231} = \begin{pmatrix} 0 \\ 0 \\ 0 \end{pmatrix}; \quad \vec{a}^{331} = \begin{pmatrix} 0 \\ 0 \\ 4 \end{pmatrix}$$

Thus the problem matrices P^1 and P^2 equal the initial problem matrix, whereas P^3 is altered.

$$P^1 + A^{132} = P^2 + A^{232} = P^{132} = P^{232} = \begin{pmatrix} -1 & 0 & 0 \\ 0 & -1 & 0 \\ 0 & 0 & 0 \end{pmatrix} = P^j$$

$$P^{332} = P^3 + A^{331} = \begin{pmatrix} -1 & 0 & 0 \\ 0 & -1 & 0 \\ 0 & 0 & 0 \end{pmatrix} + \begin{pmatrix} 0 & 0 & 0 \\ 0 & 0 & 0 \\ 0 & 0 & -1 \end{pmatrix} = \begin{pmatrix} -1 & 0 & 0 \\ 0 & -1 & 0 \\ 0 & 0 & -1 \end{pmatrix}$$

The problem vectors in the *best* and *average* scenario for the residual problem are

$$\vec{p}^{132} = P^1 \vec{s}^{131} + \vec{p}^1 + \vec{a}^{131} = \vec{p}^{232} = P^2 \vec{s}^{231} + \vec{p}^2 + \vec{a}^{231} = \begin{pmatrix} -1 & 0 & 0 \\ 0 & -1 & 0 \\ 0 & 0 & 0 \end{pmatrix} \begin{pmatrix} -10 \\ -10 \\ 0 \end{pmatrix} + \begin{pmatrix} -10 \\ -10 \\ 0 \end{pmatrix} + \begin{pmatrix} 0 \\ 0 \\ 0 \end{pmatrix} = \begin{pmatrix} 0 \\ 0 \\ 0 \end{pmatrix} = \vec{0}.$$

Obviously, the constraints concerning the fixed payments are satisfied in these scenarios.

For the problem vector in the *worst* scenario Eq. (6.24) yields

$$\vec{p}^{332} = P^3 \vec{s}^{331} + \vec{p}^3 + \vec{a}^{331} = \begin{pmatrix} -1 & 0 & 0 \\ 0 & -1 & 0 \\ 0 & 0 & 0 \end{pmatrix} \begin{pmatrix} -10 \\ -10 \\ 0 \end{pmatrix} + \begin{pmatrix} -10 \\ -10 \\ 0 \end{pmatrix} + \begin{pmatrix} 0 \\ 0 \\ 4 \end{pmatrix} = \begin{pmatrix} 0 \\ 0 \\ 4 \end{pmatrix}.$$

A feasible solution for the residual problem has to satisfy Eq. (6.11) and Eq. (6.13). A possible partial solution s^{32} ($l = 2$) for this residual problem is to sell a futures contract with a maturity of two years.[454] The payment streams for the different scenarios are the following

$$s^{32} = \left\{ \vec{s}^{132} = \begin{pmatrix} 0 \\ 0 \\ -8 \end{pmatrix}; \vec{s}^{232} = \begin{pmatrix} 0 \\ 0 \\ 0 \end{pmatrix}; \vec{s}^{332} = \begin{pmatrix} 0 \\ 0 \\ 5 \end{pmatrix} \right\}.$$

---

[453] For reasons of clarity the marginal variable is not shown in the vectors and matrices below but is only used at the end of the calculation to check whether the constraint is satisfied.

[454] Abstracting from margin payments, clearing fees, etc., there are no real cash inflows or outflows before maturity associated with the purchase of a futures contract. On futures contracts see e.g. (Steiner and Bruns 2000) or (Brealey and Myers 1996).

It can easily be shown that this partial solution satisfies Eq. (6.11) as well as Eq. (6.13) and solves the residual problem. However, this does not have to mean in turn that also a global solution has been found. The probability constraint has to be checked using the (global) solution s^3. The probability variable S^3_3 of solution s^3 can be described as $S^3_3 = [(27;0.25)(25;0.6)(23;0.15)]$. Sorting these tupels using Eq. (6.15) yields $\Theta S^3_3 = [(23;0.15;3)(25;0.6;2)(27;0.25;1)]$. Now the probabilities have to be accumulated using Eq. (6.16): $\Phi(\Theta S^3_3) = [(23;0.15;3)(25;0.75;2)(27;1;1)]$. The relevant tupel for the check on feasibility is $(23;0.15;3)$. Apparently, $s^*_3 - v_3 = 23 - 22 = 1 \geq \varepsilon$. Thus the global solution satisfies all constraints and solution s^3 is a feasible solution.

$$s^3 = s^{31} + s^{32} = \left\{ \overline{s}^{13} = \begin{pmatrix} -10 \\ -10 \\ 27 \end{pmatrix}; \overline{s}^{23} = \begin{pmatrix} -10 \\ -10 \\ 25 \end{pmatrix}; \overline{s}^{33} = \begin{pmatrix} -10 \\ -10 \\ 23 \end{pmatrix} \right\}$$

So far, only the conditions to check a probability constraint have been discussed in this section. However, there may also be desired payment streams in a setting with scenarios and a probability distribution on these scenarios that correspond to the Cases I to IV. To check a solution not only on the probability but on all constraints presented above, the following conditions have to be satisfied in order to call a solution a feasible solution.

- Check *equality and inequality constraints*:
    - *Step 1*: Check inequality constraints of the (residual) problem using the last partial solution s^{al}.
    - *Step 2*: Check equality constraints of the (residual) problem using the last partial solution s^{al}.
- Check *probability constraint*: Calculate the distribution functions of solution s^a for each necessary scenario j and point in time t.

If and only if both checks are satisfied with respect to the last partial solution s^{al} and the complete solution s^a respectively, the solution is a feasible solution s^a.

It has just formally been shown how feasible solutions can be generated in case of fixed, arbitrary, minimum and maximum payments as well as minimum payments with a minimal probability and maximum payments with a maximal probability. The formal procedure was illustrated by a comprehensive set of examples. However, there still remains an important issue: Selecting a superior solution from the set of feasible solutions (see also Fig. 40, p. 125). This will be discussed in the next section.

6.3.7 Selection of a Superior Solution

Each feasible solution is evaluated applying an upfront specified evaluation function. Based on the evaluation function and the objective function, i.e. the decision rule, the superior solution is selected from the set of feasible solutions.

In the context of financial decision-making the *net present value* (NPV) is an evaluation function that is widely used. Though customers may most of the times not understand the mechanics of the NPV there are not many alternatives when it comes to making a good decision. In contrast, customers are more likely to think in performance categories that are expressed by an *internal rate of return* (IRR). However, the IRR will often not be unique, especially if the customer problem is a bit more complicated, i.e. there are two or more changes of sign in the cash flow stream of the solution.[455] Therefore, the NPV is a prominent candidate to be used in the following to aggregate a cash flow stream in a given scenario. In decision science different alternatives and respective states of the world are usually gathered in a utility matrix. Here utility is expressed by the NPV in a first approximation. Particularly in the case of risk this has to be further considered.

Before discussing the decision rules in detail, a general rule – the *principle of dominance*[456] – normally reducing the set of feasible solutions without any loss of a potentially superior solution is presented. Solution s^2 is dominated by solution s^1 if and only if at each point in time t in each scenario the payment s_t^2 is smaller or equal to s_t^1 and at least at one point in time and in one scenario s_t^2 is smaller than s_t^1. Thus s^2 can be omitted from the set of feasible solutions. If the decision for the NPV as the objective function has already been made, s^1 dominates s^2 if and only if the NPVs of s^{j1} are greater or equal to the NPVs of s^{j2}, and if at least in one scenario the NPV of s^{j1} is greater than the NPV of s^{j2}.[457] With this rule, dominated feasible solutions can be omitted but usually more than one feasible solution will remain, hence another decision rule has to be applied.

Let $\hat{s}^a$ denote the value that is assigned to a solution s^a and $\hat{s}^{ja}$ the value that is assigned to a solution s^{ja} with respect to a specific scenario j based on the applied decision rule and the underlying evaluation function. $\hat{s}^*$ denotes the superior solution. $NPV(.)$ denotes the application of the NPV as evaluation function to a given cash flow stream.[458]

---

[455] See e.g. (Brealey and Myers 1996), (Locarek-Junge 1997). Other criteria such as *payback period* or *average return on book value* do not apply here.

[456] See e.g. (Schneider 1997).

[457] It should be mentioned though that a dominated solution should not necessarily be omitted. Although it may at best constitute a second best solution from a quantitative financial perspective, there may be qualitative factors that outweigh the quantitative disadvantage for a customer. A prominent example is the fact that many customers prefer to purchase and own their privately used home even if leasing is by far superior with respect to the financial aspects of such a deal due to utilizable tax effects. See e.g. (Buhl et al. 1999a). On psychological effects on human decision-making with respect to finance (*theory of behavioral finance*) see (Goldberg and von Nitzsch 1999), (Shefrin and Thaler 1988).

[458] The determination of an appropriate discount factor for the NPV function will not be further discussed here.

6.3.7.1   Superior Solutions under Certainty

If there is just one scenario, the optimization rule is comparably simple. If the evaluation function aggregates the cash flow stream of a solution to a scalar, just the solution alternative with the largest value based on the evaluation function is chosen. Using the NPV as the evaluation function, the feasible solution with the largest NPV is chosen. Formally, for $\hat{s}^a = NPV(s^a)$ the objective function is

$$\hat{s}^* = \max_a \hat{s}^a .$$
(6.25)

6.3.7.2   Superior Solutions under Uncertainty

Using the NPV as evaluation function in the case of different scenarios without assigned probabilities, there are a number of decision rules that may be applied.[459] Apparently, the problem of making a decision under uncertainty is that the decision has to be made with no knowledge of the likelihood of the various outcomes. Thus the chances of making less than optimal decisions under these conditions are considerable. Nevertheless, a number of rules exist given differing sets of assumptions, attitudes, and goals for the decision maker.[460] They all transform the solution vector into a scalar on which the final decision is based.

- *Criterion of Optimism* (*Maximax Criterion*): Using this criterion the best possible outcome for each feasible solution is determined and then the solution with the best of these best outcomes is selected. The Maximax Criterion assumes an unfettered optimistic perspective of the decision maker. Formally, for $\hat{s}^a = \max_j NPV(s^{ja})$ the decision rule is

$$\hat{s}^* = \max_a \max_j NPV(\hat{s}^{ja}) = \max_a \hat{s}^a .$$
(6.26)

In the context of an often risk-averse customer making decisions about his future financial position, this criterion may not fit this picture. In addition, *best* scenarios are usually not a very likely outcome since they are typically determined based on long-term historical data.[461] Thus the decision may be strongly biased by just relying on one extreme end of the spectrum of payoff values.

---

[459] On decision rules under uncertainty see e.g. (Bamberg and Coenenberg 2000), (Schneider 1997), (Pinney et al. 1992). The original references for the specific rules can be found in (Bamberg and Coenenberg 2000) and are therefore not listed in the references in this book. Note that uncertainty is not always understood as known states of the world and the absence of probabilities, see e.g. (Kreps 1988).

[460] See (Pinney et al. 1992).

[461] A common example is the information that the best one-year performance of an investment funds has been $x\%$ in the last y years.

However, since minimum cash inflows (or maximum cash outflows) can already be captured by formulating appropriate desired payment streams according to Case IV, the Maximax Criterion is not as inappropriate as it might seem at first sight.

- Criterion *of Pessimism* (*Maximin or Wald Criterion*): Using this criterion the worst possible outcome for each feasible solution is determined and then the solution with the best of these worst outcomes is selected. In contrast to the Maximax Criterion, the Maximin Criterion assumes a notoriously pessimistic perspective of the decision maker. Formally, for $\hat{s}^a = \min_j NPV\!\left(s^{ja}\right)$ the decision rule is

$$\hat{s}^* = \max_a \min_j NPV\!\left(s^{ja}\right) = \max_a \hat{s}^a. \tag{6.27}$$

In the context of a risk-averse customer the Wald Criterion seems to be better suited compared to the Maximax Criterion. However, two issues have to be raised that are not in favor of the Maximin Criterion. First, just like *best* scenarios, *worst* scenarios are usually not a very likely outcome. Hence, the decision may be strongly biased by just relying on one extreme end of the spectrum of payoff values. Thus the Maximin Criterion may particularly prevent the choice of a solution that provides for a balanced chance/risk-trade-off. Second, since minimum cash inflows (or maximum cash outflows) can already be captured by formulating appropriate desired payment streams according to Case IV, applying the Minimax Criterion seems somehow redundant. Nevertheless, if a customer is supposed to be extremely risk-averse, the Maximin Criterion is an adequate choice for the decision rule.

- *Hurwicz Criterion*: Since both the Maximin Criterion and the Maximax Criterion suffer the same shortcomings, i.e. they just look at one end of the spectrum of payoff values, the Hurwicz Criterion combines the two. Denoting the *coefficient of optimism* with $\lambda \in [0;1]$, the Hurwicz Criterion calculates a weighted average of the best and the worst outcomes for each solution. For $\lambda = 1$ the Hurwicz Criterion becomes the Maximax Criterion and for $\lambda = 0$ it becomes the Maximin Criterion. Formally, for $\hat{s}^a = \lambda \max_j NPV\!\left(s^{ja}\right) + (1-\lambda)\min_j NPV\!\left(s^{ja}\right)$ the decision rule is

$$\hat{s}^* = \max_a\!\left(\lambda \max_j NPV\!\left(s^{ja}\right) + (1-\lambda)\min_j NPV\!\left(s^{ja}\right) \right) = \max_a \hat{s}^a. \tag{6.28}$$
$$\text{s.t.} \quad \lambda \in [0;1]$$

In the context of a financial planning situation the Hurwicz Criterion has its merits since it takes a weighted perspective and allows for personal expression of the attitude towards optimism. However, as already described above, *best* and *worst* scenarios are usually not very likely. Thus the decision may be strongly biased by just relying on the extremes of both sides. Moreover, particularly due to the possibility to represent desired minimal cash inflows or maximal cash outflows, the extreme on the low end can already be captured by formulating restrictions according to Case IV.

- *Savage-Niehans-Rule* (*Minimax-Regret Principle*): A completely different perspective is taken by the Savage-Niehans-Rule by focusing on opportunity cost. First the foregone utility has to be determined, which is yielded when scenario *j* occurs and one has chosen a different alternative solution, given *j* occurs, instead of the optimal solution. Thus in a first step an opportunity cost matrix has to be determined and in a second step the solution is selected that minimizes the maximal regret. Since the Savage-Niehans-Rule is by far too complicated in the context of a financial planning consultation, the formal description is omitted here.

- *Laplace Principle*: Due to uncertainty, no probabilities can be assigned to each state of the world. The Laplace Principle assumes a uniform probability distribution on the states of the world, thus $w^j = 1/m$. Thus the outcomes in each scenario for a solution alternative can simply be summed and the largest sum is chosen as the superior solution. Formally, for $\hat{s}^a = \sum_j NPV\left(s^{ja}\right)$ the decision rule is

$$\hat{s}^* = \max_a \left(\sum_j NPV\left(s^{ja}\right) \right) = \max_a \hat{s}^a . \tag{6.29}$$

It seems a bit strange to determine feasible solutions under the assumption that no probabilities are available and after this calculation for the selection of the superior solution, probabilities are suddenly obtainable. Moreover, given there are three scenario, the *best* and the *worst* scenario will often be not as likely as the *average* scenario. Thus the Laplace Principle does not seem favorable in a financial planning consultation process.

So the Hurwicz Criterion seems to be best suited as a decision rule in case of uncertainty. It is important to note that replacing the NPVs of each scenario with utility values based on a customer's utility function, the Maximax Criterion, the Maximin Criterion, and the Savage-Niehans-Rule would still yield the same result – but not the Hurwicz Criterion and the Laplace Principle. Since most customers are assumed to be risk-averse,[462] this should be taken into account. There are a number of additional decision rules that may be applied within a setting under uncertainty that are discussed in literature.[463] Instead of discussing all of these at this point, the special situation of a financial planning consultation is dealt with.

---

[462] See e.g. (Steiner and Bruns 2000).

[463] For instance (Kramer 1967) provides another seven decision rules. He also discusses these decision rules with respect to an axiomatic treatment. From the theoretical point of view, the so-called *Krelle Rule* due to (Krelle 1968) is supposed to be the best choice under uncertainty. However, there is a high informational need not only about the states of the world but also about the customer's preferences in order to apply this rule.

This special situation is often characterized by a visualization of risk using three different scenarios ({*best*; $j = 1$};{*average*; $j = 2$};{*worst*; $j = 3$}).[464] Based on the assumption that these are the only scenarios, four interesting decision rules can be derived modifying and extending the rules presented above.

- *Average Criterion (Maxiaverage Criterion)*: Since any desired minimal cash inflow or maximal cash outflow can already be captured formulating restrictions according to Case IV and the *best* as well as the *worst* scenario will usually not occur with high probabilities, to maximize the payoff of the *average* scenario seems to be another ingenious decision rule. Formally, for $\hat{s}^a = NPV\!\left(s^{2a}\right)$

$$\hat{s}^* = \max_a NPV\!\left(s^{2a}\right) = \max_a \hat{s}^a . \tag{6.30}$$

- *Constraint Average Criterion (Constraint Maxiaverage Criterion)*: Extending the Maxiaverage Criterion, the introduction of a minimal NPV (denoted by g) in the worst scenario also seems ingenious. Formally, for $\hat{s}^a = NPV\!\left(s^{2a}\right)$ the decision rule is

$$\hat{s}^* = \max_a NPV\!\left(s^{2a}\right) = \max_a \hat{s}^a \tag{6.31}$$
$$\text{s.t.} \quad NPV\!\left(s^{3a}\right) \geq g$$

Even though the *worst* scenario can already be captured using appropriate restrictions based on Case IV, a global target value g for the NPV in this scenario can significantly improve the decision situation for a customer. Particularly if the target value is set to zero ($g = 0$), this constraint resembles a minimum performance guarantee that many customers appreciate.[465]

- *Modified Hurwicz Criterion*: Hurwicz introduced a coefficient of optimism λ to combine the worst and best outcomes. In this special setting, it may also be advantageous to modify the Hurwicz Criterion combining the *best* and the *average* scenario, since the *worst* scenario can already be taken into account using Case IV restrictions. For $\lambda = 0$ the Modified Hurwicz Criterion becomes the Average Criterion and for $\lambda = 1$ it becomes the Maximax Criterion. Formally, for $\hat{s}^a = \lambda \cdot NPV\!\left(s^{1a}\right) + (1 - \lambda) \cdot NPV\!\left(s^{2a}\right)$ the decision rule is

$$\hat{s}^* = \max_a\!\left(\lambda \cdot NPV\!\left(s^{1a}\right) + (1 - \lambda) \cdot NPV\!\left(s^{2a}\right)\right) = \max_a \hat{s}^a \tag{6.32}$$
$$\text{s.t.} \quad \lambda \in [0;1]$$

Though this modification has its merits, the applicability of this rule strongly depends on the sophistication level and mental abilities of the customer. Criticism concerning this approach may still be directed at the fact that actually just

---

[464] This implies that the cash flow stream of s^{1a} dominates s^{2a} and s^{2a} in turn dominates s^{3a}.

[465] In fact, the constraint could also be applied to all of the three scenarios. Establishing a constraint that ensures a capital guarantee is not easy since so far just cash flows and instead of assets and their values have been considered.

two of the three states of the world are included in the decision rule. The next approach will take that into account.

- *Extended Hurwicz Criterion*: Besides the already introduced coefficient of optimism λ, one could additionally introduce some kind of *coefficient of pessimism* γ and a *coefficient of neutrality* δ[466] that in combination enable a customer to include and weigh all three scenarios in the decision process. Formally, for

$$\hat{s}^a = \left[\frac{\lambda}{\lambda+\gamma+\delta} \cdot NPV\left(s^{1a}\right) + \frac{\delta}{\lambda+\gamma+\delta} \cdot NPV\left(s^{2a}\right) + \frac{\gamma}{\lambda+\gamma+\delta} \cdot NPV\left(s^{3a}\right) \right]$$ the

decision rule is

$$\hat{s}^* = \max_a \left(\frac{\lambda}{\lambda+\gamma+\delta} \cdot NPV\left(s^{1a}\right) + \frac{\delta}{\lambda+\gamma+\delta} \cdot NPV\left(s^{2a}\right) \\ + \frac{\gamma}{\lambda+\gamma+\delta} \cdot NPV\left(s^{3a}\right) \right) \tag{6.33}$$

$$= \max_a \hat{s}^a$$

s.t. $\lambda, \gamma, \delta \geq 0; \lambda+\gamma+\delta > 0$

Especially the Constraint Maxiaverage Criterion and the Extended Hurwicz Criterion appear to be best suited for a financial planning consultation. The first one impresses with its simplicity. The latter one allows a customer to express his attitude towards risk by assigning values to coefficients of optimism, pessimism and neutrality.[467] Thus all three scenarios can be included in the decision rule. Of course there is still a vast number of other decision rules that could be applied, for instance combining elements of the Constraint Maxiaverage Criterion and the Extended Hurwicz Criterion.

At this point, the number of presented and developed decision rules for the case of uncertainty shall suffice and the attention will be drawn to cases with risk instead of uncertainty. If probabilities can be assigned to each scenario, it is much easier to integrate the outcomes of each scenario to form an aggregated value. Thus no awkward decision rule has to be developed to generate a scalar, but all available information can naturally be incorporated in the decision rule.

---

[466] The coefficient of neutrality could be omitted if it can be ensured that $\alpha + \gamma \leq 1$. However, it might be more difficult for a customer to keep in mind that he implicitly has to assign a value to his attitude towards the average scenario.

[467] The only problem may be to receive consistent answers, i.e. a customer that chooses a high coefficient of optimism generally should not choose a very high coefficient of pessimism at the same time.

6.3.7.3   Superior Solutions under Risk

In case there are probabilities that are assigned to each scenario, additional decision rules can be applied. Of course, the already presented decision rules are still
valid and can be also applied within a setting under risk.[468]

- *Optimize Expected Value*: Given the decision maker is risk-neutral, a probabil-
  ity-weighted average of the outcomes of each scenario is a commonly applied
  decision rule. For $\hat{s}^a = \sum_j \left(w^j \cdot NPV\left(s^{ja}\right)\right)$ the decision rule is

$$\hat{s}^* = \max_a \left(\sum_j \left(w^j \cdot NPV\left(s^{ja}\right)\right)\right) = \max_a \hat{s}^a . \tag{6.34}$$

- *Maximize Expected Utility (Bernoulli Principle)*[469]: Since it cannot be assumed
  that private customers are generally risk-neutral – in fact, it has widely been
  empirically shown that a majority seems to be risk-averse[470] – the NPVs in the
  scenarios have to be replaced by their equivalent utility values before an aggregated expected utility value for a solution alternative s^a can be calculated. Let
  $u(.)$ denote the utility function that transforms a NPV into an utility value. For
  $\hat{s}^a = \sum_j \left(w^j \cdot u\left[NPV\left(s^{ja}\right)\right]\right)$ the decision rule is

$$\hat{s}^* = \max_a \left(\sum_j \left(w^j \cdot u\left[NPV\left(s^{ja}\right)\right]\right)\right) = \max_a \hat{s}^a . \tag{6.35}$$

The last decision rule seems to be most appropriate in a financial planning consultation process where risk is captured by using scenarios and where subjective or
objective probabilities can be assigned to each scenario. However, the difficulty
lies in the identification of the utility function of the customer.[471] Of course, elements of the decision rules can be conveniently combined to form new – more sophisticated or for a special customer target group more appropriate – decision
rules.

Having discussed the solution process on a conceptual basis, questions remain
concerning tractability of the process, the convergence of the process towards a
superior solution, and at least some ideas about a cost-benefit-calculus.

---

[468] See (Pinney et al. 1992) and particularly (Bamberg and Coenenberg 2000).
[469] The Optimize Expected Value decision rule is a special case of the Maximize Expected
Utility rule. It is often also referred to as *μ-Principle*, expressing that just the expected
value instead of the expected value and risk – for instance in form of the standard deviation – are included in the decision rule. See e.g. (Bamberg and Coenenberg 2000).
On the Bernoulli Principle also see the appendix in (Neuberger 1998).
[470] See e.g. (Steiner and Bruns 2000) and references therein.
[471] More decision rules in this context can be found in (Dinkelbach and Kleine 1996).

6.3.8 Discussion

It has been shown above that superior solutions can be produced with relatively simple algebra, thus the tractability of the process is obviously ensured. At least the determination of residual problems, the integration of several partial solutions as well as the checks on whether the constraints are satisfied can still be handled. And although the matrix algebra and the treatment of probability constraints are on a simple level, they still promise to provide good results. However, the processes for local optimizations concerning single product domains has not been covered here. Particularly, if it comes to portfolio optimization under transaction costs and taking into account tax effects, the mathematical models and the underlying problems become nearly arbitrarily complex. Nevertheless, the model contributes to an improvement in the quality of the consultation process in at least two ways: First, due to the obligatory starting point of the process with the financial problem of the customer, a product-centric view can be circumvented. Second, the model fosters the integration of already existent local optimization knowledge. Thus applications that have already been developed for a local optimization can still be used if the implementation provides for a sufficient modularization.

Talking about the convergence towards a superior solution, so far the model has not been implemented in the form presented above. Thus no empirical tests could be carried out on whether a convergence can be expected. However, there are reasons for hope that the hybrid recognition and search process converges towards qualitatively good solutions. First, combination knowledge that is already available can be incorporated in the solution process. Thus at least standard solutions that are widely offered today will be generated and in so far the model will *at least* ensure the status quo of the quality of recommendations in the financial services sector today. Second, if the principle of value additivity holds, it should be possible to generate feasible solutions that are favorable with respect to an evaluation function, i.e. they generate a positive value of the evaluation function.[472] Suppose two locally optimized partial solutions have been generated, which together do not satisfy the constraints and generate a substantially positive NPV, a global solution consisting of three partial solutions may still provide for a positive NPV even if this third partial solution – just aiming at solving the residual problem – generates a slightly negative NPV.[473] Third, in the ALLFIWIB project already mentioned above, it could be shown in a prototypical implementation that superior solutions are generated and can be expected using this approach. Although in the ALLFIWIB project just the case of certainty has been covered, since the algebra is not significantly more complicated, empirical evidence for it might be cautiously taken as a proxy for the convergence towards a superior solution of the model under uncertainty or risk. Nevertheless, this issue is certainly still a question open to further research.

---

[472] For instance a positive NPV.

[473] And most likely a feasible but standardized solution, i.e. a solution that is not tailored to a customer's specific needs and his situation, which is often offered today by financial services providers will be inferior compared to this solution.

Talking about costs and benefits of the presented model, it is far easier to estimate the costs as opposed to the benefits affiliated with the implementation of the above model. Besides the one-time implementation costs, current expenses should not be underestimated since an adaptation of the system becomes necessary as soon as relevant changes in the legal environment occur, e.g. with respect to taxation laws. Although, the costs can still be roughly estimated, the case of the benefits is far more difficult. Since particularly financial consulting services have mostly credence qualities[474], customers most likely will not be able to distinguish between better and worse recommendations – at least in the short run. Thus the implementation and introduction of the model in the consulting process has to be accompanied by a marketing campaign that draws the attention of the customers to this improved quality of the recommendations. In the long run, independent institutions regularly performing tests on the recommendation quality of financial services providers should also contribute to an increased perception as well as trust on the side of the customers. Not least the customers themselves should experience the improved quality of the recommendations and become more loyal on the one hand and become highly valuable positive opinion leaders on the other hand. Moreover, there is still one part of benefits that can be determined comparatively easily: the solutions are generated in a time and human resources saving process. Thus direct cost savings should be measurable and financial advisors can focus on trust-building activities instead of trying to determine good solutions in the back office.

Still, there is a number of limitations of the product model that are discussed in the following section.

6.3.9 Limitations and Prospects for Further Research

There are three broad issues that limit the above model to some extent. The first concerns the representation of risk, the second is affiliated with value additivity, and the third deals with convergence towards a global solution.

First, the representation of risk can be criticized. Especially the constraints that can be formulated by the customer concerning minimum cash inflows or maximum cash outflows – possibly with a specific probability – just capture shortfall risks but do not take into account any chances. With an appropriate decision rule being applied, this situation can be relaxed. If the decision rule also takes into account chances as opposed to just focusing on the downside risk, a well-balanced decision can be safeguarded. Talking about the shortfall risk, it can be faulted because it is not combined with the actual shortfall loss, once the shortfall situation occurs.[475] This is a major deficiency but could be integrated relatively easily into the model. In addition, the probabilities of occurrence were assumed to be constant in time, across all scenarios, and across all solutions. This may in some in-

---

[474] See Sec. 3.4.2.

[475] See (Steiner and Bruns 2000). A detailed representation and criticism of the shortfall risk can be found in (Albrecht 1999).

stances be an oversimplification, however, the introduction of time-specific probabilities into the model would not pose a big problem. Knowledge about the correlation between two or more financial products that may be used in an optimization process can only be implicitly used between two payment streams. Thus the opportunity of risk diversification can hardly be formalized *between* different partial solutions. Nevertheless, correlation can be accounted for explicitly *within* a partial solution. In a setting where partial solutions are calculated and proposed by independent software agents that represent a specific product domain, e.g. stocks, this does not mean a prohibitive setback for the model.[476] Important diversification effects can be captured in this way. But broadening the scope to the global financial situation of the customer is still an open research issue that should be focused on in future research efforts. The issue of risk diversification is the connection to the second major limitation of the model.

Value additivity is the basis of this model, which builds on the simple additivity of partial solutions, i.e. their payment streams, to form a global solution for a customer problem. The total value of a solution is the sum of its parts, i.e. its partial solutions. Along the same lines, a problem can be decoupled in partial problem components if necessary. (Brealey and Myers 1996) nicely point out and show that given a perfect capital market, a firm's total value is just the sum of its parts. Thus the principle of value additivity holds: Investors are not willing to pay extra for diversification effects since they can diversify in their own portfolio. But the model was developed to work on the level of the customer where diversification has to be performed and should be an important issue. As already mentioned above, locally, i.e. concerning partial solutions, diversification can be conveniently taken into account, globally not yet. Analogously, the constant marginal tax rate may in a number of cases constitute an oversimplification.[477] It is well imaginable that a partial solution generates such high tax-deductible amounts that the marginal tax rate would be lowered after the integration of this partial solution. However, this would most likely have effects on all partial solutions already integrated and also on the efficiency of the initial portfolio.

Finally, a solution process has been presented that theoretically may lead to a superior solution. However, the convergence towards a feasible solution or to a set of feasible solutions is not safeguarded. Hypothetically, one could think of the process as always generating another residual problem but never solving the initial problem. The mechanism coordinating the generation of partial solutions is therefore another interesting area for further research.[478] Questions such as:

---

[476] On state-of-the-art with respect to cooperating intelligent software agents see (Kirn 2002).

[477] However, in Germany the number of households that pay the highest marginal income tax rate is growing. Thus the assumption does not seem too far-fetched.

[478] It should be mentioned though that in the ALLFIWIB project it has already been shown empirically that convergence towards a solution can be established. See e.g. (Buhl et al. 1996), (Buhl et al. 1993), (Einsfeld and Will 1996), (Buhl and Will 1998), (König et al. 1994) and references therein.

- How many alternative solutions should optimally be calculated for a given problem?
- At which point should the solution process for one solution alternative be terminated without generating a feasible solution?
- What financial products should be taken into account for a solution based on a given customer problem?
- How can a problem be identified as suitable for existent combination knowledge?
- At which point the locally optimized partial solution should be replaced by a partial solution that just solves the residual problem?
- At which point a customer feedback loop should be incorporated, providing the customer with the opportunity to accept an unfeasible solution by altering the formulation of his initial problem?

These are just some questions as prospects for further research that will be worked on in the next couple of months at the Competence Center IT & Financial Services at the University of Augsburg.[479]

These limitations and prospects conclude the main part on the product model. In the next section, the findings will briefly be summarized.

6.3.10 Conclusion

A product model has been presented that allows for the inclusion of uncertainty and risk into the formulation of financial problems by the customer as well as into the solution process, i.e. intelligently bundling financial products to form a superior solution for a specific customer problem. The presented formal model is just a first step towards better incorporating risk in the financial planning process and facilitating the use of IT for the solution generation process. Especially customer groups with comparably structured problems and a limited problem domain such as the mass affluent segment may substantially benefit from IT-enabled financial planning concerning the solution generation process. Today, they cannot be serviced appropriately due to prohibitive high costs, but tomorrow supported by adequate applications in combination with well-trained staff, this may become a sustainable competitive advantage.

6.4 Summary

In the preceding chapter concepts for life-cycle solution provision were introduced. Based on a research framework (see Fig. 30, p. 91) that has been developed at the Competence Center IT & Financial Services at the University of Augsburg, a content and a product model were presented. Since financial services and in particular, financial products are generally not self-explanatory, appropriate informa-

---

[479] See http://www.wi-if.de.

tion of the customer is a vital part of a financial services provider's business. The proposed content model fosters the use of cost-efficient one-to-one services, thus delivering relevant content via the appropriate communication channel at the right time to a specific customer.

But information often is just a necessary embellishment, since in the end a customer's needs are nothing but an expected cash flow stream to be transformed into a desired cash flow stream with the appropriate level of risk. Due to the complexity of the solution space, this transformation function can only be fulfilled with a suitable information system. The product model described above provides for a meta language to formally describe financial problems as well as financial solutions and proposes a hybrid process of search and recognition as solution process. Both the meta language and the solution process are prerequisites to implementing the product model.

Both concepts presented in this chapter can already be implemented with state-of-the-art technology. In the next chapter a long-term outlook with respect to relevant market developments is dared.

7 Outlook: The Importance of Trust[480]

> In the long run we are all dead.
> JOHN MAYNARD KEYNES

In Chap. 5 the vision and strategy of life-cycle solution provision were laid out. In Chap. 6 two conceptual CRM models to implement a life-cycle solution provision strategy were presented that may help to increase satisfaction and loyalty of the customer to the financial services provider by generating superior solutions for customer's (latent) financial problems and providing a customer with information based on his preferences and (latent) needs. However, a misbalanced CRM strategy – not focusing on trust issues, but just on customer lock-in – will ultimately drive a financial services provider out of the market. In this chapter it is the objective to challenge the CRM business model in the financial services sector and derive important recommendations for firms operating in the market. Specifically, it will be shown that the strategy of acquiring a customer with a significant investment and locking this customer in with specially tailored services may not be sustainable, if this lock-in is based on the notion of assumed high switching costs.

7.1 Introduction

Currently, billions of dollars are invested in CRM tools and the reorganization of processes around the customer – and this trend is believed to even intensify. For instance for 2000, the expenses for CRM tools and applications are estimated to have reached US$ 3.7 billion and they are expected to soar to US$ 16.8 billion in 2003.[481] Moreover, it is estimated that revenues in the financial services industry for CRM services[482] companies will reach US$ 24.4 billion in 2004, up from a mere US$ 6.5 billion in 1999. The only industry that is estimated to generate higher revenues for CRM services companies is the "Communications/telecom/publishing" industry.[483]

---

[480] The basic idea of this chapter is based on (Kundisch 2002b). The application with respect to the financial services industry is based on joint research efforts with Werner Steck; see (Kundisch and Steck 2002).

[481] See (Anonymous 2000d).

[482] Here, CRM services include activities such as consulting, implementation, outsourcing/operations management, training, and support. See (Menzigian 2000).

[483] See (Menzigian 2000).

In the following, it will be argued why financial services providers should re-think their IT investments and detour a substantial part of these funds into trust-building activities instead of exclusively relying on earnable premiums due to the lock-in effect. In the next section, some underlying assumptions of widely applied CRM strategies are presented. Based on these findings the likely scenario of further technological developments and their impact on these CRM strategies are discussed. Special attention is drawn to the financial services sector in this con-text. Consequently, several conclusions are drawn for the financial services indus-try, all aiming at strengthening the trust relationship with the customer.

7.2   CRM Strategies and Underlying Assumptions

> Technology changes, economic laws do not.
> HAL VARIAN

> The rules change when the tools change.
> SCN EDUCATION B.V.

A lot of financial services firms currently already pursue or have recently an-nounced a strategy where the customer and his preferences, needs, and objectives is put in the center of interest and all processes are aligned around the customer. Such strategies are based on the belief that if a customer learns how to deal with the corporation and, even more important, the corporation learns how to best indi-vidually service its customers, the customer will maintain a profitable long-term relationship with this company. Due to this relationship, it is believed that corporations will be able to utilize cross-selling potential due to the knowledge the company has about the customer and charge premiums on specially tailored solu-tions which often consist – as was shown in Sec. 6.3 – of a bundle of standardized financial products.

It should have become clear in the preceding sections that in order to be able to generate solutions that can be offered to the customer at the right time and using the appropriate communication channel, at lot of knowledge – integrated over all communication channels – has to be present at the time the matching takes place. With the information in hand, the financial services provider even should often be in the situation that latent needs can be identified and addressed accordingly. An appropriately applied CRM strategy aims at achieving four business objectives:[484]

- *Increased customer loyalty*: Due to CRM measures such as qualitatively better tailored solutions with respect to the customer's specific needs and objective, customer satisfaction and trust will rise. Consequently, customer loyalty will rise and the share of wallet may ideally increase as well.[485]

---

[484]   See (Schmid et al. 2000).
[485]   Also see (Moormann 2001), (Krishnan et al. 1999).

- *Better customer selection*: Since generally 20% of the customers generate 80% of the revenues, it is important to identify and invest in the "right" customers.
- *Winning new customers*: Even if customer loyalty and retention is high, there will always be customers that switch suppliers. Therefore it is also an important part of CRM to win new customers.
- *Increased efficiency*: Enabled by appropriate IT, there are several areas where substantial efficiency gains can be realized. For instance vast amounts of data can be analyzed at low cost, sales people can focus on value-added activities, and a cost-efficient multi-channel management may be applied.

Fig. 44 depicts the generic profit structure based on successful CRM. Obviously, after a costly acquisition of a customer, constantly increasing positive cash flows are assumed.[486] The cash flow is believed to increase due to several effects, such as utilization of cross-selling potential, recommendation effect of satisfied customers, cost reductions on the side of the supplier, and an anticipated price insensitivity on the side of the customer.

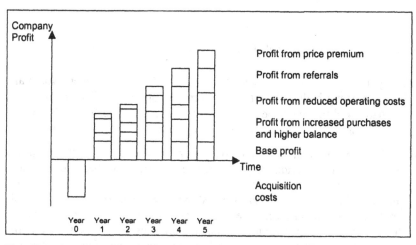

Fig. 44. Utility Derived from Long-Term Customer Relationship[487]

---

[486] For a discussion of shareholder value implications of a customer lifetime value strategy see e.g. (Dzienziol et al. 2001).

[487] See e.g. (Reichheld and Sasser 1990), (Reichheld 1997), and (Reichheld and Schefter 2000). A recent study due to (Reinartz and Krafft 2001) shows evidence that not only loyal long-life customers but also transactional short-life customers may be highly profitable for a company. Thus they conclude that it may be a "gross oversimplification to simply equate long-life customers with higher profits." However, their hypotheses are tested in the mail order business which has different service characteristics compared to the financial services industry. For specific service characteristics of financial services see Sec. 7.4.

And in fact, this profit contribution structure seems to hold for many industries.[488] Fig. 45 exemplarily shows the profit structure per customer of the credit card business in the financial services sector.

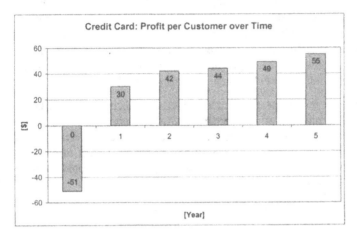

Fig. 45. Profits per Customer in Credit Card Business[489]

Certainly, this sounds like an appealing concept and many customers would already be quite happy both if their financial services provider delivered the solutions they had asked for and if they did not have the hassle of dealing with several parties. But this approach neglects some important features of human nature:

- First, a lot of people want to be able to compare their purchases with purchases of their peers. With individualized products and services this becomes increasingly difficult.[490]
- Second, more and more people are worried that companies which have a lot of information about them may misuse these data.[491] Especially high net worth individuals with sometimes extremely valuable portfolios do not want a single financial services provider to have a complete overview of their financial affairs.
- Third, a lot of people exhibit variety-seeking behavior, which means that looking for variety inherently contains utility for them.[492]

---

[488] See (Reichheld and Sasser 1990).

[489] See (Reichheld and Sasser 1990).

[490] The status quo on comparison shopping with respect to the financial services market in Germany was already discussed in Sec. 3.4.2.7, p. 48; also see (Kundisch et al. 2001). In fact, especially Internet users seem to have a preference to compare prices. According to (Arnold 2001) roughly 60% of the Internet surfers use the WWW for price comparison.

[491] See e.g. (Hagel and Rayport 1997), (Anonymous 1999a), (Hagel and Singer 1999). See (Seben 2001) and (Mabley 1999) for the connection between personalization services and privacy.

[492] See e.g. (Helmig 2001), (Gierl 1993), (Peter 1999).

- Fourth, changed income circumstances induce customers to switch a supplier.[493] There are a lot of customers who switch the financial services provider once they have reached a specific income level or value of their portfolio. In Germany many private banks with a (regionally) strong brand and a good reputation for high quality and extraordinary privacy rely on these types of customers.
- Fifth, customers want to keep some bargaining power and therefore maintain relationships to different financial services providers.[494] If a financial advisor is confronted by the customer with better offers provided by competitors, he often will also try to match the prices of these offers.
- Sixth, customers assume a positive effect on the motivation of their financial advisors, if each of them positively knows that he is in direct competition with other financial advisors and therefore constantly under pressure to perform well. Otherwise the customer might transfer some business to a rival.
- Seventh, a customer might not like to realize the fact of being locked-in making a switch to a different supplier a costly venture for him.[495]

This last issue is one of the basic underlying assumptions of (current) CRM strategies. The acquisition costs upfront of winning a new customer relationship has to pay off over time. Building up high switching costs is one of the profit sources for companies pursuing such a strategy.[496]

Switching costs can come in a variety of dimensions, which are gathered in Table 10.[497]

Table 10. Dimensions of Switching Costs

Dimension	Example
Economical	Opportunity costs of providing a company with address information.
Psychological[498]	Positive emotional relationship towards supplier based on trust, tradition or image.
Social[499]	Integration of the customer into corporate processes focusing on personal human relations
Legal[500]	Contractual long-term agreements.
Technological	Proprietary interface for data exchange.

Switching costs may also be broadly divided into *setup costs* and *takedown costs*. Setup costs include the cost of finding a replacement supplier and establishing a relationship. They also include the opportunity costs of foregoing business

---

[493] See e.g. (Gierl 1993), (Peter 1999).

[494] See e.g. (Shapiro and Varian 1998).

[495] See e.g. (Shapiro and Varian 1998), on *lock-in* see especially Chap. 5 and Chap. 6.

[496] On building-up switching costs in the financial services market see e.g. (Süchting 1998).

[497] For a slightly different categorization of switching cost components see (Tomczak and Dittrich 2000).

[498] See e.g. (Peter 1999).

[499] See e.g. (Peter 1999).

[500] See e.g. (Eifert and Pippow 2001).

with the incumbent. Takedown costs include relationship specific investments that have no value outside the relationship.[501] Concerning financial services, setup as well as takedown costs used to be high.[502] It could become a costly venture to switch the supplier of a checking account since the account number would have to be distributed and standing orders adapted accordingly. Filling in all forms to open a depot or a checking account could also become a time-consuming venture.

In the next section, the changing market environment with respect to switching costs and their impact on the importance of trust will be discussed.

7.3   Trust as a Vital Component of Switching Costs

> ...trust is a term with many meanings.
> O. WILLIAMSON

7.3.1 Customer Loyalty in the Financial Services Industry

The list above shows that there are a number of reasons why customers maintain relations with several financial services providers. In contrast, in the past most customers just maintained one house bank relationship and there was only little fluctuation of customers in the financial services sector.[503] It was common not to search for alternatives but to stay with the chosen financial services provider maybe even for a lifetime. This may stem from the fact that there simply was no alternative.[504] In the times before electronic (and telephone) banking, a customer was dependent on a branch office to perform a transaction. So the number of branch offices available for a customer was limited to the ones that could be reached without prohibitive costs.[505] Tremendous developments in IT – especially the development in Internet technologies – have changed this situation dramatically.[506] Due to the market entrance of new and purely Internet-based players like E-Trade or Charles Schwab customers are enabled to use financial services from wherever and whenever they like. The incumbents followed suit and nowadays

---

[501] See e.g. (Sengupta et al. 1997).

[502] On switching costs in the financial services industry also see (Neuberger 1998) who cites some empirical studies that provide evidence that switching costs used to be high in the U.S. market. Nevertheless, (Keller et al. 2000) refer to a study by TNS Emnid that finds that two-thirds of German universal bank customers are "wavering until ready to switch".

[503] See e.g. (Süchting and Paul 1998).

[504] See e.g. (Süchting and Paul 1998).

[505] See (Steck and Will 1998) for a search cost model illustrating this situation.

[506] (Süchting and Paul 1998) cite studies that suggest that loyalty towards a bank has suffered in the last decades. Also see Sec. 3.4. On decreasing customer loyalty towards a bank also see (Süchting 1998), (Lohmann 1997).

there is hardly a banking institution that does not offer at least basic online services.

Particularly the customers who have a high affinity for new technologies jumped at the chance to use less expensive and often better services.[507] Whereas 37% of all banking customers maintain more than one relation to a financial services provider, on the side of the home banking users there are 54% who enjoy working with more than one party (see Fig. 46). These home banking users are also more likely to switch between financial services providers. According to an Infratest-Study, only 5% of traditional banking customers switch suppliers or transfer business from the house bank to their second bank affiliation. In contrast, the share of switchers among the home banking users is twice as big.[508]

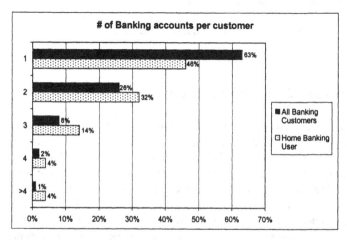

Fig. 46. Number of Banking Accounts – Banking Customers vs. Home Banking Users[509]

Interestingly, there are also the more attractive customers in terms of net income who seem to appreciate managing (at least some of) their financial dispositions using the Internet as the dotted ellipses in Fig. 47 impressively show.[510]

---

[507] See (Anonymous 2002b).

[508] See (Anonymous 2002b).

[509] Figures taken from (Institut für Demoskopie Allensbach 2002).

[510] (Keller et al. 2000) talk about wealthy customers who perform so-called *Finance Shopping*, i.e. utilizing the specific advantages – most often in terms of low prices – of several financial services providers. They also provide empirical evidence about the intensity of the relationships between German financial services providers and their customers.

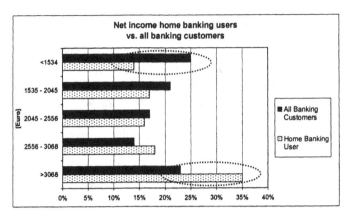

Fig. 47. Net Income – Home Banking Users vs. All Banking Customers[511]

7.3.2 PDE-Services and the Infomediary Approach

Based on the technological development specifically in applications that store and exchange information in a standardized format (e.g. XML may serve as such a global standard for data exchange on the Internet) there is now a second wave of innovation, which may even have a greater impact on the financial services sector. A growing number of (web-based) services that try to establish so-called *personal data environments* (PDE) have appeared on the market. The idea behind this is to store all personal data into an application-independent data warehouse from where it can be used whenever the customer needs it. There are already some prominent examples of approaches providing for PDE services in the market.

- *Microsoft's Passport* (http://www.passport.com) allows consumers to be able to sign-in at Passport partner firms with just a single username and login without having to fill in address fields for each company. The passport service has already an impressive list of so-called *sign-in sites* and *express purchase sites*. However, in April 2002, there is no financial services provider to be found among these companies.
- The *Liberty Alliance Project* (http://www.projectliberty.org/) works in the same direction. There are three primary goals of the project: To allow individual consumers and businesses to maintain personal information securely, to provide a universal open standard for single sign-on with decentralized authentication and open authorization from multiple providers, and to provide an open standard for network identity spanning all network devices. The Liberty Alliance Project is supported by a number of renowned companies. Founders or members from the financial services sector include American Express, Mastercard International, Citigroup, Bank of America, and Fidelity Investments. However, a first set of specifications will not be released before mid 2002.

---

[511] Figures taken from (Institut für Demoskopie Allensbach 2002).

- *memIQ* (http://www.memiq.com) – founded early 2000 by HypoVereinsbank and Vodafone Group plc. – goes a big step further compared to the two services briefly described above: It offers an intelligent electronic storage for personal documents accessible through the WWW. Particularly in the area of financial services, memIQ promises the following "Your financial records suddenly become transparent - you can see at a glance whether your insurance premium tallies with the amount deducted or your credit card bill has already been debited. In addition, retrieval and tracking of information becomes unbelievably simple – papers for your accountant are gathered in a matter of minutes – not hours."[512]
- The *Platform for Privacy Preferences Project* (P3P) (http://www.w3.org/P3P/) by the World Wide Web Consortium (W3C) is another approach that should be mentioned in this context. XML-based P3P provides an automated way for its users to gain more control over the use of personal information on websites they visit. Therefore, a user can define a personal privacy policy, i.e. preferences with respect to privacy or personal data. These preferences are automatically matched with a stated privacy policy of a P3P compliant website. There are already a lot of websites that are compliant with P3P specifications but only very few financial services providers are among these companies, such as the Kreissparkasse Köln.

As a consequence of this development it becomes increasingly easy and hassle-free for customers to transfer personal information from one financial services provider to another. Though the idea of companies serving their customer base according to their needs and really focusing on what the customer wants is appealing, customers are getting increasingly aware that the information about themselves is a highly valuable asset.[513]

It is questionable whether customers will accept in the long run that companies are getting a highly valuable asset – personalized data – for "free". Of course, customers also benefit from providing corporations with personalized information. They might save time, since they do not have to fill in address fields over and over again or they might get better-tailored solutions to their problems, but it is doubtful whether this utility outweighs the asset they are giving away for "free". Already back in 1997, Hagel and Rayport announced what they called "The coming battle for customer information".[514] With software tools becoming available and an increasing affinity for new technologies, it can be expected that customers will start keeping their own profiles and selling (temporarily) access to certain parts of these profiles to companies. Hagel and Rayport, however, believe that customers will not take care of their profiles themselves but propose the emergence of "infomediary" – corporations that act as brokers of customer information, marketing

---

[512] Shortly before this book went to press, MemIQ went bankrupt which might be a sign that the market is still not ready for such kind of services.

[513] But not only customers recognize that these data are worthy assets but also analysts tend to value companies in the Information Age according to their number of customer relationships instead of their tangible assets. See e.g. (Dzienziol et al. 2001) and references therein.

[514] See (Hagel and Rayport 1997).

it to other businesses on behalf of the consumer while protecting their privacy at the same time.[515]

The first three approaches mentioned above might evolve as infomediaries, whereas P3P focuses on providing the customer himself with a tool to manage his personal data. In the following, the question whether there will be growing number of infomediaries as business entities[516] or whether the customer becomes his own infomediary[517] will not be the center of interest, but how financial services providers should alter their current business models anticipating the shift of power towards the customer who increasingly uses such tools.[518]

Fig. 48 schematically depicts the different utility curves for a customer who switches his supplier two times. In the traditional CRM approach, the quality of individualization and hence the utility of the offered solutions steadily increase over time due to the two-way-learning and -communication process between supplier and customer. However, once a customer decides to switch the supplier, this process has to start all over again. In the infomediary setting, the customer takes all relevant data with him and ideally provides the new supplier with all necessary data to carry on at the same level of tailored solutions as the old supplier.[519]

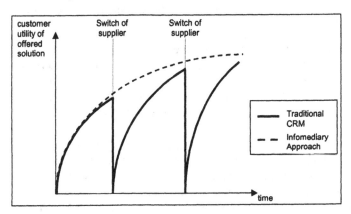

Fig. 48. Customer Utility Curves for Traditional and Infomediary Approach

Given the expected development of user-friendly applications that enable customers to maintain and continuously update their own profiles with relevant

---

[515] See e.g. (Hagel and Rayport 1997, 2000), also see (Hagel and Sacconaghi 1996), (Anonymous 1999b), (Hagel and Singer 1999).

[516] Three of the four presented value creation scenarios proposed by (Hagel and Sacconaghi 1996) assume emerging infomediaries as business entities in some form.

[517] This relates to the *customer control scenario* in (Hagel and Sacconaghi 1996) as one of four presented value-creation scenarios.

[518] (Link and Schackmann 2002) discuss possible business models with respect to PDE services.

[519] Obviously in this scenario it is assumed that the ability to generate optimal solutions based on a given set of data of a customer is the same for all suppliers, which will hardly be true in real world circumstances.

data along with the application development sketched above, a significant decline in switching costs in the technological and economical dimensions can be anticipated in the financial services sector for the years to come (on switching costs, see Table 10, p. 161).

Moreover, many relationships of customers with their financial services providers are not based on contractual long-term agreements. This is highly dependent on the financial product the customer has purchased from the financial services provider. On the one hand a checking account may be closed instantly and a portfolio may be transferred at short notice. On the other hand a mortgage loan generally is a long-term contractual agreement that can only be cancelled causing high cancellation costs before the date of maturity. It is important to note that the relationship with a financial services provider is often based on a number of contractual agreements, only some of which may be cancelled instantly.

Even though companies try to prevent the commoditization by not just providing the sheer commodity products but bundling several standardized product components into a financial solution along with consultation services, it is only the psychological and social dimensions that remain to keep customers. Thus trust – already one of the most important concepts in doing business – will get even more important and financial services firms should invest heavily in trust-building activities to keep and win customer relations.[520]

7.3.3 The Concept of Trust

In order to focus on trust-building activities, the first step is to understand the concept of trust. Astonishingly, although every business transaction is somehow based on mutual trust of the involved parties, a definition of the interdisciplinary concept of trust can hardly be found.[521]

Nevertheless, there are some constituting characteristics that may be found in almost each definition of trust:[522] Trust plays an important role in all exchange relations that include *risk* and a *dependence on the transaction partner*. If there were no risk and all actions could be performed under certainty, no trust would be necessary.[523] Risk means the opportunity of negative consequences (financial damage, personal security, loss in convenience, ...). Since honest traders are unable – or it is too expensive – to constantly check on the honesty of their trading partners, perceived risk plays a critical role in purchase decisions.[524] (Cunningham 1967) proposed a two-component model that links the *subjective probability of negative consequences* with the *extent of the negative consequences*.

---

[520] See (Barney and Hansen 1994), who examine trust as a source of competitive advantage.

[521] See (Gambetta 1988b).

[522] See (Rousseau et al. 1998).

[523] See (Lewis and Weigert 1985).

[524] See (Cunningham 1967).

Instead of trying to find an overarching definition here, following (McKnight and Chervany 2001) trust is conceptualized linking trust influencing constructs and subconstructs together (see Fig. 49). The two authors argue in a recent article "Because trust is so broad a concept, and because so many definitions have proliferated, a typology of trust constructs seems appropriate".[525]

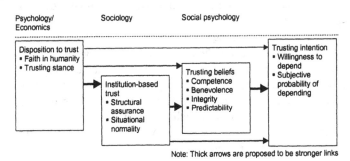

Fig. 49. Interdisciplinary Trust Constructs Model[526]

Apparently, trust is not a new concept.[527] No business transaction can be performed without trust. Though trust is already important in interpersonal relationships, with evolving sales channels that are based on the use of IT new challenges are arising. Especially in the Internet the perceived risk of negative consequences is comparatively high.[528] A consumer wanting to purchase a financial service via an electronic channel, which sometimes may even imply trade across national borders, different currencies and legal systems, must first of all trust the financial services provider.[529] This is additionally aggravated due to the fact that a web store-front can be built up relatively easily compared to a set of bricks-and-mortar branches. Thus it gets more difficult for a customer to decide about the trustworthiness of an online financial services provider upfront. (McKnight and Chervany 2001) emphasize the distinction between *trust in the supplier* of a product or service and *trust in the mechanisms of the underlying technological system*. Particularly in the financial services sector, trust in technology seems to be quite high. According to a study by the Institut für Demoskopie Allensbach, more than 8 million people (18.2% in the group of 14-64 years old) used home banking in Germany in 2001 and another 5.4 million (11%) planned to become home banking users in the near future (see Fig. 50).[530]

---

[525] See (McKnight and Chervany 2001).

[526] See (McKnight and Chervany 2001).

[527] A review on trust in economic literature can be found in (Albach 1980).

[528] See e.g. (Tan 1999).

[529] See e.g. (Jarvenpaa et al. 2000), (McKnight et al. 2000). On regulation in the EU concerning the financial services market see Sec. 3.1. On trust issues in electronic commerce also see e.g. (Dutton 2000), (Hoffman et al. 1999).

[530] See (Institut für Demoskopie Allensbach 2002).

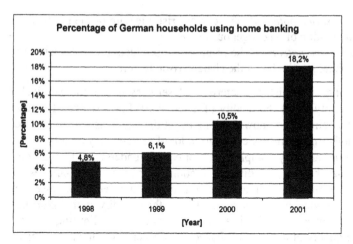

Fig. 50. Percentage of German Households Using Home Banking[531]

As it has been shown, there are the more interesting customers that perform their financial transactions online. Therefore, trust-building activities should not only be pursued offline but although it is very difficult – if not impossible – to establish a personal trust relationship over the Internet, measures should be taken to strengthen the trust in a website owner and the used technology.

Before consequences of the findings in the previous paragraphs can be derived, some special characteristics of financial services have to be discussed in the next section.

7.4 Special Characteristics of Financial Services

It has been shown that technological progress facilitates the switching of financial services providers because personal data can be transferred increasingly easily and there are a lot of new financial services providers that can now be reached at low costs using electronic communication channels. In order to find out what financial services providers can do to prevent their customers from switching, the special character of financial services and their impact on trust and trust-building activities will be discussed in this section.

Theory broadly distinguishes three dimensions of a service:[532]

1. *Potential-oriented service potential*: The ability and preparedness to produce the service, i.e. the provision and combination of input factors.

---

[531] Figures taken from (Institut für Demoskopie Allensbach 2002).

[532] See e.g. (Süchting 1994) or (Kloepfer 1999) with respect to the financial services industry. On services in general see e.g. (Corsten 2001), (Schneider 1999b), (Hardt 1996), (Thede 1992) and respective references therein.

2. *Process-oriented service potential*: The characteristic feature of the production process is the integration of an exogenous factor.
3. *Result-oriented service potential*: The result of the production process with the immateriality or intangibility being the characteristic feature.

Generally speaking, a special characteristic of services is the comparatively high ex ante uncertainty about the quality of a service.[533] For instance, if a customer wants to get a haircut and knows nothing about the hairdresser's abilities he has to trust him. In the financial services sector a lot of services rely on lots of parameters and therefore are very complex and not easy to understand. In addition, due to this complexity they are also difficult to compare, particularly if bundles of financial products, i.e. financial solutions are considered. In order to convince the customer, financial service providers try to signal their ability with luxurious branch offices for instance. *Signaling* is a well-known concept of limiting the uncertainty about the quality of a service.[534] Especially concerning immaterial financial services that even may possess credence qualities[535] it is very difficult to signal high quality. As (Spence 1976) mentions "Words are cheap, and therefore do not provide a means by which high quality sellers can differentiate their products."

It is also characteristic for services in order to be consumed that the customer himself is part of the production process as an exogenous factor.[536] Obviously, this holds not only true for the hairdresser example but also in the area of financial services where the customer and his characteristics are also an essential part of the production process. For instance, for the decision on an appropriate investment strategy the customer's attitude towards risk, the personal marginal tax rate and other customer specific parameters have to be known.

The more similar services become over time, the more the customer is able to transfer his confidence gained from one positive result into general trust in the producer. So if one haircut is good it provides strong evidence for the customer that the next ones – if made by the same person – will be good, too. A successful production process thus is a very strong signal for the producer's ability. Obviously, once a customer is convinced of the ability of a service provider there is much less reason for him to look out for other providers of this service.

The case of the financial services is much more complex. There are not only a sheer uncountable number of different financial services offered in the market, but they are also highly diverse in terms of necessary data for the production process and complexity. For instance, if a financial services provider is able to provide

---

[533] See (Engelhardt et al. 1993).

[534] (Stigler 1961) is one of the basic contributions on uncertainty about quality. There, uncertainty about quality is modeled as uncertainty about the price.

[535] See Sec. 3.4.2.

[536] Viewing the customer as an *exogenous* factor neglects the opportunity to develop the customer during the relationship with the financial services provider. It is well imaginable that for the profitability of a relationship for both partners, a specific sophistication level of the customer is optimal. Hence, considering the customer as an *endogenous* factor in the service production process is an interesting issue that is subject to further research.

hassle-free and affordable checking accounts, this is only weak evidence that the financial services provider is also a good investment advisor. Consequently, a customer does not necessarily choose the same financial services provider for his investments as for his checking account. In fact, this can have negative consequences for both financial services providers and particularly for the customer himself since both providers do not have a holistic picture of the customer and therefore are not able to tailor their products suiting the customer's preferences and needs. In addition, due to this missing holistic picture, it will be much more difficult to identify latent needs. In result, the customer will get an overall worse quality of consultancy service as well as tailored solutions of inferior quality. Customers either do not realize these disadvantages or deliberately choose to bear these disadvantages in order to circumvent the perceived disadvantages of just being with one financial services provider. With personal data being easily transferable there is basically no reason for the latter group not to evaluate alternatives. Anyway, both customer groups should be convinced with the help of trust-building activities that switching a supplier does not pay off and moreover that even reducing the number of relations with other financial services providers may be highly beneficial for the customers themselves.

These trust-building activities in the financial services sector will be the issue of the next section.

7.5 Effects on CRM Strategies for Financial Services Providers

> While there are many directions a financial services company can go today, we will only do that which supports the growth of our brand.
> KENNETH CHENNAULT, Vice-Chairman of American Express

> Consumers may be willing to pay a premium to purchase a product from a retailer they trust.
> MICHAEL D. SMITH, JOSEPH BAILEY, ERIK BRYNOLFSSON

There are a lot of components that could contribute to increasing trust in a financial services provider.[537] One of the main problems sketched above is that trust in services per se cannot be generalized in the financial services industry. There are a number of additional activities that potentially may help to foster the transfer of trust from one service to another. Each of these activities is subject to further research. The following list is just a preliminary draft of possible activities.

---

[537] On trust management in asset management for high net worth individuals see (Wicke 1997).

- A personal financial advisor may act as a product-independent *trust „medium"* for the customer.[538] Since a real personal trust relationship can hardly be built via electronic channels, the personal advisor is assigned a very special role as relationship manager. This is a strong hint that in the future financial services business will stay people business in at least some substantial parts.
- Instead of selling either single or bundled (standardized) financial products, the focus should be on selling *financial planning services* – which is an important part of the life-cycle solution provision approach described above. If there is trust in the financial planning approach, it might be easier to transfer that trust to the financial products themselves. Hence, product-independent trust may be generated.
- While focusing on *cross-selling approaches*, financial services providers should try to cross-sell products that are either somehow similar to already sold products or that complement already sold products. Trust may thus be transferred more easily from one service to the other.[539]
- Based on the life-cycle solution provision approach it is important that financial services providers focus on *comporting proactively*. Today, customers often have to identify financial problems such as liquidity bottlenecks and necessary risk provisioning on their own. It might be a substantial competitive advantage if customers recognized that a financial services provider identifies latent financial problems of the customer and at the same time proposes a tailored solution to this problem.

To summarize, financial services providers have to change their attitude towards business from being a seller of only weakly linked products to being seller of individualized solutions based on a life-cycle relationship approach.

Concerning the online presence there are a number of specific activities that may be pursued. Issues of interest for a potential investment are

- privacy policy,
- third party privacy seals (e.g. TRUSTe Privacy Program), and
- information disclosure seals (e.g. WebTrust Seal).

Apparently, the handling of private information about specific customers will be an issue of particular interest offline and even more important online. Proactively announcing the privacy policy and offering/enabling customers to access their personal profile at the supplier's site might become common in a few years, but today it might be a first mover advantage that could be exploited.[540] In addition

---

[538] The importance of personal contact is supported by (Zeithaml 1984). He states the hypothesis that "consumers seek and rely more on information from personal sources than from nonperson sources when evaluating services prior to purchase." He also cites some empirical studies that underpin this hypothesis.

[539] On cross-selling probabilities with respect to financial services see (Stracke and Geitner 1992).

[540] For a different point of view on the importance of privacy statements and seals based on empirical findings see (Spiekermann et al. 2001).

- reputation and brand building activities,
- reliability seals, security seals (e.g. VeriSign Secure Site Program), and
- site quality

are also important factors. Guarantees and return policies are frequently also named in such lists, too. However, they are only applicable in a very narrow scope in the financial services sector due to the (sometimes) speculative, intangible, and non-storable characteristics of the services. Besides these comparably precise recommendations, there are another two conclusions of a more general and visionary nature, respectively.

Financial services firms should not rely on profit contribution structures as presented in Fig. 44 (p. 159) and Fig. 45 (p. 160). Such a strategy could easily lead to profitability troubles in the long run. Just imagine companies act following this profit structure: Investing in a relationship with high acquisition costs at the beginning of the relationship – a decoy offer that does not generate any margin in the short run, i.e. no shareholder value – and expecting constantly increasing profit contributions in the future ultimately will drive a company out of business. If consumers switch suppliers at comparatively low costs, they might tend to utilize several decoy offers at different companies instead of establishing a long-term relationship with one company. In this case, the initial acquisition costs will never amortize. As a consequence, focusing on the bottom line for every single deal will become more important in the future.[541]

As already discussed in the section dealing with the emergence of the infomediaries, many financial services providers already own two highly valuable assets that in combination may be turned into an extremely profitable business opportunity. One the one hand they already own vast amounts of (personal) information about their customers and on the other hand customers trust their (prime) financial services provider at least more than most other companies they are doing business with. In addition, the financial services industry as an IT intense industry has already accumulated a lot of specially-skilled employees that may deal with lots of data. Likewise most financial institutions have already been operating for years in a market where privacy is essential and many of them have built up a good reputation and brand over the years – at least in their regional markets.[542] In the light of shrinking margins, more transparent markets, and an increasing commoditization of financial products, turning this trust into a business opportunity might even become a vital contributor to a financial services provider's profits in the future. Offering trust-based services such as digitalization, management, and structuring of personal data to form an effective and efficient PDE as a service for customers might be in high demand in the future. The potential of such a service shall be clarified by an example:

---

[541] This may be achieved easier with the proposed pricing approach in Sec. 5.2.7.

[542] In 2001, there are just four financial services brands (Citibank, American Express, Merrill Lynch, Goldman Sachs) among the top 100 brands and none of them belongs to a German firm; see (Anonymous 2001c). Interbrand, a leading brand consultancy, states that the "financial services sector is notoriously lacking strong brands"; see (Anonymous 2001a).

Example 7.1: Mr. Smith uses the personal data environment services offered by his financial services firm. At the end of the year the necessary documents to make the annual tax declaration can be printed at a single-mouse click. The hassle of searching relevant documents has vanished. Even his tax declaration itself can be finished at a single mouse-click. This service not only saves him a lot of time and effort but also the costs of his tax consultant.

This visionary example concludes the main body of this chapter. In the following section the findings will be briefly summarized before a general summary of the whole contribution as well as issues that are subject to further research will be presented in the last chapter.

7.6 Summary

The real battle for customer relationship in the financial services industry has just begun and many firms acknowledge that the customer and his preferences, needs and objectives should be put in the center of interest. Effectively applied CRM strategies might help to service customers better and to establish a profitable long-term relationship between the financial services provider and the consumer. However, due to an anticipated decline in switching costs, business models just relying on customer lock-in will not be sustainable. Focusing on the acquisition of customers with heavy investments at the beginning of a relationship and charging premiums in the future because of high switching costs that have been built up by CRM methods are supposed to be unprofitable in the long run.

In such an environment and anticipated development the concept of trust becomes vital. Financial services firms should therefore proactively invest in trust-building activities. Moreover, taking into account the bottom line of every single deal with a customer will gain importance due to these lowered (economical) switching costs. By and large the financial services industry is in the convenient position of becoming trusted infomediaries because of the already established and relatively strong trust relationships with their customers. In fact, it is well imaginable that trust or so-called PDE services may contribute more to a bank's bottom line in the long run compared to transaction commissions.

It remains to be seen whether advances in IS development are fast enough to already allow a customer in the near future to conveniently manage a highly valuable asset – his personal information – on his own. With respect to the anticipated realizable scale effects it seems to be more likely that special infomediaries or financial services providers acting as infomediaries emerge, which may successfully offer their trust-based services.

8 Summary and Outlook

Innovate or die.
PETER DRUCKER on Financial Services, 1999

The starting point for this book was the observation that (German) financial services firms have not been able to generate an adequate return for their shareholders in the business with private customers in recent years. Therefore, the development of a vision, a complementing strategy as well as exemplary implementation concepts that provide a firm operating in this market with a sustainable competitive advantage was the center of interest. In the following, the main findings of the analysis and, finally, primary prospects for further research will be presented.

8.1 Conclusion

In *Chap. 1* a short description of the status of the business with private customers in the German financial services market is given and the problem statement is introduced for the research that has been conducted.

Important technical terms that are widely used throughout the book were defined in *Chap. 2*. It includes on the one hand the definition of financial services providers as well as their offered products and services and on the other hand the definition of financial problems and related strategic (solution) concepts.

Four major mega-trends – trends with the most significant impact on the financial services market in the years to come – were considered in *Chap. 3*. Due to *regulation* efforts by the EU the European financial services market is increasingly being turned into a level playing field for European financial services providers resulting in improved consumer protection and transparency on the one hand and in intensified competition on the other hand. Although this makes the European/German financial services market a difficult market to operate in, *society changes* open interesting new business opportunities for financial services providers. Since especially in Germany pay-as-you-go pensions schemes will not be able to cover the expenses of future pensioners, private retirement planning becomes more and more popular. The recently introduced state-supported private pensions scheme (*Riester-Rente*) – despite of all its problems – has also increased customer's sensibility with respect to this topic. Another interesting development are the changing *working life conditions*, which keep creating more and more need for individualized solutions instead of standardized products for a customer's financial problems. Finally, it has been shown that due to increasing transparency caused by *new means of communication*, particularly the Internet and standardized data exchange protocols such as XML, prices for standardized financial commodity products are driven down to marginal costs. In a search cost model, it has been shown that customers can be expected to ever more use simultaneous search engines, intensifying the pressure on margins. Thus the European/German financial services market is characterized by new business opportunities arising due to society changes and changing working life conditions on the one hand and dramatically intensifying competition, increasing transparency, and ever more empowered customers on the other hand.

Based on these findings, in *Chap. 4* two generic strategies – *cost leadership* and *differentiation* – are analyzed in more detail. To become a cost leader, enormous scale effects have to be realized. This explains the wave of mergers that could be observed in recent years in the financial services market. However, supported by lots of empirical evidence, particularly a cost-driven merger is a defensive strategy and a high risk venture in a dynamically evolving market environment. Thus differentiation seems to be a potentially superior strategy that may provide a sustainable competitive advantage in this environment. Taking into account the analyzed mega-trends, a *life-cycle solution provision strategy* is proposed and developed in more detail in the next chapter.

Chap. 5 starts out with a description of the relatively poor status quo of customer segmentation strategies in the financial services market and its potential impact on the bottom line. Consequently a vision and strategic building blocks to implement this vision are presented. These comprise the following:

- *One-stop shopping*: A successful solution provider has to offer the whole range of financial services in order to be able to generate superior and integral solutions to customer problems.
- *Individualization*: A fitting solution to a customer problem can only be generated by integrating the customer into the production process.
- *Strategy of Choice*: Customers should not be segmented – e.g. by their income or value of assets – but they should have the choice between several qualities of service.
- *Multi-Channel Approach*: A relationship manager and solution provider has to deliver its financial products and services through multiple channels to the customer. However, sound business decisions about the provision of distribution channels as well as about the combinations of financial services and respective channels have to be made.
- *Life-cycle Consultation Approach*: Independently from the chosen or offered level of service, the underlying approach for each served customer is the notion of a life-cycle consideration. In the extreme, each single buy or sell decision has to be made in the light of its expected global consequences on the customer's situation. Thus a financial planning approach is the basis for the interaction of the relationship manager with the customer, be it an information system or a personal financial advisor at the customer interface.

- *Customer Lifetime Value*: Customer acquisition and retention efforts are based on the expected customer lifetime value and thus have to be individually sound business decisions with respect to each (potential) customer.
- *Pricing*: To stop cross-subsidization – especially between transaction and consultation services – a new pricing scheme has to be gradually introduced. Based on the strategy of choice, customers have to be directly charged for services with a higher quality.

Since the financial services industry is an information industry, IT plays a very important role in implementation of the strategy. Therefore, two concepts are presented in the next chapter.

The two concepts presented in Chap. 6 particularly contribute to the strategic building blocks *individualization* and *life-cycle consultation approach*. Firstly, an IT-enabled *content model* is developed that facilitates to deliver the right content at the right time using the appropriate communication channel. Thus individual informational needs of a specific customer can be satisfied and at the same time the customer might be sensitized for certain topics and latent needs may be aroused resulting in cross-selling opportunities. To achieve this, customer preferences are matched with content meta data and a multi-channel distribution process is applied to the result set. First steps of this model have already been realized at the Deutsche Bank's Private Banking website. Secondly, a *product model* that supports a cash flow based (life-cycle) financial planning approach is presented. The model allows for a depiction of various desired cash flow structures of a specific customer. For this purpose, a formal meta language to represent financial problems as well as financial solutions has been developed, which may be applied in a hybrid process of search and recognition as solution process. The main contribution of this concept lies in the inclusion of uncertainty and risk in the problem formulation as well as in the solution process, which is important for a financial planning consultation and thus may significantly improve the quality of consultation services.

In *Chap. 7* a long-term outlook with respect to relevant market developments is dared. Extrapolating the advances in IT and especially PDE services, it can assumed that switching costs will be significantly reduced in the years to come. This makes the *concept of trust* even more important in the business where many products and services possess credence qualities. Theoretical considerations imply that commonly assumed rising profit contribution structures over time may not be valid in the future anymore and financial services firms have to focus on both trust-building activities on the one hand and the bottom line impact of each single transaction on the other hand. Moreover, the analysis reveals that financial services providers are in the comfortable position of possibly becoming trusted PDE service providers, turning a threat into a business opportunity with a potential profit contribution that may be higher than their traditional core business.

8.2   Prospects for Further Research

Throughout the book various areas have been identified that offer promising prospects for further research. The future work of the author at the Competence Center IT & Financial Services at the University of Augsburg will be guided by the following three primary themes:

- Development of a *channel model* in combination with an *extension of the content model* to realize further steps of the individualized multi-channel content distribution vision.
- *Extension of the product model* in terms of an endogenous tax rate and a more detailed analysis of risk diversification effects. Moreover, coordination mechanisms within the hybrid process of search and recognition will receive more attention.
- Development of a customer-focused and *IT-based financial planning application* targeting mass affluent and retail customers and tapping a business opportunity largely unexploited so far.

It remains to be seen whether financial services providers will be able to transform themselves from product oriented administration institutions to flexible customer and needs oriented solution providers. The question is whether they have a real choice at all, or – as Peter Drucker put it – they can only "innovate or die".

List of Abbreviations

ALLFIWIB	Unterstützung von **Allfi**nanz-Angebotsprozessen mit verteilten **wissens**basierten Systemen (Project name)
API	Application programming interface
ATM	Automatic teller machine
B2C	Business-to-customer
B2B	Business-to-business
CAPM	Capital Asset Pricing Model
CEO	Chief Executive Officer
CFO	Chief Financial Officer
CFP	Certified Financial Planner
CLV	Customer lifetime value
CPA	Certified Public Accountant
CPU	Central processing unit
CR	Concentration ratio
CRM	Customer relationship management
DC	Defined contribution
DESA	Department of Economic and Social Affairs
DFG	Deutsche Forschungsgemeinschaft (German national science foundation)
DM	Deutschmark
ECB	European Central Bank
e.g.	For example
FAN	Forschergruppe Augsburg Nürnberg (research group Augsburg Nuremberg)
GDP	Gross Domestic Product
GSM	Global System for Mobile Communications
GVU	Graphic, Visualization & Usability Center
HBCI	Home Banking Computer Interface
HHI	Herfindahl-Hirschman Index
HNWI	High Net Worth Individuals
HTTP	Hypertext transfer protocol
HTTPS	Hypertext transfer protocol secured socket layer
Hypo-Bank	Bayerische Hypotheken- und Wechsel-Bank AG
HypoVereinsbank	Bayerische Hypo- und Vereinsbank AG
i.e.	that is
IF	Information filtering
IP	Internet protocol

IR	Information retrieval
IRR	Internal rate of return
IS	Information system
ISO/OSI	International Standard Organization/Open Systems Interconnection
ISP	Internet service provider
ISSM	Incremental Searcher Satisfaction Model
IT	Information technology
ITRS	International Technology Roadmap for Semiconductors
KonTraG	Gesetz zur Kontrolle und Transparenz im Unternehmensbereich
KWG	Gesetz über das Kreditwesen
LBBW	Landesbank Baden-Württemberg
M&A	Mergers and acquisitions
MMR	Maximal Marginal Relevance
MB	Megabyte
NASDAQ	National Association of Securities Dealers Automated Quotation
NEMAX	Neuer-Markt-Index
NPV	Net present value
P3P	Platform for Privacy Preferences
PangV	Preisangabenverordnung
PAYG	Pay-as-you-go
PC	Personal computer
PDE	Personal data environment
PDF	Portable document format
PGP	Pretty good privacy
pm	post meridiem
POP	Point of presence
SMS	Short message service
SMTP	Simple mail transfer protocol
SSL	Secured socket layer
UCITS	Undertakings for collective investment in transferable securities
U.S.	United States (of America)
VDAX	Deutscher Volatilitätsindex
Vereinsbank	Bayerische Vereinsbank AG
W3C	World Wide Web Consortium
WAP	Wireless application protocol
WKWI	Wissenschaftliche Kommission Wirtschaftsinformatik
WWW	World wide web
XML	Extensible markup language

List of Figures

List of Tables

References

Abby E (1999) A Generation of Freelancers. The New York Times, August 15, Sec. 3: Money and Business/Financial Desk, p.13

ACM (1992) Special issue on information filtering. Communications of the ACM, Number 12, 35

Albach H (1980) Vertrauen in der ökonomischen Literatur. Zeitschrift für die gesamte Staatswissenschaft 136: 2–11

Albert H (2000) Interaktives Customer Relationship Management im Multi-Dialog-Mix. Die Bank, Number 5, pp. 352–354

Albrecht T (1999) Asset Allocation und Zeithorizont. Uhlenbruch, Bad Soden

Ancona D, Kochan TA, Scully M, van Maanen J, Westney DE, Kolb DM, Dutton JE, Ashford SJ (1999) Managing for the future: organizational behavior & processes. South-Western College Publishing, Cincinnati

Anderson S, Renault R (1999) Pricing, Product Diversity, and Search Costs: A Bertrand-Chamberlain-Diamond Model. The Rand Journal of Economics 30: 719–735

Ando RK, Boguraev BK, Byrd RJ, Neff MS (2000) Multi-document Summarization by Visualizing Topical Content. In: Proceedings of ANLP/NAACL 2000 Workshop on Summarization. Seattle, USA, pp. 79–88

Anonymous (1995) Leere Versprechen: Jedes dritte Beratungsgespräch war „mangelhaft" oder „sehr mangelhaft". FINANZtest, Number 5, pp. 14–20

Anonymous (1997a) Zwischen Zaudern und Zocken. FINANZtest, Number 12, pp. 12–20

Anonymous (1997b) Vereinsbank und Hypo schließen sich zusammen. Süddeutsche Zeitung, Number 166, 07/22/1997, p. 1

Anonymous (1998a) Das goldene Los. Der Spiegel, Number 17, pp. 78–96

Anonymous (1998b) HypoVereinsbank kostet Bereinigung von Altlasten 3,5 Milliarden DM. Süddeutsche Zeitung, Number 249, October 29, p. 23

Anonymous (1998c) The end of jobs for life? The Economist, February 21, Issue 8056, 346: 76

Anonymous (1999a) The end of privacy: The surveillance society. The Economist, May 1, Issue 8117, 351: 21–23

Anonymous (1999b) Survey: Business and the Internet: The rise of the infomediary. The Economist, June 26, Issue 8125, 351: B21–B24

Anonymous (2000a) Financial modernization: The Gramm-Leach-Bliley Act: An executive summary. Kentucky Banker Magazine, Issue 876, pp. 12–13

Anonymous (2000b) Baufinanzierungsberatung: Passt selten. FINANZtest, Number 2, pp. 12–17

Anonymous (2000c) Anlageberatung: Völlig verschnitten. FINANZtest, Number 5, pp. 12–19

Anonymous (2000d) Kundenbindungs-Systeme auf dem Vormarsch. Electronic Commerce Info Net, available at http://www.ecin.de/news/2000/01/25/01000/

Anonymous (2000e) Survey online finance: The virtual threat. The Economist, May 20, Issue 8171, 355: SO5–SO8

Anonymous (2001a) Bank on the brand. Business Papers No 1, available at http://www.brandchannel.com/images/papers/Bankonthebrand.pdf

Anonymous (2001b) Der Markt der Finanzanlagen: Daten, Fakten, Trends. Focus, March 2001, available at http://www.medialine.de/marktanalysen

Anonymous (2001c) The 100 Top Brands. Business Week, August 6, pp. 60–64

Anonymous (2001d) Consors & Co. im Netz gefragt. Electronic Commerce Info Net, available at http://www.ecin.de/ news/2001/01/12/01403/index.html

Anonymous (2001e) Schlechte Beratung. FINANZtest, Number 9, p. 23

Anonymous (2002a) Survey: Time to grow up. The Economist, February 16, Issue 8260, 362: S3–S5

Anonymous (2002b) FOCUS Marktanalyse: Keditinstitute. Availabe at http://medialine.focus.de/PM1D/PM1DD/PM1DDC/PM1DDCU/PM1DDCUC/pm1ddcuc.htm

Anonymous (2002c) Getting Basel right: Bank capital. The Economist, February 23, Issue 8261, 362: 16

Anonymous (2002d) Multichannel-Shopper mit Spendierhosen. Electronic Commerce Info Net, avilable at http://www.ecin.de/news/2002/01/30/03834/

Anonymous (2002e) Risikomanagement bekommt größere Bedeutung: In der Gefahr rufen Konzerne nach dem Staat. Handelsblatt, February 5, p. 13

Arnold O, Faisst W, Härtling M, Sieber P (1995) Virtuelle Unternehmen als Unternehmenstyp der Zukunft. HMD 32: 8–23

Arnold W (2001) Internet und Online-Banking: Weiter auf Wachstumskurs. In: inter/esse, Informationen, Daten, Hintergründe, 9/2001, pp. 6–8, available at http://www.bdb.de/pic/artikelpic/112001/ie-09-01.pdf

Auerbach AJ, Reihus D (1988) Taxes and the Merger Decision. In: Coffee JC, Lowenstein L, Rose-Ackerman S (eds) Knights, Raiders & Targets, The Impact of the Hostile Takeover. Oxford University Press, New York, pp. 157–187

Ausfelder R, Kühne G, Wöhler J (1999) Attraktives Geschäftsfeld Affluent Banking. Die Bank, Number 8, pp. 526–529

Avery RJ (1996) Determinants of Search for Nondurable Goods: An Empirical Assessment of the Economics of Information Theory. The Journal of Consumer Affairs 30: 390–420

Arrow KJ (1951) Alternative Approaches to the Theory of Choice in Risk-Taking Situations. Econometrica 19: 404–437

Baeza-Yates R, Ribeiro-Neto B (1999) Modern information retrieval. Addison-Wesley, Harlow

Baker WE (1992) The network organization in theory and practice. In: Nohria N, Eccles RG (eds) Networks and organizations. Harvard Business School Press, Boston, pp. 397–429

Bakos Y (1991) A Strategic Analysis of Electronic Marketplaces. MIS Quarterly 15: 295–310

Bakos Y (1997) Reducing Buyer Search Costs – Implications for Electronic Marketplaces. Management Science 43: 1676–1692

Bakos Y (1998) The Emerging Role of Electronic Marketplaces on the Internet. Communications of the ACM 41: 35–42

Bamberg G, Coenenberg AG (2000) Entscheidungslehre. 10th Edition, Vahlen, München

Bamberg G, Dorfleitner G (2001) Fat Tails and Traditional Capital Market Theory. Arbeitspapier 177/2001 des Instituts für Statistik und Mathematische Wirtschaftstheorie der Universität Augsburg

Bank for International Settlements (1999) International Banking and Financial Market Developments. BIS Quarterly Review, August 1999, Bank for International Settlements, Monetary and Economic Department, Basel, available at http://www.bis.org

Bank for International Settlements (2001) Electronic finance: a new perspective and challenges. BIS Paper No 7, November 2001, Bank for International Settlements, available at http://www.bis.org

Barney JB, Hansen MH (1994) Trustworthiness as a source of competitive advantage. Strategic Management Journal 15: 175–190

Barton P (2001) Förderung der Servicequalität von Banken: Selbstbewertung als innovatives Managementinstrument. Bankakademie-Verlag, Frankfurt am Main

Basler Bankenvereinigung (1999) Multi-channel Distribution im Banking: Tagungsband zum 6. Basler Bankentag, 19. November 1998. Paul Haupt, Bern

BBE Unternehmensberatung (2001) Mehr Millionäre in Deutschland. BBE Unternehmensberatung, February 15, available at http://www.bbeberatung.com/NEWS/welcome_details.asp?Index=17

Beatty SE, Smith SM (1987) External Search Effort: An Investigation Across Several Product Categories. Journal of Consumer Research 14: 83–95

Beitel P, Schiereck D (2001) Value creation at the ongoing consolidation of the European banking market. Institute for Mergers and Acquisitions (IMA), Working Paper No. 05/01

Bekier MM, Flur DK, Singham SJ (2000) A future for bricks and mortar. The McKinsey Quarterly, Number 3, pp. 78–85

Bekier MM, Bogardus AJ, Oldham T (2001a) Mastering revenue growth in M&A. McKinsey on Finance, Summer 2001, pp. 1–5

Bekier MM, Bogardus AJ, Oldham T (2001b) Why mergers fail. The McKinsey Quarterly, Number 4, pp. 6–9

Bellman R (1957) Dynamic Programming. Princeton University Press, Princeton

Bennett RA (2001) Glass-Steagall revisited. USBanker 111: 6

Berger AN, Hunter WC, Timme SG (1993) The efficiency of financial institutions: A review and preview of research past, present and future. Journal of Banking & Finance 17: 221–249

Berger AN, Kashyap AK, Scalise JM (1995) The transformation of the US banking industry: What a long, strange trip it's been. Brookings Papers on Economic Activity 2: 55–218

Berger FC, van Bommel P, van der Weide TP (1999) Ranking Strategies for Navigation Based Query Formulation. Journal of Intelligent Information Systems 12: 5–25

Bernet B (1999) Warum fusionieren Banken? In: Siegwart H, Neugebauer G (eds) Mega-Fusionen: Analysen, Kontroversen, Perspektiven. 2nd Edition, Paul Haupt, Bern, pp. 131–145

Bernhardt R, Hofferbert-Junge B (2002) Vertriebskanäle: Koexistenz oder Konkurrenz? Computerwoche, Number 4, January 25, pp. 42–43

Bertrand JLF (1883) Théorie mathématique de la richesse social par Léon Walras: Recherches sur les principes mathématiques de la théorie des richesse par Augustin Cournot. Journal des savants 67: 499–508

Betsch O (1999) Irrtümer und Wahrheiten zum Retailbanking. bank und markt, Number 4, 28: 18–24

Bibel W (1993) Wissensrepräsentation und Inferenz, Eine grundlegende Einführung. Vieweg, Braunschweig

Bitz M (1995) Finanzdienstleistungen. 2nd Edition, Oldenbourg, München

Blattberg RC, Getz G, Thomas JS (2001) Customer Equity: Building and Managing Relationships as Valuable Assets. Harvard Business School Press, Boston

Böckhoff M, Stracke G (1999) Der Finanzplaner: Handbuch der privaten Finanzplanung und individuellen Finanzberatung. Sauer, Heidelberg

Börner CJ (1998) Die Konzentration im Bankenwesen – Ursache und Folgen. In: Büschgen HE (ed) Finanzplatz Deutschland an der Schwelle zum 21. Jahrhundert. Fritz Knapp, Frankfurt am Main, pp. 29–45

Bowen JW, Hedges RB (1993) Increasing Service Quality in Retail Banking. Journal of Retail Banking 15: 21–28

Brealey RA, Myers SC (1996) Principles of Corporate Finance. 5th Edition, McGraw-Hill, New York

Breuer RE (2002) Entwicklungslinien des europäischen Kapitalmarkts und Implikationen für das Geschäftsmodell einer großen Bank. Die Betriebswirtschaft 62: 202–210

Brown J, Goolsbee A (2000) Does the Internet Make Markets More Competitive? Evidence from the Life Insurance Industry. National Bureau of Economic Research Working Paper No. 7996

Brunner WL, Vollath J (1993) Finanzdienstleistungen. Schäffer-Poeschl, Stuttgart

Brunner WL (1993) Die Güte der Kundenberatung als Wettbewerbsfaktor. In: Brunner WL, Vollath J (eds) Finanzdienstleistungen, Schäffer-Poeschl, Stuttgart, pp. 752–768

Brynjolfsson E, Smith M (2000) Frictionless Commerce? A comparison of Internet and Conventional Retailers. Management Science 46: 563–585

Buhl HU, König HJ, Will A (1993): ALLFIWIB: Distributed Knowledge Based Systems for Customer Support in Financial Services. In: Karmann A, Mosler K, Schader M, Uebe G (eds) Operations Research '92. Physica, Heidelberg, pp. 537–540

Buhl HU, Roemer M, Sandbiller K (1996) Verteiltes Suchen und Erkennen zur Erstellung von Finanzdienstleistungen. KI Künstliche Intelligent 10: 17–25

Buhl HU, Will A (1998) Economic aspects of electronic commerce in financial services and advantageous steps to extended offers in internet banking. In: Blanning RW, King DR (eds) Proceedings of the 31st Annual Hawai'i International Conference on System Sciences HICSS. Los Alamitos, USA, Vol. 4, pp. 282–289

Buhl HU, Hinrichs JW, Satzger G, Schneider J (1999a) Leasing selbstgenutzter Wohnimmobilien. Die Betriebswirtschaft 59: 316–331

Buhl HU, Sandbiller K, Will A, Wolfersberger P (1999b) Zur Vorteilhaftigkeit von Zerobonds. Zeitschrift für Betriebswirtschaft 69: 83–114

Buhl HU, Visser V, Will A (1999c) Virtualisierung des Bankgeschäfts. Wirtschaftsinformatik 41: 116–123

Buhl HU, Kundisch D, Steck W, Leinfelder (2000a) IT-Enabled Sophistication Banking. In: Werthner H, Bichler M, Mahrer H (eds) Proceedings of the 8th European Conference on Information Systems ECIS 2000. Vienna, Austria, pp. 789–795

Buhl HU, Schneider J, Tretter B (2000b) Performanceattribution im Private Banking. Die Bank, Number 5, pp. 318–323

Buhl HU, Wolfersberger HP (2000a) Neue Perspektiven im Online- und Multichannel Banking. In: Locarek-Junge H, Walter B (eds) Banken im Wandel: Direktbanken und Direct Banking. Berlin-Verlag, Berlin, pp. 247–268

Buhl HU, Wolfersberger HP (2000b) One-to-one Banking. In: von Riekeberg M, Stenke K (eds) Banken 2000 – Projekte und Perspektiven. Gabler, Wiesbaden, pp.189–211

Buhl HU, Kundisch D, Steck W, Leinfelder A (2001) IT-Enabled Sophistication Banking. In: Werthner H, Bichler M (eds) Lectures in E-Commerce. Springer, Wien, pp. 27–46

Buhl HU, Kundisch D, Steck W (2002) Sophistication Banking als erfolgreiche Strategie im Informationszeitalter. Zeitschrift für Betriebswirtschaft, Ergänzungsheft 2/2002, 72:1–12

Bühler W (1993) Kundenzufriedenheit im Privatkundengeschäft. Die Bank, Number 9, pp. 511–519

Bühler W (1995) Quality Banking: Modewort oder neue Wettbewerbsphilosophie? Service Fachverlag, Wien

Bühler W (1997) Service-Versionen als Marketing-Vision für Banken. In: Hörter S, Wagner A (eds) Visionen im Bankmanagement: Festschrift für Professor Leo Schuster. Beck, München, pp. 249–260

Bühler W, Breyer M, Bruckner B, Csacsinovits J, Nader G, Palleschitz R, Royer K (1999) Forschungsprojekte am Institut für Kreditwirtschaft im Überblick. In: Schneider H (ed) Betriebswirtschaftliche Forschung an der Wirtschaftsuniversität: Konezpte, Befunde und Ausblick. Ueberreuter, Wien, pp. 33–50

Bühler W (2000a) Zweiklassensystem – Ultima Ratio der Privatkundensegmentierung? Die Bank, Number 11, pp. 748–753

Bühler W (2000b) Kundenbindung durch Wahlangebotsstrategien. Die Bank, Number 12, pp. 846–851

Bühler W (2000c) Mehrertragschancen durch Service-Differenzierung im Retailgeschäft. Österreichisches Bankarchiv 48: 887–893

Bülow S (1995) Netzwerk-Organisation für Allfinanzanbieter. Deutscher Universitätsverlag, Wiesbaden

Burdett K, Coles M (1995) Steady State Price Distributions in a Noisy Search Equilibrium. Journal of Economic Theory 72: 1–32

Bürkner HP, Grebe M (2001) Non-Banks im europäischen Finanzdienstleistungsgeschäft. In: Rolfes B, Fischer TR (eds) Handbuch der europäischen Finanzdienstleistungsindustrie. Fritz Knapp, Frankfurt am Main, pp. 118–128

Büschgen HE (1991) Bankbetriebslehre: Bankgeschäfte und Bankmanagement. Gabler, Wiesbaden

Buzzell RD, Gale BT (1989) The PIMS Principles: Linking Strategy to Performance. Free Press, New York

Bylinsky G (2000) Hot New Technologies for American Factories. Fortune, June 26, 142: 288A–288K

Cain JM, Fahey JJ (2000) Banks and Insurance Companies – Together in the New Millennium. The Business Lawyer 55: 1409–1425

Calomiris CW (1995) Pricing margins: Competition is the driver. Journal of Retail Banking Services 17: 59–62

Calomiris CW (1999) Gauging the efficiency of bank consolidation during a merger wave. Journal of Banking & Finance 23: 615–621

Carbonell J, Goldstein J (1998) The Use of MMR: Diversity-Based Reranking for reordering Documents and Producing Summaries. In: Croft WB, Moffat A, van Rijsbergen

CJ, Wilkinson R, Zobel J (eds) Proceedings of the 21st Annual International ACM SIGIR Conference on Research and Development in Information Retrieval, pp. 335–336

Carlton DW, Perloff JM (1994) Modern industrial organization. 2nd Edition, HarperCollins College Publishers, New York

Chandler GD, Goodrich JW, White DE (1984) Developing Winning Distribution Strategies. The Bankers Magazine, Nov.-Dec., pp. 30–40

Corsten H (2001) Dienstleistungsmanagement: Einführung. 4th Edition, Oldenbourg, München

Covey S (1990) Seven Habits of Highly Effective People. Fireside Books, New York

Coyne KP, Subramaniam S (1996) Bringing discipline to Strategy. The McKinsey Quarterly, Number 4, pp. 14–25

Cunningham SM (1967) The Major Dimensions of Perceived Risk. In: Cox DF (ed) Risk Taking and Information Handling in Consumer Behavior. Harvard University Press, Boston, pp. 82–108

Darby MR, Karni E (1973) Free Competition and the Optimal Amount of Fraud. Journal of Law and Economics 16: 67–88

Daum J (2000) Generation Y: When the Internet generation is joining your workforce you better be prepared. News, November 10, available at http://www.juergendaum.com/news/11_10_2000.htm

Davidow WH, Malone MS (1992) The virtual corporation: Structuring and revitalizing the corporation for the 21st century. Harper Collins, New York

Davis D, Holt C (1996) Consumer Search Cost and Market Performance. Economic Inquiry 34: 133–151

DeGroot MH (1970) Optimal Statistical Decisions. McGraw-Hill, New York

Deutsche Bundesbank (2001) The performance of German credit institutions in 2000. Deutsche Bundesbank Monthly Report, September 2001, pp. 15–50

Deutsche Bundesbank (2002) Banking supervision in the Federal Republic of Germany. III. Development of banking supervision after the Second World War. Available at http://www.bundesbank.de/en/banken/aufsicht/uebersicht/uebersicht3.htm

Devlin JF (1995) Technology and innovation in retail banking distribution. International Journal of Bank Marketing, Number 4, 13: 19–25

Diamond PA (1971) A Model of Price Adjustment. Journal of Economic Theory 3: 156–168

Diamond PA (1989) Search Theory. In: Eatwell J, Milgate M, Newman P (eds) The New Palgrave: allocation, information and markets. Macmillan Press Limited, London, pp. 271–286

Dinkelbach W, Kleine A (1996) Elemente einer betriebswirtschaftlichen Entscheidungslehre. Springer, Berlin

Domschke W, Drexl A (1996) Logistik: Standorte. Oldenbourg, München

Drucker P (1990) The emerging theory of manufacturing. Harvard Business Review, May-June, 68: 94–102

Drucker P (1999) Drucker on financial services: Innovate or die. The Economist, September 25, Issue 8138, 352: 25–28

Dutton P (2000) Trust Issues in E-Commerce. Presented at the 6th Australasian Women in Computing Workshop, Brisbane, available at www.sqi.gu.edu.au/wic2000/docs/Dutton.pdf

Dwyer FR (1989) Customer Lifetime Valuation to Support Marketing Decision Making. Journal of Direct Marketing 3: 8–15

Dzienziol J, Schroeder N, Wolf C (2001) Kundenwertorientierte Unternehmenssteuerung. In: Buhl HU, Kreyer N, Steck W (eds) e-finance – Innovative Problemlösungen für Informationssysteme in der Finanzwirtschaft. Springer, Berlin, pp. 63–86

Dzienziol J, Eberhardt M, Renz A, Schackmann J (2002) Multi-Channel Pricing for Financial Services. In: Proceedings of the 35ᵗʰ Annual Hawai'i International Conference on System Sciences HICSS. Big Island, USA

Dzienziol J, Kundisch D (2002) Einbezug von Risiko bei der Problem- und Lösungsrepräsentation im Rahmen von IT-basiertem Financial Planning. WI-110, Diskussionspapiere des Instituts für Betriebswirtschaftslehre der Universität Augsburg, available at http://www.wi-if.de

Eder R (2002) Financial Planning – Eigenständige Bepreisung in Theorie und Praxis. Österreichisches Bankarchiv 50: 116–124

Edwards K, Bauer M, Lutfiyya H, Widgery R (2001) Determining Factors that Influence Electronic Commerce Performance for Dynamic Content Generation. In: Proceedings of the International Conference on Internet Computing IC 2001, pp. 1041–1047

Eifert D, Pippow I (2001) Erfolgswirkungen von One-to-one Marketing – Eine empirische Analyse. In: Buhl HU, Huther A, Reitwiesner B (eds) Information Age Economy. Physica, Heidelberg, pp. 265–278

Eilenberger G, Burr W (1997) Zur Virtualisierung von Banken: Konsequenzen des Electronic Banking für Bankorganisation und Bankwettbewerb. In: Hörter S, Wagner A (eds) Visionen im Bankmanagement: Festschrift für Professor Leo Schuster. Beck, München, pp. 183–216

Einsfeld U, Will A (1996) Blackboardbasierte Systemunterstützung von Allfinanzangebotsprozessen. KI Künstliche Intelligenz 10: 49–54

Elbracht-Hülseweh B (1985) Problemlösungsverhalten und Problemlösungsmethoden bei schlechtstrukturierten Problemen. Studienverlag Dr. N. Brockmeyer, Bochum

eMarketer (2002) eGlobal Report. eMarketer eReport January 2002, available at http://www.emarketer.com/ereports/eglobal/welcome.html

Engel-Flechsig S, Maennel F, Tettenborn A (2001) Beck'scher IuKDG-Kommentar. Beck, München

Engelhardt WH, Kleinaltenkamp M, Reckenfelderbäumer M (1993) Leistungsbündel als Absatzobjekte. Schmalenbachs Zeitschrift für betriebswirtschaftliche Forschung 45: 395–426

Epple MH, Ramin J (1993) Bedürfnisse und Einstellungen in einzelnen Lebensphasen. BankInformation und Genossenschaftsforum, 7/93, pp. 42–45

Essayan M, Rutstein C, Wetenhall P (2002) Activate and Integrate: Optimizing the Value of Online Banking. Opportunities for Action in Financial Services, The Boston Consulting Group, available at http://www.bcg.com

Evans PB, Wurster TS (1997) Strategy and the New Economics of Information. Harvard Business Review, September-October, 75: 71–82

European Central Bank (2000a) EU Banks' Margins and Credit Standards. European Central Bank, December 2000, available at http://www.ecb.de

European Central Bank (2000b) Mergers and Acquisitions involving the EU Banking industry – facts and implications. European Central Bank, December 2000, available at http://www.ecb.de

Ferstl OK, Sinz EJ (2001) Grundlagen der Wirtschaftsinformatik, Bd.1. 4th Edition, Oldenbourg, München

Fisher I (1930) The Theory of Interest. Macmillan, New York.

Fischer TR, Rolfes B (2001) Finanzdienstleistungen in einem vereinten Europa. In: Rolfes B, Fischer TR (eds) Handbuch der europäischen Finanzdienstleistungsindustrie. Fritz Knapp, Frankfurt am Main, pp. 1–10

Flieger M, Frischmuth R (2002) Betriebliche Altersversorgung: Geschäftspotenzial für Filialbanken. Die Bank, Number 2, pp. 104–109

Flur DK, Mendonca LT, Nakache P (1997) Personal financial services: A question of channels. The McKinsey Quarterly, Number 3, pp. 116–125

Focarelli D, Pozzolo AF (2001) The patterns of cross-border bank mergers and shareholdings in OECD countries. Journal of Banking & Finance 25: 2305–2337

Frank M, Kundisch D, Schell A (2000) Elektronischer Vertrieb von Dienstleistungen: Der optimale Serverstandort als Warehouse Location Problem. In: Bodendorf F, Grauer M (eds) Verbundtagung Wirtschaftsinformatik 2000. Shaker, Aachen, pp. 208–222

Frey M (2000) Global-E verknüpft Märkte und Kunden. Information Management & Consulting 15: 79–81

Fridgen M, Schackmann J, Volkert S (2000a) Preference based customer models for electronic banking. In: Werthner H, Bichler M, Mahrer H (eds) Proceedings of the 8th European Conference on Information Systems ECIS 2000. Vienna, Austria, pp. 819–825

Fridgen M, Volkert S, Haarnagell M, Marko D, Zimmermann S (2000b) Kundenmodell für eCRM – Repräsentation individueller Einstellungen. Presented at FAN 2000, Siegen

Fridgen M (2003) Kundeninteraktion in der Mehrkanalwelt – kundenzentrisches Wirtschaften und kundenzentrische Informationssysteme (working title). Dissertation at the University of Augsburg, forthcoming

Fridgen M, Steck W (2002) Customer Tracking in the Internet: New Perspectives on Web Site Controlling. Quarterly Journal of Electronic Commerce 3: 235–245

Friedman M (1957a) A Theory of the Consumption Function. Princeton University Press, Princeton

Friedman M (1957b) The Permanent Income Hypothesis: Comment. The American Economic Review 48: 990–991

Fuchs HJ, Girke M (2002) Wachstumsmarkt Wealth Management. Die Bank, Number 2, pp. 90–95

Furash EE (1994) The Information Advantage. The Journal of Commercial Lending, December 1994, pp. 214–224

Gagnebin G (2001) Entwicklungsperspektiven im Private Banking aus europäischer Sicht. In: Rolfes B, Fischer TR (eds) Handbuch der europäischen Finanzdienstleistungsindustrie. Fritz Knapp, Frankfurt am Main, pp. 470–478

Gambetta D (1988a) Trust: Making and Breaking cooperative relations. Blackwell Publishers, New York

Gambetta D (1988b) Can we trust Trust? In: Gambetta D (ed) Trust: Making and Breaking cooperative relations. Blackwell Publishers, New York, pp. 213–237

Garner RJ, Coplan RB, Raasch BJ, Ratner CL (1996) Ernst & Young's Personal Financial Planning Guide. 2nd Edition, John Wiley & Sons, New York

Gebhardt G, Gerke W, Steiner M (1993) Ziele und Aufgaben des Finanzmanagements. In: Gebhardt G, Gerke W, Steiner M (eds) Handbuch des Finanzmanagements, C. H. Beck, München, pp. 1–23

Geiger H (1993) Das Allfinanzkonzept der deutschen Sparkassenorganisation. In: Brunner WL, Vollath J (eds) Finanzdienstleistungen. Schäffer-Poeschl, Stuttgart, pp. 500–521

Gierl H (1993) Zufriedene Kunden als Markenwechsler. Absatzwirtschaft 36: 90–94

Gilmore JH, Pine BJ (2000) Markets of One: Creating Customer-Unique Value through Mass Customization. Harvard Business School Press, Boston

Gölz R, Göppl F (1999) Electronic Commerce: Entwicklungspfade und Differenzierungsstrategien. technologie & management 48: 26–29

Goldberg J, von Nitzsch R (1999) Behavioral Finance: Gewinnen mit Kompetenz. Finanzbuch Verlag, München

Greco J (1999) Going the distance for MBA candidates. The Journal of Business Strategy 20: 30–34

GVU (1998) GVU's 10th WWW User Survey. Available at http://www.gvu.gatech.edu/user_surveys/survey-1998-10

Gulati R, Garino J (2000) Get the Right Mix of Bricks & Clicks. Harvard Business Review, May-June, 78: 107–114

Günter B, Helm S (2001) Kundenwert: Grundlagen – Innovative Konzepte – Praktische Umsetzungen. Gabler, Wiesbaden

Gutenberg E (1953) Zum "Methodenstreit". Zeitschrift für handelswirtschaftliche Forschung 5: 327–356

Hagel J, Sacconaghi AM (1996) Who will benefit from virtual information. The McKinsey Quarterly, Number 3, pp. 22–37

Hagel J, Rayport JF (1997) The Coming Battle for Customer Information. The McKinsey Quarterly, Number 3, pp. 65–76

Hagel J, Rayport JF (2000) The new infomediaries. The McKinsey Quarterly, Number 3, Strategy in the new Economy, pp. 119–128

Hagel J, Singer M (1999) Private Lives. The McKinsey Quarterly, Number 1, pp. 6–15

Hansen HR (1995) Conceptual framework and guidelines for the implementation of mass information systems. Information & Management 28: 125–142

Hardt P (1996) Organisation dienstleistungsorientierter Unternehmen. Deutscher Universitätsverlag, Wiesbaden

Hassels M (1997) Data-Based Marekting – Voraussetzung für bedarfsgerechte Produktbündelung. In: Rolfes B, Schierenbeck H, Schüller S (eds) Das Privatkundengeschäft – Die Achillesferse deutscher Kreditinstitute. Fritz Knapp, Frankfurt am Main, pp. 125–138

Haubrich JG (1989) Financial Intermediation: Delegated Monitoring and Long-Term Relationships. Journal of Banking & Finance 13: 9–20

Hawkes A (1995) Relationship Marketing in the Financial Services Industry. Available at http://www.managingchange.co.uk/guestcon/aha111fr.doc

Heigl A (2001) 3rd Generation: Wie sich von der Alterung profitieren lässt. Volkswirtschaft, HypoVereinsbank, May 2001, available at http://www.hvb.de

Helm S, Günter B (2001) Kundenwert – eine Einführung in die theoretischen und praktischen Herausforderungen der Bewertung von Kundenbeziehungen. In: Günter B, Helm S (eds) Kundenwert: Grundlagen – Innovative Konzepte – Praktische Umsetzungen. Gabler, Wiesbaden, pp. 3–35

Helmig B (2001) Variety Seeking Behavior. Die Betriebswirtschaft 61: 727–730

Henzler HA (1992) Vision und Führung. In: Hahn D, Taylor B (eds) Strategische Unternehmensplanung – Strategische Unternehmensführung. 6th Edition, Physica, Heidelberg, pp. 289–302

Herrhausen A (1988) Strategische Führung – Mehr als nur Strategie. In: Henzler HA (ed) Handbuch Strategische Führung. Gabler, Wiesbaden, pp. 59–68

Hey JD (1981) Economics in Disequilibrium. Martin Robertson, Oxford

Hoffman DL, Novak TP, Peralta M (1999) Building Consumer Trust Online. Communications of the ACM 42: 80–85

Holmsen CA, Paler RN, Simon PR, Weberg PK (1998) Retail Banking: Managing Competition Among Your Own Channels. The McKinsey Quarterly, Number 1, pp. 82–93

Homburg C (2001) Kundenzufriedenheit: Konzepte – Methoden – Erfahrungen. 4th Edition, Gabler, Wiesbaden

Huemer F (1991) Mergers & acquisitions: strategische und finanzielle Analyse von Unternehmensübernahmen. Peter Lang, Frankfurt am Main

Huther A (2003) Integriertes Chancen- und Risikomanagement für Real- und Finanzinvestitionen – Evaluation und Weiterentwicklung finanzwirtschaftlicher, insbesondere portfolioorientierter Methoden und Konzepte für ein integriertes Chancen- und Risikomanagementsystem (Rendite-/Risikosteuerung) in der Industrieunternehmung. Dissertation at the University of Augsburg, February 2003

Instenberg-Schieck G (1999) Multi-channel Banking – die Wege zum Kunden. Die Bank, Number 9, pp. 602–607

Institut für Demoskopie Allensbach (2002) Zunahme beim Homebanking: Mit dem Homebanking steigt die Zahl an Bankverbindungen. allensbacher berichte, Nr. 4

James M, Mendonca LT, Peters J, Wilson G (1997) Playing to the endgame in financial services. The McKinsey Quarterly, Number 4, pp. 170–185

Jansen DE (1992) Allfinanz 2000: das Handbuch der Kapitalanlage und Vermögensbildung. Luchterhand, Neuwied

Jansen S (2001) Mergers & Acquisitions: Unternehmensakquisitionen und -kooperationen – Eine strategische, organisatorische und kapitalmarkttheoretische Einführung. 4th Edition, Gabler, Wiesbaden

Jarvenpaa SL, Tractinsky N, Vitale M (2000) Consumer Trust in an Internet Store. Information Technology and Management 1: 45–71

Jervis FR (1971) The Economics of Mergers. Routledge & Kegan Paul, London

Kaindl H (1989): Problemlösen durch heuristische Suche in der artificial intelligence. Springer, Wien

Kaufmann H (1999) Der Euro wird Mega-Fusionen fördern – Beispiele aus dem Finanzsektor. In: Siegwart H, Neugebauer G (eds) Mega-Fusionen: Analysen, Kontroversen, Perspektiven. 2nd Edition, Paul Haupt, Bern, pp. 499–514

Kay IT, Shelton M (2000) The people problem in mergers. The McKinsey Quarterly, Number 4, pp. 27–37

Keller B, Lerch S, Matzke S (2000) Umfrage: Kundenbindung und Wechselbereitschaft. Die Bank, Number 6, pp. 376–381

Kerscher B (1998) Telekommunikation im Bankgeschäft: Ein ganzheitliches Gestaltungskonzept für innovative Telekommunikationssysteme im elektronischen Bankgeschäft. Physica, Heidelberg

Kießling W, Balke WT, Wagner M (2001) Personalized Content Syndication in a Preference World. In: Proceedings of the EnCKompass Workshop on E-Content Management EnCKompass 2001. Eindhoven, The Netherlands, pp. 3–6

Kirn S, Weinhardt C (1994) Künstliche Intelligenz in der Finanzberatung: Grundlagen – Konzepte – Anwendungen. Gabler, Wiesbaden

Kirn S (2002) Kooperierende intelligente Softwareagenten. Wirtschaftsinformatik 44: 53–63

Klein HK (1971) Heuristische Entscheidungsmodelle. Gabler, Wiesbaden

Klein R, Nathanson-Loidl D (2000) Der Kunde in der Fusion – Nutznießer oder Opfer. Die Bank, Number 3, pp. 168–172

Kloepfer J (1999) Marketing für die Private Finanzplanung: Vermarktung einer innovativen, komplexen Beratungsdienstleistung. Deutscher Universitätsverlag, Wiesbaden

Knight FH (1921) Risk, Uncertainty, and Profit. The University of Chicago Press, Chicago

Knöbel U (1997) Kundenwertmanagement im Retail Banking: Kundenprofitabilitätsanalyse und Customer-Life-Cycle Costing am Beispiel einer Universalbank. Rosch-Buch-Druckerei GmbH, Scheßlitz

Kogut, CA (1990) Consumer Search Behavior and Sunk Costs. Journal of Economic Behavior & Organization 14: 381–392

Kohlhaussen M (1999) Die aktuelle Fusionswelle im europäischen Bankenwesen – Vortrag im Rahmen der Studienrichtung "Investment banking". CWG-Dialog, Number 4, pp. 1–6

Kohn M, Shavell S (1974) The Theory of Search. Journal of Economic Theory 9: 93–123

Kollenda B (1992): Allfinanzanbieter und ihre Privatkunden. Gabler, Wiesbaden

König HJ, Roemer M, Sandbiller K, Weinhardt C, Will A (1994) Ein verteiltes Problemlösungssystem für die Allfinanz-Kundenberatung. In: Kirn S, Weinhardt C (eds) Künstliche Intelligenz in der Finanzberatung. Gabler, Wiesbaden, pp. 225–237

Kopper H (1998) Perspektiven der Universalbanken. In: Büschgen HE (ed) Finanzplatz Deutschland an der Schwelle zum 21. Jahrhundert. Fritz Knapp, Frankfurt am Main, pp. 47–54

Körner V, Zimmermann HD (2000) Management of customer relationship in business media – The case of the financial industry. In: Proceedings of the 33rd Hawai'i International Conference on System Science HICSS. Maui, USA

Krafft M, Albers S (2000) Ansätze zur Segmentierung von Kunden – Wie geeignet sind herkömmliche Konzepte? Schmalenbachs Zeitschrift für betriebswirtschaftliche Forschung 52: 515–536

Krapp M (2000) Kooperation und Konkurrenz in Prinzipal-Agent-Beziehungen. Deutscher Universitätsverlag, Wiesbaden

Kramer G (1967) Entscheidungsproblem, Entscheidungskriterien bei völliger Ungewissheit und Chernoffsches Axiomensystem. Metrika 11: 15–38

Krämer HP (2002) Kreissparkasse Köln: Wie werden die Margen besser? bank und markt, Number 4, pp. 22–25

Kraus PJ (2002) Mehr Rendite bei weniger Risiko. bankmagazin, Number 5, pp. 24–28

Krelle W (1968) Präferenz- und Entscheidungstheorie. J.C.B. Mohr (Paul Siebeck), Tübingen

Kreps DM (1988) Notes on the Theory of Choice. Westview Press, Boulder

Krishnan MS, Ramaswamy V, Meyer MC, Damien P (1999) Customer Satisfaction for Financial Services: The Role of Products, Services and Information Technology. Management Science 45: 1194–1209

Kruschew W (1999) Private Finanzplanung: die neue Dimension für anspruchsvolle Anleger. Gabler, Wiesbaden

Kuhl M, Stöber O (2001) Data Warehousing und Customer Relationship Management als Grundlagen des wertortierten Kundenmanagements. In: Günter B, Helm S (eds)

Kundenwert: Grundlagen – Innovative Konzepte – Praktische Umsetzungen. Gabler, Wiesbaden

Kulkarni S (2000) The Influence of Information Technology on Information Asymmetry in Product Markets. Journal of Business and Economic Studies 6: 55–71

Kundisch D (2000) Buyer Search Behavior in an Electronic Commodity Market: Consumer's Decision for a Sequential or Simultaneous Search Method. In: Kim SH, Sheng O, Lee JK, Whinston AB, Schmid B (eds) Proceedings of the 2nd International Conference on Electronic Commerce ICEC2000. Seoul, Korea, pp. 88–93

Kundisch D, Wolfersberger P, Calaminus D, Klöpfer E (2000) Ein Contentmodell für den Multichannel Vertrieb von Finanzdienstleistungen. Presented at FAN 2000, Siegen

Kundisch D, Wolfersberger P, Calaminus D, Klöpfer E (2001a) Enabling eCCRM: Content Model and Management for Financial eServices. In: Sprague R (ed) Proceedings of the 34th Annual Hawai'i International Conference on System Sciences HICSS. Maui, USA

Kundisch D, Wolfersberger P, Klöpfer E (2001b) Enabling Customer Relationship Management: Multi-Channel Content Model and Management for Financial e-Services. The International Journal on Media Management 3: 91–104

Kundisch D (2001c) Ein Beitrag zur Vorteilhaftigkeit von Online-Immobilienfinanzierungen mit KfW-Darlehen. WI-101, Diskussionspapiere des Instituts für Betriebswirtschaftslehre der Universität Augsburg, available at http://www.wi-if.de

Kundisch D, Dzienziol J, Eberhardt M, Pinnow M (2001d) Vergleichsmöglichkeiten für Finanzdienstleistungsangebote im WWW. Wirtschaftsinformatik 43: 305–315

Kundisch D (2002a) Beratungsqualität bei Finanzdienstleistern am Beispiel von Online-Immobilienfinanzierungen mit KfW-Darlehen. In: Weinhardt C, Holtmann C (eds) E-Commerce: Netze, Märkte, Technologien. Physica, Heidelberg, pp. 159–179

Kundisch D (2002b) Building Trust - The Most Important CRM Strategy? In: Proceedings of the 3rd World Congress on the Management of Electronic Commerce. Hamilton, Canada

Kundisch D, Steck W (2002) Trust and Switching Costs in the Financial Services Industry. In: Mastoriakis N, Mladenov V (eds) Recent Advances in Computers, Computing and Communications. WSEAS Press, Athen, pp. 92–97

Kundisch D, Dzienziol J (2003) Formalization of Financial Problems and Solutions under Risk as an Essential Requirement for IT-based Financial Planning. In. Proceedings of the 36th Hawai'i International Conference on System Sciences HICSS. Waikoloa, USA

Lang G, Welzel P (1996) Efficiency and technical progress in banking – Empirical results for a panel of German cooperative banks. Journal of Banking & Finance 20: 1003–1023

Laternser S (2000) Vermögensverwaltung – Quo vadis? "Branding", "Bundling", "Unbundling", … In: Britzelmaier B, Geberl S (eds) Wandel im Finanzdienstleistungssektor: 1. Liechtensteinisches Finanzdienstleistungs-Symposium an der Fachhochschule Liechtenstein. Physica, Heidelberg, pp. 111–118

Laubacher RJ, Malone TJ (1997) Two Scenarios for 21st Century Organizations: Shifting Networks of Small Firms or All-Encompassing "Virtual Countries"? Sloan School of Management, Massachusetts Institute of Technology, MIT Initiative on Inventing the Organizations of the 21st Century, Working Paper 21C WP #001

Laux H, Liermann F (1997) Grundlagen der Organisation: Die Steuerung von Entscheidungen als Grundproblem der Betriebswirtschaftslehre. 4th Edition, Springer, Berlin

Lawrence DB (1999) The Economic Value of Information. Springer, New York

Lee HG (1998) Do electronic markets lower the price of goods? Communications of the ACM 41: 73–80

Lehmann AP (1998) Qualität und Produktivität im Dienstleistungsmanagement: strategische Handlungsfelder im Versicherungs- und Finanzdienstleistungswettbewerb. Gabler, Wiesbaden

Leibenstein H (1966) Allocative efficiency vs. "X-Efficiency". The American Economic Review 56: 392–415

Lenat DB (1983) The role of heuristics in learning by discovery: Three case studies. In: Michalski RS, Carbonell JG, Mitchell TM (eds) Machine Learning: An Artificial Intelligence Approach. Tioga Presse, Palo Alto, pp. 243–306

Lewis DJ, Weigert A (1985) Trust as a Social Reality. Social Forces 63: 967–985

Link H, Schackmann J (2002) Intermediaries for the Provision of Mass Customized Digital Goods in Electronic Commerce. WI-111, Diskussionspapiere des Instituts für Betriebswirtschaftslehre der Universität Augsburg, available at http://www.wi-if.de

Lintner J (1965) The Valuation of Risk Assets and the Selection of Risky Investments in Stock Portfolios and Capital Budgets. Review of Economics and Statistics 47: 13–37

Lipstein AD (1984) Marketing Financial Services. In: Sametz AW (ed) The Emerging Financial Industry: Implications for Insurance Products, Portfolios, and Planning. Lexington Books, Lexington, pp. 49–54

Locarek-Junge H (1997) Finanzmathematik: Lehr- und Übungsbuch. Oldenbourg, München

Lohmann F (1997) Loyalität von Bankkunden: Bestimmungsgrößen und Gestaltungsmöglichkeiten. Deutscher Universitätsverlag, Wiesbaden

Looser U (1999) Was Fusionen erfolgreich macht. In: Siegwart H, Neugebauer G (eds) Mega-Fusionen: Analysen, Kontroversen, Perspektiven. 2nd Edition, Paul Haupt, Bern, pp. 265–274

Lucius O (2002) CFP® - ein Gütesiegel im Interesse der Kunden. Österreichisches Bankarchiv 50: 345–346

Ma WY, Bedner I, Chang G, Kuchinsky A, Zhang H (2000) A framework for adaptive content delivery in heterogeneous network environments. In: Proceedings of Multimedia Computing and Networking 2000 MMCN00. San Jose, USA, pp. 86–100

Mabley K (1999) Privacy vs. Personalization: A Delicate Balance. Cyber Dialogue, available at http://www.cyberdialogue.com

Macharzina K (1999) Unternehmensführung: das internationale Managementwissen. 3rd Edition, Gabler, Wiesbaden

Mädche A, Staab S, Studer R (2001) Ontologien. Wirtschaftsinformatik 43: 393–395

Magnus JR, Neudecker H (1988) Matrix differential calculus with applications in statistics and econometrics. John Wiley & Sons, Chichester

Maguire A, Dyer A, Orlander P (2001) Untapped Riches: The Myths and Realities of Wealth Management. Opportunities for Action in Financial Services, The Boston Consulting Group, available at http://www.bcg.com

Mainzer K (1999) Computernetze und virtuelle Realität: Leben in der Wissensgesellschaft. Springer, Berlin

Malone TW, Laubacher RJ (1998) The Dawn of the E-Lance Economy. Harvard Business Review, September-October, 76: 145–152

Markowitz H (1959) Portfolio Selection: Efficient Diversification of Investments. John Wiley & Sons, New York

McCall J (1965) The economics of information and optimal stopping rules. Journal of Business 38: 300–317

McKnight DH, Choudhury V, Kacmar C (2000) Trust in e-commerce vendors: a two-stage model. In: Proceedings of the 21st International Conference on Information Systems. Brisbane, Australia

McKnight DH, Chervany NL (2001) Conceptualizing Trust: A Typology and E-Commerce Customer Relationships Model. In: Sprague R (ed) Proceedings of the 34th Hawai'i International Conference on System Sciences HICSS. Maui, USA

Meier G (2000) Beratungsorientierte Kommissionen im Private Banking. In: Britzelmaier B, Geberl S (eds) Wandel im Finanzdienstleistungssektor: 1. Liechtensteinisches Finanzdienstleistungs-Symposium an der Fachhochschule Liechtenstein. Physica, Heidelberg, pp. 135–138

Menzigian K (2000) Worldwide CRM Services Market Forecast and Analysis, 1999 – 2004. IDC Research, Document #: 22441, July 2000

Mertens P, Faisst W (1995) Virtuelle Unternehmen, eine Organisationsstruktur für die Zukunft? technologie & management 44: 61–68

Mertens P, Griese J, Ehrenberg D (1998) Virtuelle Unternehmen und Informationsverarbeitung. Springer, Berlin

Mertens P, Höhl M (1999) Wie lernt der Computer den Menschen kennen? Bestandsaufnahme und Experimente zur Benutzermodellierung in der Wirtschaftsinformatik. In: Scheer AW, Nüttgens M (eds) Electronic Business Engineering. Physica, Heidelberg

Mertens P, Bodendorf F, König W, Picot A, Schumann M (2001) Grundzüge der Wirtschaftsinformatik. 7th Edition, Springer, Berlin

Merton RC (1992) Continuous-Time Finance. Blackwell Publishers, Cambridge

Merz M (1999) Electronic Commerce: Marktmodell, Anwendungen und Technologien. dpunkt, Heidelberg

Milbourn TT, Boot AWA, Thakor AV (1999) Megamergers and expanded scope: Theories of bank size and activity diversity. Journal of Banking & Finance 23: 195–214

Modigliani F, Brumberg R (1954) Utility analysis and the consumption function: An interpretation of cross-section data. In: Kurihara KK (ed) Post-Keynesian Economics. Rutgers University Press, New Brunswick, pp. 388–436

Monroe KB (1990) Pricing: Making Profitable Decisions. McGraw-Hill, New York.

Moormann J (2001) Bankvertrieb im digitalen Zeitalter. In: Moormann J, Rossbach P (eds) Customer Relationship Management in Banken. Bankakademie Verlag, Frankfurt am Main, pp. 3–20

Moorthy S, Ratchford BT, Talukdar D (1997) Consumer Information Search Revisited: Theory and Empirical Analysis. Journal of Consumer Research 23: 263–277

Muench T, Todd J, Bunyan C, Cain L (2001) Selling financial services by mail, telephone and the Internet – Commissioners Byrne and Bolkestein welcome political agreement in the Council. September 27, available at http://europa.eu.int/comm/internal_market/en/finances/consumer/01-1325.htm

Nader G (1995) Zufriedenheit mit Finanzdienstleistungen: Erfolgswirksamkeit, Messung und Modellierung. Springer, Wien

Negroponte N (1995) Being Digital. Vintage Books, New York

Nelson P (1970) Information and consumer behavior. Journal of Political Economy 78: 311–329

Neuberger D (1998) Mikroökonomik der Bank: Eine industrieökonomische Perspektive. Vahlen, München

Neumann K (1975) Operations Research Verfahren Band I. Carl Hanser, München

NFO Infratest (2001a) Monitoring Informationswirtschaft, 3. Faktenbericht 2001 (Band I), Chartbericht zum 3. Faktenbericht 2001 (Band II). Im Auftrag des Bundesministerium für Wirtschaft und Technology, eine Sekundärstudie von NFO Infratest, August 2001, 01.16.20302.020. München, Germany

NFO Infratest (2001b) Euro.net 8. The European Internet User Monitor. Omnibus Demographics Europe (PR). Conducted by NFO Infratest (Munich), NOP (London) and TMO (Paris). Wave 8, publishing: July/August 2001. Available at http://www.nfoeurope.com/euronet/de/PR_Omnibus_3L.pdf

Niehans J (1983) Financial Innovation, multinational banking, and monetary policy. Journal of Banking & Finance 7: 537–551

Nowak D (1999) Lebensweltorientierte Zielgruppenbildung im Finanzmarkt. In: Herrmann A, Jasny R, Vetter I (eds) Kundenorientierung von Banken: Strategien für Kundennähe und effektives Beziehungsmanagement. Frankfurter Allgemeine Buch, Frankfurt am Main, pp. 60–79

OECD (1998) Industrial Performance and Competitiveness in an Era of Globalisation and Technological Change. The OECD Observer, No. 210, February/March, p. 55

Palm-dos-Reis A, Zahedi F (1999) Designing personalized intelligent financial decision support systems. Decision Support Systems 26: 31–47

Parja B, Campbell KE, Finnegan CM (2000) MoneyTalks: The Road Ahead for Online Financial Services Providers. Wit Capital, Industry Report, February 2000, available at http://www.witcapital.com

Pau LF, Gianotti C (1990) Economic and financial knowledge-based processing. Springer, Heidelberg

Penzel HG, Pietig C (2000) MergerGuide: Handbuch für die Integration von Banken. Gabler, Wiesbaden

Peter SI (1999) Kundenbindung als Marketingziel: Identifikation und Analyse zentraler Determinanten. 2nd Edition, Gabler, Wiesbaden

Peppers D, Rogers M (1997) The One to One Future: Building Relationships One Customer at a Time. Currency/Doubleday, New York

Perridon L, Steiner M (2002) Finanzwirtschaft der Unternehmung. 11th Edition, Vahlen, München

Piller F, Schoder D (1999) Mass Customization und Electronic Commerce. Zeitschrift für Betriebswirtschaft 69: 1111–1136

Piller F, Zanner S (2001) Mass Customization und Personalisierung im Electronic Business. Das Wirtschaftsstudium 30: 88–96

Pine BJ, Peppers D, Rogers M (1995) Do You Want to Keep Your Customers Forever? Harvard Business Review, March-April, 73: 103–114

Pinney WE, McWillams DB, Atchinson M (1992) Management Science: An Introduction to Quantitative Analysis for Management. 3rd Edition, McGraw-Hill, New York

Popp S (1998) Strukturwandel bei Banken – Verbesserung des Shareholder-Value durch konsequente Kundenorientierung im Privatkundengeschäft von Kreditinstituten – Eine empirische Studie anhand eines Vergleichs zweier Institutsgruppen. Verlag Managementwissen Zukunft, Remseck

Porter M (1985) Competitive Advantage: creating and sustaining superior performance. Free Press, New York

Porter M (1996) What is Strategy? Harvard Business Review, November-December, 74: 61–78

Porter M (1998) Competitive advantage: Techniques for analyzing industries and competitors. Simon & Schuster, New York

Probst A, Wenger D (1998) Elektronische Kundenintegration: Marketing, Beratung & Verkauf, Support und Kommunikation. Vieweg, Braunschweig

Quartapelle AQ, Larsen G (1996) Kundenzufriedenheit. Springer, Berlin

Radev DR, Jing H, Budzikowska M (2000) Centroid-based summarization of multiple documents: sentence extraction, utility-based evaluation, and user studies. In: Proceedings of ANLP/NAACL 2000 Workshop on Summarization. Seattle, USA, pp. 21–29

Rahman SM, Bignall RJ (2001) Internet Commerce and Software Agents: Cases, Technologies and Opportunities. Idea Group Publishing, Hershey

Randle WM (1995) Who Will Guard the Gates to the Financial Services Industry? Bank Marketing, April, 27: 19–22

Rasch S, Lintner A (2001) The Multichannel Consumer: The Need to Integrate Online and Offline Channels in Europe. The Boston Consulting Group, July 2001, available at http://www.bcg.com

Rehkugler H, Voigt M, Kraus B, Otterbach A (1992) Die Qualität der Anlageberater. Die Bank, Number 6, pp. 316–322

Rehkugler H, Zimmermann HG (1994) Neuronale Netze in der Ökonomie, Grundlagen und finanzwirtschaftliche Anwendungen. Vahlen, München

Reichheld FF, Sasser WE (1990) Zero Defections: Quality comes to Services. Harvard Business Review, September-October, 68: 105–111

Reichheld FF (1997) Der Loyalitätseffekt. Campus, Frankfurt am Main

Reichheld FF, Schefter P (2000) E-Loyalty: Your Secret Weapon on the Web. Harvard Business Review, July-August, 78: 105–113

Reinartz WJ, Krafft M (2001) Überprüfung des Zusammenhangs von Kundenbindungsdauer von Kundenertragswert. Zeitschrift für Betriebswirtschafslehre 71: 1263–1281

Reitinger W, Stracke G, Tilmes R (1997a) Gewinne durch Financial Planning (I). Die Bank, Number 10, pp. 580–585

Reitinger W, Stracke G, Tilmes R (1997b) Gewinne durch Financial Planning (II). Die Bank, Number 11, pp. 658–662

Reitwiesner B (2001) Integrierte Rendite-/Risikosteuerung in der Industrieunternehmung: Betriebswirtschaftliche Konzeption und Umsetzung auf der Basis von Standardsoftware. Deutscher Universitätsverlag, Wiesbaden

Rhodes D, Rocco I, Buerkner HP (1999) Exploiting the Next Wave of Banking Consolidation in Europe. Opportunities for Action in Financial Services, The Boston Consulting Group, available at http://www.bcg.com

Richter J (2001) Grundsätze ordnungsmäßiger Finanzberatung: Normensystem zur Gestaltung und Prüfung von Finanzberatungen. Uhlenbruch, Bad Soden/Ts.

Robben M (2001) Internetnutzung – ja wo surfen sie denn? Electronic Commerce InfoNet ECIN, March 22, available at http://www.ecin.de/marktbarometer/internetnutzung

Rockafellar RT, Wets RJB (1991) Scenario and policy aggregation in optimization under uncertainty. Mathematics of Operations Research 16: 119–147

Rockart JF, Short JE (1991) The networked organization and the management of interdependence. In: Morton MSS (ed) The corporation of the 1990s: Information technology and organizational transformation. Oxford University Press, New York, pp. 189–219

Roemer M (1998) Direktvertrieb kundenindividueller Finanzdienstleistungen: Ökonomische Analyse und systemtechnische Gestaltung. Physica, Heidelberg

Romano NC (2001) Customer Relations Management Research: An Assessment of Sub Field Development and Maturity. In: Sprague R (ed) Proceedings of the 34th Annual Hawai'i International Conference on System Sciences HICSS. Maui, USA

Rolfes B, Schierenbeck H, Schüller S (1997) Das Privatkundengeschäft – Die Achillesferse deutscher Kreditinstitute. Fritz Knapp, Frankfurt am Main

Rolfes B (2001) Finanzdienstleistungen im europäischen Markt – Strukturentwicklung und strategische Konsequenzen. In: Tietmeyer H, Rolfes B (eds) Globalisierung der Finanzindustrie: Beiträge zum Duisburger Banken-Symposium. Gabler, Wiesbaden, pp. 37–60

Rothschild M (1975) Searching for the Lowest Price When the Distribution of Prices Is Unknown. Journal of Political Economy 82: 689–711

Rousseau DM, Sitkin SB, Burt RS, Camerer C (1998) Not so Different After All: A Cross-Discipline View of Trust. Academy of Management Review 23: 39–44

Rudolf-Sipötz E (2001) Kundenwert: Konzeption – Determinanten – Management. Thexis, St. Gallen

Rust RT, Zeithaml VA, Lemon KN (2000) Driving Customer Equity: How Customer Lifetime Value is Reshaping Corporate Strategy. The Free Press, New York

Salop S, Stiglitz J (1977) Bargains and Rip-offs: A Model of Monopolistically Competitive Price Dispersion. Review of Economic Studies 44: 493–510

Salop S, Stiglitz J (1982) The Theory of Sales: A Simple Model of Equilibrium Price Dispersion with Identical Agents. The American Economic Review 72: 1121–1130

Salmons J, Babitsky T (2002) The Nanocorp, Atomic Theory and the Network Effect. Organizing Principles and Scale in Small Is Good Business Webs. Available at http://sohodojo.com/nanocorp-atoms-network-effect.html

Samuelson PA, Nordhaus WD (1998) Economics. 16th Edition, Irwin/McGraw-Hill, Boston

Sandbiller K, Weinhardt C, Will A (1992) Cooperative Agents Solving Financial Problems: A Scenario. Contribution to the Meeting of the working group "Verteilte Künstliche Intelligenz" of the GI, 17. – 18.12.1992

Satzger G, Kundisch D (2002) Der Zusammenhang zwischen Investitionsentscheidung, Finanzierung und steuerlichem Totalerfolg. WI-70, Diskussionspapiere des Instituts für Betriebswirtschaftslehre der Universität Augsburg, available at http://www.wi-if.de

Schackmann J (2002) Individualisierung und Personalisierung – Eine ökonomische Analyse unter besonderer Berücksichtigung der Informationstechnologie und des Electronic Commerce. Dissertation at the University of Augsburg, July 2002

Scheer O (1989) Potentialorientierte Analyse und Steuerung des Privatkundengeschäfts von Banken. Wissenschaftsverlag Vauk, Kiel

Schenk H (2000) On the Performance of Banking Mergers: Some Propositions and Policy Implications; The impact of mergers and acquisitions in Finance on workers, consumers and shareholders. Background Report, UNI-Europa, Brussels/Geneva, pp. 24–43

Schierenbeck H (1997) Qualitätsmanagement im Privatkundengeschäft. In: Rolfes B, Schierenbeck H, Schüller S (eds) Das Privatkundengeschäft – Die Achillesferse deutscher Kreditinstitute. Fritz Knapp, Frankfurt am Main, pp. 139–172

Schierenbeck H (1999a) Bankenzusammenschlüsse – Konsequenzen für die Geschäftspolitik. In: Siegwart H, Neugebauer G (eds) Mega-Fusionen: Analysen, Kontroversen, Perspektiven. 2nd Edition, Paul Haupt, Bern, pp. 275–286

Schierenbeck H (1999b) Die Vertriebskanäle der Zukunft im Privatkundengeschäft. In: Basler Bankenvereinigung (1999) Multi-channel Distribution im Banking: Tagungsband zum 6. Basler Bankentag, 19. November 1998. Paul Haupt, Bern, pp. 3–49

Schmid RE, Bach V, Österle H (2000) Mit Customer Relationship Management zum Prozessportal. In: Bach V, Österle H (eds) Customer Relationship Management in der Praxis. Springer, Berlin, pp. 3–55

Schmidt A (2002) Finanzmärkte in einer Ageing Society. Die Bank, Number 4, pp. 228–232

Schmitz R (1993) Mergers & Acquisitions-Beratung als Bankdienstleistung: Grundlagen und Probleme. Deutscher Universitätsverlag, Wiesbaden

Schmoll A, Ronzal W (2001) Neue Wege zum Kunden: Multi-Channel-Vertrieb im Bankgeschäft. Gabler, Wiesbaden

Schneider D (1997) Betriebswirtschaftslehre Band 3 Theorie der Unternehmung. Oldenbourg, München

Schneider J, Buhl HU (1999) Simultane Optimierung der Zahlungsströme von Leasingverträgen und deren Refinanzierung. Zeitschrift für Betriebswirtschaft, Ergänzungsheft 3, 69: 19–39

Schneider J (1999a) Finanzanalysen in der Investitions- und Finanzierungsberatung: Potential und problemadäquate Systemunterstützung. Physica, Heidelberg

Schneider M (1999b) Innovation von Dienstleistungen: Organisation von Innovationsprozessen in Universalbanken. Deutscher Universitätsverlag, Wiesbaden

Schumann M, Hess T (1999) Content-Management für Online-Informationsangebote. In: Schumann M, Hess T (eds) Medienunternehmen im digitalen Zeitalter. Gabler, Wiesbaden, pp. 69–87

Schüller S, Riedl M (2000) Multi-channel Management – die Vertriebsherausforderung im Retail Banking. Die Bank, Number 12, pp. 828–832

Schüller S (2001) Privatkundengeschäft in Europa. In: Tietmeyer H, Rolfes B (eds) Globalisierung der Finanzindustrie: Beiträge zum Duisburger Banken-Symposium. Gabler, Wiesbaden, pp. 61–77

Schulte-Noelle H (1998) Der Finanzdienstleistungsmarkt aus Sicht der Versicherungsunternehmen. In: Büschgen HE (ed) Finanzplatz Deutschland an der Schwelle zum 21. Jahrhundert. Fritz Knapp, Frankfurt am Main, pp. 109–122

Schütte M, Höfle K (1998) Anforderungsprofil und Qualifikationsentwicklung von Privatkundenbetreuern. In: Süchting J, Heitmüller HM (eds) Handbuch des Bankmarketing. 3rd Edition, Gabler, Wiesbaden, pp. 217–240

Seben L (2001) Privacy Plus Personalization Equals Sales. CRMDaily.com, May 10, available at http//www.crmdaily.com

Seebauer R (1993) Banken und Versicherungen als Finanzdienstleister im Jahr 2000. In: Brunner WL, Vollath J (eds) Finanzdienstleistungen. Schäffer-Poeschl, Stuttgart, pp. 740–747

Seidel GR (1995) Kritische Erfolgsfaktoren bei Unternehmensübernahmen: Eine Analyse der US-Bankenbranche. Deutscher Universitätsverlag, Wiesbaden

Sengupta S, Krapfel RE, Pusateri MA (1997) Switching costs in key account relationships. The Journal of Personal Selling & Sales Management 17: 9–16

Sestina JE (1991) Fee-only financial planning: how to make it work for you. Dearborn Financial Publishing, Chicago

Shapiro C, Varian H (1998) Information Rules. Harvard Business School Press, Boston

Sharpe WF (1964) Capital Asset prices: A Theory of Market Equilibrium under Conditions of Risk. Journal of Finance 19: 425–442

Shefrin HM, Thaler RH (1988) The Behavioral Life-Cycle Hypothesis. Economic Inquiry 26: 609–643

Shy O (1997) Industrial Organization. 3rd Printing, MIT Press, Cambridge

Siegel JJ (1998) Stocks for the long run. 2nd Edition, McGraw-Hill, New York

Skiera B, Lambrecht A (2000) Erlösmodelle im Internet. In: Albers S, Herrmann A (eds) Handbuch Projektmanagement. Gabler, Wiesbaden

Smith M, Bailey J, Brynjolfsson, E (2000) Understanding Digital Markets: Review and Assessment. In: Brynjolfsson E, Kahin B (eds) Understanding the Digital Economy: Data, Tools, and Research. MIT Press, Cambridge, pp 99–136

Spence M (1976) Informational Aspects of Market Structure. Quarterly Journal of Economics 90: 592–597

Spiekermann S, Großklags J, Berendt B (2001) Stated Privacy Preferences vs. Actual Behaviour in EC Environments: a Reality Check. In: Buhl HU, Kreyer N, Steck W (eds) e-finance – Innovative Problemlösungen für Informationssysteme in der Finanzwirtschaft. Springer, Berlin, pp. 129–147

Spremann K (1996) Wirtschaft, Investition und Finanzierung. 5th Edition, Oldenbourg, München

Spremann K, Buermeyer (1997) Zur Dimensionierung von Banken. In: Hörter S, Wagner A (eds) Visionen im Bankmanagement: Festschrift für Professor Leo Schuster. Beck, München, pp. 169–179

Spremann K, Winhart S (1998) Anlageberatung und Lebenszyklus. Finanzmarkt und Portfolio Management 12: 150–169

Spremann K (1999) Vermögensverwaltung. Oldenbourg, München

Spremann K (2000) Für jede Lebensphase die passende Investition wählen. Finanz und Wirtschaft, Number 19, August 03, p. 24

Stahl DO (1989) Oligopolistic Pricing with Sequential Consumer Search. The American Economic Review 79: 700–712

Stahl HK, Hinterhuber HH, Friedrich SA, Matzler K (2000) Kundenzufriedenheit und Kundenwert. In: Hinterhuber HH, Matzler K (eds) Kundenorientierte Unternehmensführung: Kundenorientierung – Kundenzufriedenheit – Kundenbindung. 2nd Edition, Gabler, Wiesbaden

Stam N (1999) Moore's Law will continue to drive computing. PC Magazine, May 22

Statistisches Bundesamt (2000) Bevölkerung: Bevölkerungsentwicklung Deutschlands bis zum Jahre 2050, Ergebnisse der 9. koordinierten Bevölkerungsvorausberechnung. Statistisches Bundesamt, available at http://www.destatis.de/download/veroe/ bevoe.pdf

Steck W, Will A (1998) Suche im WWW: Nachfragerverhalten und Implikationen für Anbieter. In: Scheer AW, Nüttgens M (eds) Electronic Business Engineering – 4. Internationale Tagung Wirtschaftsinformatik 1999. Physica, Heidelberg, pp. 289–307

Steck W (2003) Ansätze zur wirtschaftlichen Gestaltung der Individualisierung von Kundenbeziehungen im Finanzdienstleistungsbereich. Dissertation at the University of Augsburg, February 2003

Steiner A (1999) Data Warehouse and Data Mining. In: Moormann J, Fischer T (eds) Handbuch Informationstechnologie in Banken. Gabler, Wiesbaden, pp. 317–328

Steiner M, Bruns C (2000) Wertpapiermanagement. 7th Edition, Schäffer-Poeschl, Stuttgart

Stigler G (1961) The Economics of Information. Journal of Political Economy 69: 213–225

Stiglitz JE (1989) Imperfect Information in the Product Market. In: Schmalensee R, Willig RD (eds) Handbook of Industrial Organization. Elsevier Science Publishers, North Holland, pp 769–847

Stracke G, Geitner D (1992) Finanzdienstleistungen: Handbuch über den Markt und die Anbieter. Verlag Recht und Wirtschaft GmbH, Heidelberg

Straub E (1990) Electronic Banking: Die elektronische Schnittstelle zwischen Banken und Kunden. Paul Haupt, Bern

Streim H (1975) Heuristische Lösungsverfahren – Versuch einer Begriffsklärung. Zeitschrift für Operations Research 19: 143–162

Süchting J (1994) Vertrieb von Finanzdienstleistungen auf dem Markt für Privatkunden. Die Bank, Number 8, pp. 449–457

Süchting J (1998) Die Theorie der Bankloyalität – (immer noch) eine Basis zum Verständnis der Absatzbeziehungen von Kreditinstituten. In: Süchting J, Heitmüller HM (eds) Handbuch des Bankmarketing. 3rd Edition, Gabler, Wiesbaden, pp. 1–24

Süchting J, Paul S (1998) Bankmanagement. 4th Edition, Schäffer-Poeschl, Stuttgart

Tan SJ (1999) Strategies for Reducing Consumers' Risk Aversion in Internet Shopping. Journal of Consumer Marketing 16: 163–180

Tapscott D, Ticoll D, Lowy A (2000) Digital Capital: Harnessing the Power of Business Webs. Harvard Business School Press, Boston

Telser LG (1973) Searching for the Lowest Price. American Economic Association 63: 40–49

Tenhagen HJ (2000) Contra zu ‚Banken – ist der Kunde König?'. Die Bank, Number 8, p. 511

Thede J (1992) Finanzdienstleistungen und Absatzwege im deutschen Privatkundenmarkt. Wissenschaftsverlag Vauk, Kiel

Tilmes R (2000) Financial Planning im Private Banking: Kundenorientierte Gestaltung einer Beratungsdienstleistung. Uhlenbruch, Bad Soden/Ts.

Tirole J (1988) The Theory of Industrial Organization. MIT Press, Cambridge

Toffler A. (1980) The third wave. Random House, New York

Tomczak T, Dittrich S (2000) Kundenbindung - bestehende Kundenpotentiale langfristig nutzen. In: Hinterhuber H, Matzler K (eds) Kundenorientierte Unternehmensführung: Kundenorientierung – Kundenzufriedenheit – Kundenbindung. Gabler, Wiesbaden, pp. 103–126

Tomczak T, Rudolf-Sipötz E (2001) Bestimmungsfaktoren des Kundenwerts: Ergebnisse einer branchenübergreifenden Studie. In: Günter B, Helm S (2001) Kundenwert: Grundlagen – Innovative Konzepte – Praktische Umsetzungen. Gabler, Wiesbaden, pp. 127–154

Train KE (1991) Optimal Regulation: The Economic Theory of natural Monopoly. 5th Printing. MIT Press, Cambridge

Ulrich W (1976) Einführung in die heuristischen Methoden des Problemlösens. Das Wirtschaftsstudium 5: 251–256

Urbany JE (1986) An Experimental Examination of the Economics of Information. Journal of Consumer Research 13: 257–271

U.S. Department of Commerce (2002) Evans: Census Data Show America is Online. U.S. Department of Commerce, Press release, February 5, available at http://osecnt13.osec.doc.gov/public.nsf/docs/Evans-Census-Online

van Bommel P, van der Weide TP (1998) Multi Media Information Filtering on the WWW. In: Proceedings of the World Automation Congress WAC'98. TSI Press, Anchorage

van der Weide TP, Huibers TWC, van Bommel P (1998) The Incremental Searcher Satisfaction Model for Information Retrieval. The Computer Journal 41: 311–318

van der Weide TP, van Bommel P (1998) Individual and Collective Approaches for Searcher Satisfaction in IR. Technical Report CSI-R9819

van Rijsbergen CJ (1990) Information Retrieval. Butterworths, London

Varian H (1999) Economics and Search. Keynote Address at the 22nd International conference on Research and Development in Information Retrieval SIGIR'99

Viner N, Rhodes D, Dumas DR, Ivanov S (2000) Making Mergers Work: Turning a Big Deal into a Good Deal. Opportunities for Action in Financial Services, The Boston Consulting Group, available at http://www.bcg.com

Vitányi P (2001) The quantum computing challenge. In: Wilhelm R (ed) Informatics: 10 years back, 10 years ahead. Springer, Heidelberg

Volkert S (2003) Wissensrepräsentation und Software-Architekturen für Customer Relationship Management (working title). Dissertation at the University of Augsburg, forthcoming

Wagner M, Holland S, Kießling W (1999) Towards Self-tuning Multimedia Delivery for Advanced Internet Services. In: Proceedings of the First International Workshop on Multimedia Intelligent Storage and Retrieval Management (MISRM'99) in conjunction with ACM Multimedia Conference 1999. Orlando, USA

Wagner PJ (1991) Die Bildung von Allfinanzkonzernen: Grundlagen und Ansatzpunkte der Integration von Bank und Versicherung in einem Allfinanzkonzern. Peter Lang, Bern

Wang S, Xia Y (2002) Portfolio Selection and Asset Pricing. Springer, Berlin

Watson I, Maver C, Latimore D (2000) The Customer Speaks: 3,300 Internet Users Tell Us What They Want form Retail Financial Services. Strategy Report, Mainspring, September 25

Weikum G (2001) The Web in 2010: Challenges and Opportunities for Database Research. In: Wilhelm R (ed) Informatics – 10 years back, 10 years ahead. Springer, Heidelberg, pp. 1–23

Weimer T, Wißkirchen C (1999) Sechs Thesen zur Fusionswelle im Bankenbereich. Die Bank, Number 11, pp. 758–764

Weitzman ML (1979) Optimal Search for the Best Alternative. Econometrica 47: 641–654

Werbach K (2000) Syndication: The Emerging Model for Business in the Internet Era. Harvard Business Review, May-June, 78: 85–93

Wigand R, Picot A, Reichwald R (1997) Information, Organization, and Management: Expanding Markets and Corporate Boundaries. John Wiley & Sons, New York

Whinston A, Stahl D, Choi SY (1997) The Economics of Electronic Commerce. Macmillan Technical Publishing, Indianapolis

Wicke JM (1997) Individuelle Vermögensverwaltung für Privatkunden: Konzepte für das Management von Vermögensverwaltungs-Gesellschaften. Deutscher Universitätsverlag, Wiesbaden

Wiemann HU (1993) Herausforderungen an das Vermögensanlagegeschäft der Banken in den neunziger Jahren. In: Brunner WL, Vollath J (eds) Finanzdienstleistungen. Schäffer-Poeschl, Stuttgart, pp. 157–173

Wilde LL (1980) The Economics of Consumer Information Acquisition. Journal of Business 53: S143–S158

Will A (1995) Die Erstellung von Allfinanzprodukten: Produktgestaltung und verteiltes Problemlösen. Deutscher Universitätsverlag, Wiesbaden

Will A (1999) Individuelle Finanzdienstleistungen auf Netzmärkten – Ökonomische Analyse und Angebotsgestaltung. Habilitationsschrift, Wirtschafts- und Sozialwissenschaftliche Fakultät der Universität Augsburg

WKWI (1994) Wissenschaftliche Kommission Wirtschaftsinformatik (WKWI) im Verband der Hochschullehrer für Betriebswirtschaft e.V.: Profil der Wirtschaftsinformatik. Wirtschaftsinformatik 36: 80–81

Woywod A (1997) Verfeinerung von Expertisesystemen durch Benutzermodellierung. Peter Lang, Frankfurt am Main

Wolfersberger HP (2002) Analyse und innovative Gestaltungskonzepte zur Erlangung nachhaltiger strategischer Wettbewerbsvorteile für Finanzdienstleister. Dissertation, Universität Augsburg

Wölfing D, Mehlmann OF (1999) Multi-Channel-Konzepte für den multimedialen Marktplatz. In: Moormann J, Fischer T (eds) Handbuch Informationstechnologie in Banken. Gabler, Wiesbaden, pp. 105–124

Wondergem BCM, van Bommel P, Huibers TWC, van der Weide TP (1997) Towards an Agent-Based Retrieval Engine. In: Furner J, Harper DJ (eds) Proceedings of the 19th BCS-IRSG Colloquium on IR Research. Aberdeen, Scotland, pp. 126–144

Wondergem BCM, van Bommel P, Huibers TWC, van der Weide TP (1998) Agents in Cyberspace – Towards a Framework for Multi-Agent Systems in Information Discovery. In: Proceedings of the 20th BCS-IRSG Colloquium on IR Research. Grenoble, France

Woodhouse I, Weatherill B (2001) European Private Banking / Wealth Management Survey 2000/2001 – Executive Summary. PricewaterhouseCoopers, available at http://www.pwc.com

Yang Y (1999) An evaluation of statistical approaches to text categorization. Journal of Information Retrieval 1: 67–88

Yang Y, Liu X (1999) A re-examination of text categorization methods. In: Hearst M, Gey F, Tong R (eds) Proceedings of 22nd International conference on Research and Development in Information Retrieval SIGIR'99. Berkeley, USA, pp. 42–49

Yang Y, Chen J, Zhang H (2000) Adaptive delivery of HTML Contents. In: Poster Proceedings of 9th International World Wide Web Conference. Amsterdam, The Netherlands, pp. 24–25

Zeithaml VA (1984) How Consumer Evaluation Processes Differ between Goods and Services. In: Lovelock (ed) Services Marketing: Text, Cases, & Readings. Prentice-Hall, Englewood Cliffs, pp. 191–199